WRITING THE MODERN MYSTERY

SPECIAL KUDOS FROM SOME OF THE MYSTERY AUTHORS BARBARA NORVILLE HAS WORKED WITH

"This book would have saved me three years in establishing my career as a mystery writer. The only thing Barbara Norville does better than edit mystery novels is to tell you how to write and sell them. She knows perhaps better than anyone in the mystery publishing business the elements of a first-rate mystery novel. What sets her apart is her ability to instruct the writer on how to incorporate these elements into his or her manuscript."
—Richard Forrest, *Death Under the Lilacs, A Child's Garden of Death, The Killing Edge*

" 'I love your book, Barbara Norville told me when she bought my first novel, but it needs a little work. Now, line one, page one . . .' I had fallen into the clutches of the best mystery editor in New York. Reading *Writing the Modern Mystery* was like running into an old friend, professor and drill sergeant rolled into one inspired package. Two pages in, I started outlining a new detective story."
—Justin Scott, *Rampage, The Shipkiller, Many Happy Returns*

"She has turned dozens of promising writers into money-earning professional writers. She is one of the great editors of our time. If you want to learn the craft and the art of writing mysteries, sit down to sessions of work with her through this book. You will be inspired as well as instructed."

—William M. Green, *The Romanov Connection*, *The Man Who Called Himself Devlin*, *See How They Run*

"For the novelist of suspense and detective fiction, Norville's wonderfully instructive and fun-to-read book has all the necessary guideposts to writing a polished bestseller. I sincerely wish I'd had her book to learn from before I wrote my own suspense story, for then it might just have been great instead of good, might have *made* that bestseller list."

—Beth de Bilio, *Vendetta Con Brio*

"For anyone interested in writing a mystery, or simply better understanding the genre, *Writing the Modern Mystery* has to be the book to turn to. It is practical—filled with clearly developed examples; and encouraging—leading the novice to believe in himself. As I read the book, I could hear her talking; the wit and forthright tone complement the content."

—James MacDougall, *Death and the Maiden*, *Weasel Hunt*

"Barbara's book smells of the kitchen where good things are prepared, and her recipe works. Just add one egg (your own creative genius) and season to taste with battle, murder, sudden death, and red ruin for a gourmet's delight and immortal mystification."

—Will Cooper, *Death Has a Thousand Doors*

More kudos appear on the back of the jacket.

WRITING the MODERN MYSTERY

Barbara Norville

Cincinnati, Ohio

About the Author

For ten years Barbara Norville was the editor of the prestigious Inner Sanctum Mysteries at Simon & Schuster. She then went on to create her own mystery line at the venerable publishing house of Bobbs-Merrill. During her twenty-years-plus career, she has worked with more than 150 writers, giving many of them their start and turning new authors into professionals. She has also introduced English and French authors to American audiences. A good many of the authors she has worked with were given Edgar Awards (granted by Mystery Writers of America for the best mystery or best first mystery of the year) or its British equivalent, the Silver Dagger Award.

Ms. Norville now teaches at Brooklyn College.

Writing the Modern Mystery. Copyright © 1986 by Barbara Norville. Printed and bound in the United States of America. All rights reserved. No part of this book may be reproduced in any form or by any electronic or mechanical means including information storage and retrieval systems without permission in writing from the publisher, except by a reviewer, who may quote brief passages in a review. Published by Writer's Digest Books, an imprint of F&W Publications, 1507 Dana Ave., Cincinnati, OH 45207. First edition. First paperback printing 1992.

96 95 94 93 92   5 4 3 2 1

Library of Congress Cataloging-in-Publication Data

Norville, Barbara, 1923-
    Writing the modern mystery.
    Bibliography:p.
    Includes index.
    1. Detective and mystery stories—Authorship. I. Title.
PN3377.5.D4N67   1986   808'.02   86-15795
ISBN 0-89879-523-0

Design by Christine Aulicino

*I want to express my gratitude to all
the authors I have worked with, for it
is they who have taught me my trade.*

CONTENTS

WRITING THE MODERN MYSTERY

A WORD TO THE ASPIRING WRITER

IN THE TWENTY YEARS that I spent editing mysteries, approximately 4,000 manuscripts came across my desk. Of those, I accepted about 400, or 10 percent. This does not mean that the remaining 3,600 were not publishable. Some of them were simply not to my taste; editors do have biases. I would not, for example, take on a manuscript that depicted prolonged cruelty to children—or to anyone, for that matter. I accepted few books that portrayed psychos; it is a rare author, in my opinion, who can get into the mind of one.

I did not exercise my biases often. Most of the manuscripts were just not well enough thought through *before they were written*. Even those that were—the 400—did not come to me in absolutely perfect shape. All of them, to some extent, needed work. This is understandable because there are a lot of elements that go into writing a mystery, and they do not get the same degree of attention. One author would have a well-wrought plot and only moderately successful characters. Another would have good characters but needed to shore up weak motivation. It was my aim to teach them *as soon as possible* to think through those areas they were weak in, and I did it with a three-pronged approach: 1) to undo bad habits before they became entrenched; 2) to put authors on the right track; and 3) to urge them to go beyond their self-conceived limitations. I set standards for them that were practical, flexible and achievable.

Throughout the years I found the same errors appearing over and over. Although every author presented different problems, they all shared, in one area or another, the same *inexperience*. As one author after another appeared, and as one problem after another was explored, pinned down and solved, I developed a set of blueprints that proved serviceable to them and to me.

Perhaps my sharing these blueprints with you will help you become more aware of what goes into the writing of a mystery novel that makes it acceptable to a publisher and welcomed by readers.

In writing this book, I have, of course, included suggestions on manipulating suspense, plotting, developing characters, researching backgrounds, and other important mechanics used in writing mystery novels. I have also felt it was significant to include a chapter on style. The authors I worked with appreciated my comments on how to make their prose suspenseful, incisive and persuasive. I come close to being idiosyncratic in my insistence that a well-written mystery is as much to be desired as good writing is in any field. Believe me, the most ingenious plot falters and the most colorful characters fade if you do not have a command of words to stir your audience.

There is something else I have tried for in writing this book. Granted, I cannot talk to each of you individually but in putting down these words I have thought of how I could reach you as individuals. I have imagined you sitting in my office, your manuscript and my notes spread out on the desk. In this vignette, you are asking the questions and I am giving you the best answers I can. Our meetings are friendly, informal and productive for both of us. I hope this vision comes across in the pages you are about to read.

WHAT IS A MYSTERY?

MYSTERY WAS FIRST DEFINED by the Greeks with the word *mysterion*, meaning "to keep silence." It came from the verb *myein*, to be closed (i.e., the eyes or the lips). In early Christian times—and to this day, actually—it was assigned as a religious truth, that mankind could know the "truth" by revelation alone and could not ever fully understand it. In the Middle Ages, it took on yet another character—that of a morality play which ferreted out evil, to the chagrin of the wrongdoer, the elation of the ferreter and the enlightenment of the audience. The wrongdoer was found out, he was mocked, and therefore shunned. An apt punishment.

The modern mystery has its roots in the morality play. Instead of sins of pride, sloth, envy, and so on, today's literary culprit works in a sterner framework of felonious assault against his neighbor and crimes against entire populaces. He is not only to be shunned but condemned. The stakes are higher and the punishments harsher. The morality inherent in modern-day mysteries is no less fervent. Wrong-doing is still a recognized antisocial act and must be dealt with by society. We still take pleasure in unveiling criminous deeds against one person or our milieu. Part of the satisfaction is because we have a code of laws that we can live with comfortably. We, as a whole society, can agree to condemn the one. In totalitarian countries, the one can condemn the whole. (In those countries only recently emerging from totalitarian rule, the jury is still out.) In a democracy the entire nation, through its courtroom surrogates, serves as judge and jury. Just as we extol the beauties of our bountiful land with song and verse, we celebrate our even-handed judicial heritage — our collective morality — with the mystery story.

As mediaevalists "enlightened" by lacing their plays with singing and dancing in the churchyard, mystery writers keep their readers turning the pages with devices that also entertain: near-genius villains, foible-filled heroes and funky heroines, eerie and exotic settings, outlandish maneuverings, sparky dialogue, and stage businesses that become trademarks of the authors or their characters. These devices lighten the basic "crime and punishment" theme. They lend variety and color. They sometimes, fortuitously, turn out to be integral parts of the plot. These ancillary elements make mystery writing an entertainment for the author, too.

If the morality play was meant to raise alarums about the transgressions of the fifteenth century, the modern-day mystery writer certainly mirrors the mayhem of the twentieth century. Not everyone can become a hotshot crime reporter on a big newspaper daily. Not every writer wants to. Mystery writers especially would rather take the raw material from their imaginations and create their own crimes and to solve them without the help of computers, the FBI or the local psychic. They can create a far more credible story, more gut-satisfying situations, when they're not bound by reality. The elements are the same: a crime, a victim, a perpetrator, germane facts and a solution. But in the prismatic world of the mystery, the good storyteller manipulates these elements to draw out the story to its last intrinsic word's worth, to keep the reader in suspense.

We're going to talk about these elements. We're going to list them, describe them and pinpoint their uses. When this is done, you will know what goes into writing a mystery. The only elements that you need to supply are a strong desire to write one and a steady confidence in your own talent.

CHAPTER 1

GENRES
WITHIN THE GENRE

EVERY SO OFTEN I will read in a mystery review column that "So-and-So's mystery is good enough to qualify as a mainstream novel" or "is novel-like in structure" or "is far better written than one expects in this field." This seems condescending. Why couldn't the reviewer have said, "This is a well-written, well-structured mystery"? It is true that there will always be some mysteries that are better written or more solidly constructed than others, but if a mystery is an especially good example of its kind, must it be taken out of its kind? Is this the reward reviewers deem appropriate? Frog into prince? Sow's ear into silk purse? Is the mystery essentially a scullery maid who, by the magic of the reviewers' praise, becomes queen for a day? I would be willing to bet such reviewers are either stringers or were borrowed from the sports page.

Apparently these reviewers are unaware that half the books on *The New York Times* Best Sellers list are murder mysteries. A recent one is John Gregory Dunne's *True Confessions,* which featured two brothers—a monsignor and a police detective—and the murder of a prostitute, and which became a very good movie. *The Name of the Rose* by Umberto Eco was also on the Best Sellers list for many weeks. It is a novel about medieval morality which encompasses seven murders in its six hundred pages.

In his preface to *The Mystery Story* (edited by John Ball), William D. McElroy estimates that there have been fifty thousand mystery stories published. Multiply each reading by a modest ten thousand and you have 500 million readers since the inception of the genre. There is no doubt that the mystery has held its own in the field of literature. As it brings in more and more variation within its form to keep abreast of its time, it will continue to attract talented authors and avid readers.

The mystery is neither above nor below other kinds of writing. It is simply itself. It is characterized by its own rules and is judged by its use of those rules. It makes no claim to being a deliberate reflection of our age, a novel of manners or a mirror held up to life. It is, as Graham Greene said, "an entertainment."

It is not an easy genre to write in. It has strict guidelines—introduce your action quickly, play fair, have a believable solution, and many others. It involves a great deal of juggling to accommodate motivation and subsequent actions. There is no such thing as a simple, "linear" plot in a mystery, though a good mystery reads that way. You may start with A and go to C before you can bring in B, and then introduce E, which is a subplot of D. This example is an exaggeration, but not by much. The point is that it would be wise for you, as a beginning writer, to work out the plot from the beginning through the middle and to the end before you begin writing. A mystery is essentially a novel of action with a theme and must work toward a resolution of that theme. There is no room for loose ends or irrelevant material, and there is absolutely no changing course in midstream.

Creating mystery characters also involves rules. Characters, once described, must be consistent in their attitudes and their actions. They must be rounded enough to be believable, but because they are essentially agents for forwarding the action, "deep" psychological character studies tend to draw the interest away from the theme and blunt the thrust of working toward a solution. The characters in the mystery field are important for what they do or for what they represent more than for who they are. Of course, their actions spring from who they are, but they must be tailored to fit the theme of the book.

Background has grown increasingly important as the subgenres have expanded, and as a greater number of authors with wider interests are attracted to the mystery field. Like characters, background is tailored to fit the theme, for background, however exotic or crammed with expertise, is meant to create a mood that will enhance the theme.

What is meant by *theme*? Theme can be broken down into two elements. The first is the choice of the crime—say, murder. The second is the author's attitude toward the crime—here, of murder. Will the story end with the cool, dispassionate workings of justice? Does the author want the wronged characters to claim an eye for an eye? Will some of the characters "deserve" to die? Are *all* murders senseless? Or just some? An author's personal, pragmatic view of crime will work its way in and be most dramatically portrayed in mystery writing.

Fortunately, as we shall see, there is wide latitude for operating within these rules. The rules themselves are basically very simple, and if adhered to, in spirit at least, offer solid springboards for many variations.

With the proliferation of subgenres, the term "mystery" is almost a misnomer now, but it does serve, for brevity's sake, to identify all novels that deal exclusively with crime and punishment. Publishers are getting out from under this umbrella and are calling the subgenres by their own names: detective, caper, romantic suspense, police procedurals, etc. This is good merchandising because it identifies the kinds of ambience, characters and even plots the reader can expect.

The identification of the kinds of crime markets means latitude for you, too. You can create a "world" you are comfortable with, using characters you "know" best and the kinds of mean streets they would "naturally" walk down. You can choose your own subgenre.

Eight modern subgenres are popular reading in the mystery field. I will describe them as I have absorbed them from my own reading and editing. Perhaps one of them will pique your interest enough to try it out. Remember that each of them offers as many variations as there are readers of this book, and you will certainly have your own input to offer—your own uniqueness.

I have not included adventure and spy novels, which have more to do with exploitative deeds than with whodunit, nor have I included horror novels, which fall into the gothic. I have deliberately left out the locked-room mystery, which had its heyday in the thirties and forties with writers like John Dickson Carr and Ellery Queen. The locked-room device played an important part of the plot with these earlier writers, but contemporary authors, writing for a more sophisticated audience, have soft-pedaled the means of entry and exit—the howdunit—in favor of the interplay of their characters—the whodunit and whydunit. At this writing I can think of only two authors who have used this purely cerebral exercise of howdunit, and then only in a modest way: Richard Forrest, in *A Child's Garden of Death*, and Orania Papazoglou, in *Sweet, Savage Death*.

I have also not touched upon the *roman à clef*, in which real-life events are transmuted into novelistic form, as in Meyer Levin's *Com-*

pulsion, a fictionalized version of the Loeb-Leopold case. It has always been my impression that the real events of a murder case are more interesting to read than their reshaping into fiction. If you remember, Levin's novel became the basis for Alfred Hitchcock's movie production of *Rope,* and the two young men in the movie could not have been further from what the real murderers were like. Probably the most famous example we have of a *roman à clef* is Edgar Allan Poe's *The Mystery of Marie Rôget,* which he based on newspaper accounts of the murder of a young woman, Mary Cecilia Rogers, whose body was found in the New Jersey swamps. Her murder was never solved—not even by Poe!

THE PRIVATE EYE NOVEL

An author I know who writes police procedurals sneers at the private eye novel. "Unrealistic," she says, of the main character. "A real private eye doesn't have the manpower or the facilities to do the work of the police. At best, he serves subpoenas or tails wandering husbands." She is comparing apples to oranges. Real-life detectives perform vital services that the police would not be in a position to perform. They are hired in cases of industrial espionage, they are go-betweens in kidnappings and jewel thefts, they zero in on missing persons more specifically than police APBs can. Like the police, they have electronics equipment, polygraphs, fingerprint kits and sketch artists. And, of course, they are licensed and bonded to ensure the client a fair shake. The essential difference here, the operative word is: *private.* Some cases are simply not within the province of the police, and some clients prefer to keep their problems within the family.

As for the private eye novel being "unrealistic," again the sneering author misses the point. Nobody has ever claimed that the private eye novel has to *be* realistic to *seem* realistic. And it provides a marvelous scope for writers by working both horizontally and vertically.

By *horizontally,* I mean the private eye covers a lot of ground—by car, foot and plane; he goes into nursing homes, morgues, bars, brothels, girls' schools and consulates—anywhere there are people. The mobile private eye has an unlimited range of milieu.

By *vertically,* I mean when the private eye meets these people, he digs down and gets underneath their surfaces and discovers facets that would not be brought out in police interrogations—everything from voyeurism to incest—and which provide clues that are germane to the case.

In the literature of the past, the private eye was often a parody. He drank and wenched hard and consorted with seedy characters. His methods were not much different from those of the culprits he was tracking; he often worked outside the law. Since those early, crude days, the private eye has grown up. He has been given attributes that make him a more rounded, more interesting human being. He seldom has a wife but is either divorced or has a sometimes-live-in girlfriend. He is hardly ever promiscuous. He is literate, likes music, appreciates art and goes hunting and fishing. He dresses well but casually and knows his way around dessert spoons. He is often a college graduate. Sometimes he is an ex-cop, a background which provides either bitterness about his past or convenient contacts with old buddies still on the force.

He is psychologically more complex than his predecessors, yet less urbane and more flappable. He has the potential for violence, but more often violence is done to him. As I have mentioned, he is hardly ever a family man, in order to remain a freewheeling agent, but he has a deep sense of family which gets transmuted into a custodial role toward his clients; he needs people who need his protection.

There is one school that says the private eye should be outwardly colorful, to give him uniquely identifying marks, especially if he is to become a series character: He has a physical prowess that attracts violence to him; he uses the jargon of the street in dealing with the street people; he wears outlandish clothes, loves children, has a garage full of vintage cars.

Another school emphasizes an exotic background for him: He is a familiar figure in Las Vegas. He is around the racetrack a lot. He has an office near the wholesale fruit and vegetable markets. He is a theater buff.

A third school is concerned only peripherally with his outer traits: He could pass unnoticed in a crowd (which is a plus in his trade). It is his unusual interior makeup that is most relevant. This character is an extremely independent person, too much so at times. He has the offbeat, slightly eccentric insight of the born loner and he sometimes thinks of himself as a born loser. He states his hefty fee up front at the first client interview; thereafter, money is simply something he spends to find out what he wants to know. If he sits around a plush bar sipping Courvoisier, you can bet he is on a stake-out for a Mr. Big. He is sybaritic and he is not a good businessman.

He is intelligent, of course. He is analytical when facts need to be correlated. He is intuitive when impressions need sorting out. He is extremely observant of his surroundings, whether it is to describe a scam operation, a stolen-goods warehouse, or a pair of scruffy shoes. He is acutely aware of people's mannerisms, speech and clothes. He is aware of complexions, body odors, body language, dental work and nervous tics. And he is lavish in his desire to share these observations with the reader. Not only does he keep a sharp eye open for these items, which could turn out to be clues, he is also a born chronicler.

The primary attribute of the private eye is his unique sense of justice, and this is the *theme* of all private eye novels. Because he is licensed by the state, he knows the law and respects it for its inhibitory restrictions as much as for its safeguarding purposes, and he usually stays within the law to protect his license. But his private ideas of what is legal and what is not transcend the written statutes if the law goes against his own conscience or is at variance with his client's interests. For instance, if his client is being wrongly subjected to a police vendetta, he will hide the client until he proves the client's innocence, at great risk to himself. He is a Knight Errant in windbreaker and corduroys.

Sometimes the private eye will have a partner—Keogh & Cudahy, Pvt. Investigators. This means splitting up the action as well as the rewards. It means working the plot on a double level, which can increase the tension or water it down. The partner could be a girlfriend, though usually in a minor role. This (mostly) excludes her as a suspect and offers a valid reason for including love and/or sex. This gives an added dimension to the private eye and helps to pad out the story.

I use *pad* advisedly. Seldom is the love interest an integral part of the story. It is used as a breathing space between sleuthing episodes. The private eye will cook an exotic meal for the girlfriend prior to or after taking her to bed. Period. She is occasionally used in a subplot when the bad guys kidnap her for leverage. Love and sex are background only, and not nearly as important a background as the layout of the warehouse containing the stolen merchandise or The Strip where he prowls at night. As the private eye becomes more fleshed out and the milieu becomes more diverse, the unimportance of the sex theme is the last bulwark of the classic detective form. The Knight Errant, it seems, still wants his Lady Fair sitting demurely under the canopy, and not jousting at the tourney with him.

This composite portrait of the private eye, private investigator, detective—whatever you choose to call him—is based on a lot of reading, but is in no way meant to seem complete. Each author will develop his or her own ideal private eye—will add to this portrait or disagree with it. It is meant only as a primer.

There are four authors I would recommend in this subgenre: First is John D. MacDonald, whose detective, Travis McGee, has appeared in twenty books (by present count), all of which contain a color in their titles. MacDonald's books have solid plotting and easy-flow narration; he is a master craftsman. McGee, however, can be parodistically macho at times. Robert B. Parker's plotting is not as tight and his private eye, Spenser, is a cream puff of a detective who spends as many pages proving how emotionally vulnerable he is as he spends chasing down culprits. Lawrence Block's private eye, Matthew Scudder, is a recovering alcoholic, and he seems to me to be a more genuinely vulnerable human being. Jack Livingston's detective, Joe Binney, faces another interesting handicap: he is deaf.

What about the distaff side—the woman detective? She first appeared in print some 125 years ago. The first, a Mrs. Paschal, saw the light of day in 1861 (or 1864, depending on which literary historian you read). The writer was anonymous. At least a dozen other English writers followed with their women detectives. In the United States, Louisa May Alcott supported her indigent family by writing mysteries for a decade or so before she wrote *Little Women*. Penny thrillers were a thriving market for the "female detective," short stories of terrible doings and brave, resourceful heroines. Many of the characters were ensconced in full-length novels, as well.

Women detectives abound in the twentieth century, too. Among the women writers of the thirties and forties who created them were Mary Roberts Rinehart, Mignon G. Eberhart, Leslie Ford and Josephine Tey. Among the men creating women detectives were Stuart Palmer, Paul Gallico, Rex Stout and Erle Stanley Gardner writing as A. A. Fair. In the fifties and sixties, Joyce Porter, Dorothy Uhnak and Lillian O'Donnell developed colorful women detectives. There are many creators of female detective characters whom I have not listed, but these authors' women seem to me the most memorable.

Certainly the most enduring such writer is Agatha Christie. Jane Marple made her novel-length debut in 1930. Like Mrs. Christie herself, Miss Marple was the product of the waning years of the Victorian era. Both ladies gracefully combined the stalwart values of the nineteenth century with the pragmatism of the twentieth century for more than three decades. In *The Body in the Library* (1942), Miss Marple is described as "an old lady, with a sweet, placid, spinsterish face and a mind that has plumbed the depths of human iniquity." Miss Marple was only about sixty then,* yet throughout the book she is described as "old"—at an age to be shelved, yet still kicking; a Victorian throwback. She comes across as snobbish, shrewd and, when the occasion calls for it, compassionate. She has no visible means of support, yet she lives moderately well. Aside from a nebulous nephew, she has no family. It is as if she were wrapped in a cocoon to observe life rather than to live it. In her cases it is only her clues that prove to be germane, yet the actual legwork and confrontations are performed by the police and other characters. Depending on how you view her, Miss Marple is a cop-out as a character or is intelligently unobtrusive.

Creators of modern-day women detectives have shown far more leeway with their characters. Their detectives drink, smoke, go to bed with their lovers, and often share their most personal thoughts with the reader. They are on scene constantly. Like their counterparts of a hundred years ago, they are intelligent and courageous. Like their modern-day male counterparts, they are careful chroniclers when it comes to describing characters, moods and scenes. They are subjected to violence and they carry licensed guns which they use as a last resort. They are inclined to pay attention to their hair and clothes, and they are aware of the difference between an appreciatively appraising look and a leer. (But then you will find chauvinistic peccadilloes on the spear side: the macho male detective who *does* leer and who is proud of his eighty-dollar jogging shoes.) Like their brethren, they solve their cases by hard, slogging work and occasional flashes of insight.

I think three authors who have created women private eyes within the last five years are worth mentioning. Sara Paretsky has created V. I. Warshawski, who works out of Chicago and has a good eye for her environment. In her first book, her detective seemed to place an inordinate emphasis on her clothes in the same chapter in which she bettered a grown man at karate. She was an uneasy amalgam of derring-do and feminine wiles. As Ms. Paretsky has written more, she has become more confident and so has her detective. Marcia Muller's private eye, Sharon McCone, is an attractive, freewheeling young woman who has a nice balance of sweetness and cynicism and a good sense of her San Francisco Bay Area background. A third, Sue Grafton, gives her

*In *The Mirror Crack'd* (1962), twenty years later, Miss Marple is depicted as an octogenarian. This is the book, by the way, that Mrs. Christie dedicated to Margaret Rutherford, who played a marvelous Miss Marple on the screen.

mysteries "alphabetical" titles (*A Is For Alibi*, *B Is For Burglar*, etc.). Her private eye, Kinsey Millhone, is a laid-back southern California divorcée and ex-cop who drives a beat-up VW, wears jeans and boots on the job and carries a .32 automatic. She keeps her action going with interviews over a wide territory. The precise descriptions of her characters and her detailed local color reinforce her solid story lines.

The opening scene for too many private eye novels in the past began like this: He (yes, he) is sitting at his desk, flipping through unpaid bills and junk mail, when this beautiful blonde/redhead/brunette walks sinuously into his office. . . . Eventually the story develops and events come tumbling across the pages to their satisfying denouement. Such an opening today would be a parody of a parody, or should be.

Consider it a challenge to introduce the private eye in an original way. For instance, the crime takes place first and the private eye is introduced in chapter 2. Or the private eye witnesses a crime. Or if you want the first encounter with the client to open the book, arrange a meeting in a restaurant or in a park. Better yet, open in the client's home; the reader will learn more sooner about the client. Granted, a private eye's office is the base of operations, but he or she is by nature a mobile operator.

Mobility is an operative word for the structure of this genre. I heard one mystery editor at a symposium complain that the private eye novel was "just one interview after another." It is more than that. There is a constant searching out of suspects, victims, police, records, murder weapons, getaway cars, motives, crime scenes; a constant backtracking and double-checking. In subplots, the private eye is made privy to family skeletons and current sins which are relevant or red herrings, according to the person being interviewed. Yes, there are many contacts between the private eye and the people in the case, but there is no need to apologize for this dynamic structure. Characterization, color and action are accomplished in these contacts.

There is one other detective category—the amateur. And this breaks into two subcategories.

The first is the professional person who discovers a crime that takes place in his or her field of expertise, a field colorful enough to attract the reader. The professional person may not go to the police, or the police may not want to cooperate because there is no body of evidence. Out of professional pride and interest, it is up to the protagonist to track down the culprit, who is often another professional.

What kinds of professionals appear in mysteries? Just about any kind you can imagine, and some you would probably never think of as suitable sleuths.

Here is a short list of the professionals I have encountered in my readings. There is no reason they cannot be used again, and, besides, these forty-five barely scratch the surface.

Actor	Meter Reader
Antiques dealer	Nurse
Aircraft pilot	Opera star
Banker	Paramedic
Bartender	Pathologist
Chef	Pawnbroker
Clairvoyant	Philatelist
College student	Postal inspector
Cryptographer	Priest
Deep sea/scuba diver	Professor
Dentist	Psychologist
Diplomat	Psychiatrist
Doctor	Publisher
Engineer	Rabbi
Enologist	Sailor
Fashion designer	Scientist
Fisherman (commercial)	Sports figure
Hospital administrator	Stripteaser
Janitor	TV/radio personality
Journalist	Veterinarian
Lawyer	Wrangler
Librarian	Writer
Madam	

Authors have chosen their professionals as protagonists by one of three methods:

1. The authors themselves are professionals. They are familiar with their fields and the procedures and vocabularies that go with them. John R. Feegel, who writes convincingly of doctors and lawyers, is himself a doctor *and* a lawyer. Justin Scott, some of whose books are set at sea, is an expert small-boat sailor. There have been mysteries that have featured writers as the hero or her-

oine, and who could better describe this kind of protagonist than a writer?

2. The second method involves research; you haunt hospitals or read law tomes or take a short course in cryptography. You ask people in these fields for advice and reading lists on their subjects. You immerse yourself so thoroughly that when it comes to writing the book, your expertise does not read like short lectures interspersed here and there, but rather flows out of the book's theme. We will get into this second method in more detail in the chapter on background.

3. The third method uses a much simpler approach than the other two but is just as demanding: observing everyday people in your life, or people you have at least a nodding acquaintance with. They do not necessarily need to be among the obvious professionals, but their jobs are specific ones: janitor, pawnbroker, clergy, bartender. They have their own bodies of job knowledge which are more easily grasped and just as open to plot ideas.

To give you a notion of how professionals are used as amateur sleuths, here are two ideas for opening scenes. Each kicks off with an intriguing problem arising from their backgrounds:

An antiques dealer had been given a Hepplewhite chest on consignment from an estate that had been broken up by the death of a well-known collector. Examining the chest, the dealer found a note between a drawer bottom and its frame. The note read

> In the event of my untimely death, pls follow thru on L249. Sotheby.
> 6/8. Will know what to do.

The figures, of course, were the number of a lot to be sold by the famous auction house, Sotheby Parke Bernet, on June 8th—three days from then. But *who* will know *what* to do? Puzzled and concerned, the dealer attended the auction, only to learn that lot 249 had been withdrawn.

Two retired seamen were hired to sail a thirty-six-foot Albin trawler down the Intracoastal Waterway from Norfolk to Miami. As they headed for a night's anchorage in Marsh Harbor, South Carolina, they saw a body dumped into the water and two figures run back to a Jaguar parked on the pier. The next morning the Charleston *News & Courier* reported that a prominent yachtsman had died by drowning, and that a suicide note had been found in his study. The man, according to the coroner's report, had ingested an appreciable amount of barbiturates shortly before his death.

Because the crimes are peculiar to their settings, the solutions must also arise from those settings, as well as from the professional's expertise. The antiques dealer knew everybody in the trade, including the shady ones. The seamen knew their tides and so were solid witnesses to the fact that the yachtsman didn't drown in the same area of the harbor where the body was discovered.

Recent mysteries using professional amateurs are *Asia Rip* by George Foy, in which the sleuth is a commercial fisherman; *Billingsgate Shoal* by Rick Boyer, which features a dentist as the protagonist; and *An Equal Opportunity Death* by Susan Dunlap, whose heroine is a meter reader for a utilities company.

The second kind of amateur detective is the plain, ordinary citizen who is the victim of fate.

He stumbles upon a crime in progress and, by being a Good Samaritan, gets involved. He chases the criminal away and becomes a target for revenge, or is used by the cops as a judas goat, or seeks his own revenge.

Or, he is in the way of a ruthless Somebody who wants to use his business as a drug drop or a money laundry, and finds himself dealing with the local Mafia.

Or, his house is the only one standing in the way of a greedy contractor. If it is his entire neighborhood that stands in the way, he becomes the vulnerable leader of a citizen's group.

The crime does not have to be murder, nor does the amateur detective have to retaliate in kind if it is. That would be a heavy burden to lay on an ordinary citizen and, realistically, he is not equipped to deal with it, though his pursuer(s) may have murderous intentions. What can be dealt with in a realistic way is to bring out attributes he didn't know he had: bravery, resourcefulness and a deep-down anger that is aroused by the injustice of the situation. These attributes are developed in proportion to the danger that threatens him, and doubled when his loved ones are threatened. If the private eye is the Knight Errant, the private citizen is the Good Shepherd. Other threats are more minor but fit in with the amateur's role of nonsuperman. His job is in jeopardy, he loses face with his colleagues, he shakes the faith of his family, he damages his health, he wrecks his bank account. Not earthshaking, but rough enough for a guy on a fixed salary and a need to get along with his peers and reestablish his status quo.

His status quo includes fixing the toaster (finally!), resuming Sunday morning golf, spending time with his clients and his family—the normal activities he has sacrificed during the time his life has been turned upside down. The reader can identify with a man like this, but keep in mind that he has a little something extra that lets him rise to the uncommon challenge, that makes him worth writing about.

Two good examples of the "ordinary man" taking the law into his own hands are *Death Wish* by Brian Garfield and *Fighting Back* by Charles Alverson.

Because the mystery field is still festooned with chauvinism, the heroine has been pretty much relegated to the genre of romantic suspense, with the muscular male coming in the nick of to save her from a fate worse than. The authors of the few really good Jane Citizen novels have turned the so-called vulnerabilities around by giving the heroine options. Lacking physical prowess, she has no compunctions about ignoring the rules that males have established. She may be just as reluctant to kill someone, but lacking muscle, she feels she has the right to a gun, knife or baseball bat to equalize the struggle. Or, forgoing the blood-in-the-eye instinct, she calls upon her brain—and there, at least in mysteries, she is more than equal to her slow-witted adversaries.

While a man's castle, business or honor is his stake, a woman's stakes have been her body and her children. Rape has a built-in backlash; it is difficult to prove and the most difficult felony to prosecute successfully. The defense attorney's classic tactic is to malign the woman's reputation: She allegedly sleeps around. She dresses "sexy." Whatever the circumstances, she was asking for it. Until recently, a woman's alleged promiscuity *was* admissible evidence. Her past deeds, if any, are now protected by rape-shield laws in all 50 states, and on May 20, 1990, the Supreme Court backed this ruling. Still, many rape cases go unreported because of threats or unwanted publicity and never reach the courts, leaving her high and dry and her assailant scott-free.

How does she avenge herself? The woman can work an entrapment scam, where the rapist ends up accused of another crime, this one court-sure because he had been so cocksure. If you consider rape a capital crime, you can have the woman do away with the rapist when he comes back to rape her again. This offers you a good balance for the book: the first rape, the second attempt and the murder, balanced against the disposal of the body. This could be the book's resolution, or you could add other complications which further justify her act. Her satisfaction—and the reader's—in bringing the rapist to a kind of justice is enhanced by the pleasure of revenge against both the man and the legal system.

A more complicated set of maneuvers is used when the woman's children are threatened. They are unwitting victims and the emotions of surprise, fright and bewilderment work to the threatener's advantage. The mother must deal with the children's reactions as well as safeguarding the children physically. But first she must deal with her own reactions. What are the threat and the who and the why? If she sorts out these answers in a short time, she will be more able to cope with the situation. If she is kept in the dark about the who, what and why, going on the offensive is going to be more difficult for her. In fact, it isn't fair to the mother character to leave her so unarmed, nor to the reader who wants to see a fair fight, not a victim dumped into an emotional bath that verges on bathos. We all know that the mother is going to win out in the long run, so she must be given the wit and strength to do so. If possible, she enlists the help of the older children, usually teenagers. This gives the author additional characters to work with. The children, by their very age, develop into something more than they were at the story's beginning. They get a crash course in maturity.

The variant of this plot is the use of the husband as a secondary character. This brings about yet another set of emotions: Whose mode of action is the better? The analytical father's or the instinctual tiger-mother's? If the threatener isn't a psychopath from out of the blue, then the most abrasive question in this subplot is: Was it the husband/father's fault that this situation came about? Is it *his* enemy taking vengeance on the entire family? When the threat has been defused and their lives return to normal, will family relations have to be rebuilt? (A fairly good portrayal of a Jane Citizen fighting the odds is in Carolyn Crane's *Woman Vanishes*.)

THE POLICE PROCEDURAL NOVEL

Next to stories about doctors and lawyers, stories about police run a close third, probably because they affect our lines in much the same ways that the other two do: all three represent bastions of safety and order, and so they are figures of authority.

We have an uneasy alliance with the police. Because they are guardians of the law, we set them up on pedestals, but because we are

leery of arbitrary law enforcement, we give them clay feet. We cheer
when a cop saves a child from a burning building and we gloat when a
crooked cop is exposed.

A good police procedural novel capitalizes on this dichotomy and
does its best to maintain a balance between effective and ineffective police work. More often, though, cops are shown in a good light. They
are portrayed as hardworking, honest people who slog along like any
nine-to-fiver, with a few miracles to their credit every now and then.
The occasional portrayal of the dishonest cop highlights the honesty of
the others.

The police procedural author has to be something of a sociologist
because the precinct is a microcosm of the world at large—here, of the
seedier aspects of the world. The author has to have a sense of community and a feeling for the interactions of the kinds of people in it. If the
community is a homogeneous one, there will be a relatively stable order to it. If it is made up of diverse groups, which happens especially in
large cities, there is going to be a conflict of values and a constant maneuvering in the pecking order, and the result produces clashes of
priorities. The precinct cops, who are the monitors of these clashes,
have to be streetwise. They have to know when to act tough and when
to show compassion. They have to learn to deal with pressures within
themselves: when to tighten up and when to hang loose. There is a
constant interplay of tension, both on the street and in themselves.
This tension, adeptly balanced, keeps both the cops and the readers on
their toes.

If this is the genre you want to work in, then it would be well to get
to know your cop on the beat and to make visits to your precinct house.
Police departments have community affairs officers, either at police
headquarters or at the precinct house itself. Both HQ personnel and
precinct officers helped me put together the information I have gar-
nered for this chapter, information based on a city of 2.6 million population. If your city or town is smaller, your information may be different
from mine, but not appreciably so.

There are four main elements that go into a police procedural novel. They are 1) the precinct, 2) the precinct house, 3) the police and 4)
the criminals, victims and the rest of the population. Which of these
you lay out first is a matter of personal judgment. You may have an
idea for a specific cop or a series of crimes peculiar to that precinct or
maybe the interdepartmental politics and the foul-ups it causes. Initially, it doesn't matter in which order you develop these elements in your

mind. The final product will show your preference—or nonpreference—anyway.

Let us start with the precinct. It is the biggest and, on the surface, the most complex. First, give it a name: Central, South, Midtown, Greenwood, 84th. How big is it? How many square miles or square blocks does it encompass? This is determined by a combination of factors: population, crime rate and the potential hazards in the area—airports, parks, highways, wherever there is a transient population.

Furnish the precinct. Give it grocery stores, liquor stores, book stores, hardware stores, TV and stereo shops, dress shops, betting parlors, massage parlors, ice cream parlors, newsstands, bars, Laundromats, cleaners, movie houses, theaters, restaurants, fast-food joints, churches, schools, hospitals and firehouses.

You will have transportation: bus lines, subways, els, taxi stands, parking lots and public garages. What are the times of light and heavy traffic?

Are there parks, freeways, thruways, highways? Winding, tree-lined avenues or straight-as-die, potholed streets? Are they named First or Thirty-fifth or Dubois Avenue and Watermelon Lane?

Does your area have single-family homes, apartment houses, projects, hotels, slums, light industry or a mixture?

What is the weather like? Do your people freeze in winter and swelter in summer? Or is it mild year-round?

What is the ethnic makeup? Are the people predominantly Irish, Polish, Jewish, Hispanic, Black? Artsy, all-American, wealthy, middle-class, blue-collar? Is the area safe, dangerous, noisy, quiet? Do the citizens look upon cops as their natural enemies or do they invite them in for morning coffee? Are the people crime-conscious and cooperative or just crime-conscious?

You may want to lay the precinct out in a diorama, or you can add any of these components as you develop your plot. For instance, a hold-up in a liquor store puts that component on the map. Interviewing a mugging victim introduces the emergency room of a hospital. A cop tailing a suspect will stop at a newsstand to buy a pack of gum to cover his cover. You can open a scene on an icy street in front of the precinct house. The action might start with raiding a massage parlor. You need to have a general idea of the area and then zero in on specific locations. For instance, you have probably been in many liquor stores, but now you will go in with a discriminating eye to check out a liquor store's location on the block, the floor plan, the number of employees, where the cash register is, how the counters are lined up and whether the window displays hide the action from the street. The more details you describe, the more realistic the scene will be and the more easily you can move your characters around. By *describe*, I mean you will have those details in your head, whether they go down on paper or not. Diagrams are a good idea.

The precinct is going to be your arena, and it will contain all of the crimes that happen in it.

I have read many police procedural novels, but to get a feel for the real thing, I went to my precinct house and spent part of an afternoon looking around and talking with the officers on watch. (I called first.)

It is a two-story brick-and-glass building located on a quiet street where the cops park their cars halfway on the sidewalk, like deputies' horses lined up at the tethering post. On the ground floor is a large, open area, fifty feet by thirty, with a twenty-foot ceiling. Along one wall is a long counter, serviced by half a dozen men and women officers working on reports and answering phones. Opposite the counter is a recessed waiting room which contains three carefully aligned rows of battered plastic chairs in nursery school colors. Behind them are flashy vending machines with the usual junk food. On one wall there is a large bulletin board thumbtacked with "Wanted" flyers. The entire area doubles as the muster room for roll call. The walls are painted institutional green and there is a faint, institutional Lysol smell. The years of transient traffic have imbued the area with a tired look, but the sunlight streams across the linoleum floor. Off to the sides are doors leading to the captain's office, the Records and Administration Section, and the branch office for the district attorney.

A scuffed stairway leads to the low-ceilinged second floor: the Investigating (interrogation) Unit, the Senior Citizens' Robbery Unit, the Pedophilia Squadroom, the detectives' bullpen, a mesh-enclosed holding cell and a fingerprint and photo lab. There is a small room set off by itself for juvenile interrogation. On the wall opposite the door is a blockletter sign:

JUVENILE REPORTS *NOT* AUTHORIZED
1) felonies 2) unlawful assemblies 3) photographable misdemeanors

AUTHORIZED FOR
1) petit larceny 2) stranded 3) runaways
4) missing 5) prostitution 6) drugs*

*I was told that when a juvenile reaches his or her sixteenth birthday, all records are destroyed.

The rooms range from large and airy to shoebox-windowless and are furnished with nondescript desks, chairs and filing cabinets. Everywhere are the ubiquitous bulletin boards with their flyers, regulations and announcements of intramural social events.

I was given a rundown on the precinct's arsenal: the official sidearm is a .38-caliber, six-shot Smith & Wesson or Colt revolver with a four-inch barrel. Plainclothes (known as "soft" clothes) officers' .38s have two-inch barrels for easier concealment. For heavy action—riots and snipers—they use .357-caliber or 9-millimeter sidearms for better firepower, along with shotguns and rifles and tear gas.

Patrol officers use walkie-talkies for radio communications; they also use them now in squad cars for better mobility. The radios are tuned to the precinct's area frequency. Officers in the precinct I visited use computers for administration and personnel and have a tie-in with a statewide computer for checking for stolen vehicles and other property and for wanted or missing persons.

And they fill out a variety of forms. The UF61 is a complaint form, which records the crime. An arrest form follows, based on the UF61, which in turn is followed by a DD5, the detectives' field report on the crime. There is a monthly activity report which lists an officer's formal contacts and summonses.

A suspect is apprehended on the basis of a complaint form and is brought in and booked on an arrest form. Then the arrestee is searched, fingerprinted, photographed, and put in a holding cell. The prints, along with a query for outstanding warrants, are fed into the statewide computer. With all data in, the arresting officer then speaks to the assistant district attorney down the hall concerning arraignment and bail. Depending on the computer printout and the nature of the crime, the suspect is kept in jail, allowed bail, or released on his or her own recognizance. The officer may eventually appear in court as a witness, but from here on the legal system takes over from the police.

This is a once-over-lightly treatment of the goings-on in a particular precinct house, but it should be enough to give you a foundation for your own questions when you visit a precinct yourself.

When you have the precinct diorama in place and when you have the precinct house layout thumbtacked in your mind or on *your* bulletin board, you can start thinking about the characters. As I have said, your idea for a novel may be triggered by a personality or an event, so the sequence of priorities I am putting down here is meant only as an overall blueprint. By all means, establish your own priorities; switch them around according to your own inspiration. Just keep in mind that the police procedural novel is documentary fiction and that, although the characters are the most important element, they must have convincing backgrounds.

An important part of the background, of course, is the roles the characters are assigned. Here is the *dramatis personae* for my precinct:

Commanding Officer, either a deputy inspector or a captain.

Administrative Lieutenant, who functions under the commanding officer.

Integrity Control (ICO) Lieutenant, who is in charge of personnel and records.

Five Watch Lieutenants, who see to the everyday running of the precinct.

Ten Sergeants. Two are anticrime softclothes persons; the other eight are on patrol in uniform.

One hundred forty-three patrol officers—on foot and in the ten squad cars, on the four traffic scooters and in a van (for picking up merchandise from unlicensed peddlers).

These 161 men and women oversee a steady precinct population of fifty-eight thousand, with twice that many transients. They work in eight-hour watches, 365 days of the year.

Profiling the police, like describing the precinct house, should involve field work. Try making friends with the cop on your beat. He or she might be cagey at first; loyalty, public relations and discretion will restrict the cop to complimenting you on your coffee and doughnuts. But if you assure this minion of the law that by the time the incidents get put down on paper not even the sergeant would recognize them, the cop will unbend. After all, who doesn't like talking about themselves, especially if it involves recounting daring exploits, near misses or babies delivered?

On the reverse side of the coin I have talked with one cop who delighted in running down one of her dumb colleagues—the one who almost got her shot. Another one I talked to said he had to get on the pad because of peer pressure, even though it went against his grain.

If you are interested in filling in the seedier side of law enforcement, there was a spate of nonfiction books on police corruption published in the seventies. You can find them in *Books in Print* and the *Subject Catalog* in your library under "Police Corruption." As I have said earlier in this chapter, the few bad guys make the good guys look even better, and it will add dimension to your profiles.

The slant of many cops' social lives is peculiar to their profession. Some officers claim they don't mix well with "civilians," including their own families. They have high-pressure jobs and their tensions often spill over into their private lives, and only other cops can understand this. Even when they are not tense, they can run into trouble. One cop told me a story to illustrate this point. "I go to parties only where there are going to be other cops, and I'll tell you why." He described a social gathering where *he* was accosted by a belligerent drunk, yet *he* was the one who was asked to leave. His host was apologetic but he "knew" that the sober cop was inherently more dangerous than the belligerent drunk. I mentioned earlier that our good citizens give the police clay feet. This host turned clay into mud.

The rogue cop is an interesting facet of the police procedural, but he is seldom the protagonist. His presence represents chaos in the social order and, as in all escapist literature, we want to end up with a balancing of the scales. Consequently, the majority of the characters are steady and knowledgeable human beings. Some of them have harmless little quirks or slightly peculiar physical features which make them identifiable from one book to the next. They have happy family lives or love affairs or are divorced or homosexual. They look upon the dishonest act with indignation or cynicism. They arm themselves with ghoulish senses of humor. They are crude and cruel, idealistic and softhearted—human emotions that, in them, show up in extra-sharp relief.

The fourth element of the police procedural encompasses the criminals, victims and other characters who are peripheral to the crimes. Once you have the background under your belt, this fourth element is an open road. You can set up *any* kind of crime. In fact, you can have lots of them, and should. However, do not load up to the point of confusion; your book then becomes a welter of names, and some of the crimes will get short shrift, dramatically speaking. The most effective structure I have seen has been to have one major crime running through the book, with lesser crimes to lighten the load. You can start with a crime or with a criminal and victim. However you do it, the three must ring true to the circumstances:

• A foxy lady is done in and the murderer, it is soon discovered,

is the rejected lover. But because he is the son of a powerful politico, the cops have to tread carefully and work doubly hard to make
a court-sure case. This is worth a lot of pages on the lady's shady
background and the colorful politico.

• You can spin out a story with a series of murders. Here, dere-
licts are being knocked off with disturbing regularity. It will take at
least two murders to establish a pattern, and the cops are in and
out of skidrow hotels *ad nauseam* talking with a lot of grungy characters. The murderer turns out to be a psycho ("I felt sorry for
them")—the most difficult kind of criminal to fathom and the
most difficult one to write about.

• A middle-aged, upright citizen is found stuffed in the trunk
of his car. His business partner, another upright citizen, has been
cooking the company's books and to avoid discovery, has dis-
posed of his partner in a way that suggests a gangland killing,
thus throwing the cops off for pages and pages. The seemingly ordinary person who makes one big sortie into crime packs a lot of
wallop as a character.

Along with the major criminals and victims are the minor ones
who serve to give variety and relief, sometimes comic relief, and
their crimes nowhere near match the intensity of the major ones.
They, too, can be drawn out at some length and can take on the appearance of a bright ribbon woven into the somber overall tapes-
try:

• An enterprising housewife has learned to milk the Laundro-
mat machines in the area.

• An inept numbers runner tries to take over a new territory.

• A local contractor is short-changing the nuns on the new St.
Bartholomew School for Indigent Boys, using shoddy materials
and scare tactics.

These minor crimes are usually allocated to the secondary detectives,
but on occasion they go to the primary detective as a thorn in his or her
side. ("As if I didn't have enough . . .")

"Peripheral" is a slight misnomer for the characters who are not
directly involved with the major crime—the witnesses, snitches, relatives, employers, *et al.* Each provides a piece of the puzzle. Some of
them have vital information. A few turn out to be dead ends (a form of
red herring). Like the private eye, the police do a lot of interviewing,
which allows you to introduce a colorful rogues' gallery.

There are three authors whose police procedural novels are well
worth reading because each of them handles this subgenre in a unique

way. Dorothy Uhnak has written three excellent books in this field: *The Bait*, *The Witness* and *The Ledger*. They feature a policewoman, Christie Opara, a widow with a small son. Mrs. Uhnak was herself a policewoman and her background and procedures ring with authenticity. Ed McBain's 87th Precinct series—there are well over a dozen books of them—will give you a flavor of a busy, large-city precinct. Dell Shannon has written many books in a series featuring Lt. Luis Mendoza of the Los Angeles Police Department. All three authors skillfully interlock the working and personal lives of their officers.

HEISTS, CAPERS AND KIDNAPPINGS:

The Busy Triumvirate

The smash-and-grab burglary of a small jewelry store is done in a matter of minutes. The burglar takes the half dozen bracelets to a local fence, who gives him forty cents on the dollar, and that is that until the burglar runs out of beer money again.

The heist is a smash-and-grab many times magnified. It involves a great deal of planning and, usually, backup money to implement the scheme. It has a cast of characters ranging in number from three to ten. The higher the stakes, the better guarded they are and the more difficult is the undertaking—and the more inventive the plot can be.

Here are the elements that go into the heist novel:

1. The target
2. The mastermind
3. The mastermind's cohorts
4. The expense money
5. The equipment
6. Diagrams and schedules
7. The heist
8. The getaway
9. The disposal of the equipment
10. The dividing of the spoils
11. The dispersal of the gang
12. The final outcome

This is a sound blueprint for the perfect heist, and once in a while newspaper headlines will report that just such a perfect crime did take place. But fiction readers want a final balancing out and the robbers caught in the end, no matter how much they have been cheered on during the heist. We will discuss the ways they are caught. First, though, let us briefly explore the twelve steps.

The target. The hallmarks of a heist are ingenuity and daring, and so, proportionately, the rewards must be great. The target is worth millions and is eagerly coveted by high-type fences representing special markets. It can be currency for the well-connected money launderer, paintings for an Arab sheik, stocks and bonds for an international broker, guns for an African republic. Because of its great worth, the target is housed in an "impregnable fortress" of some kind: a steel vault with four-foot walls, a museum with an alarm in every display case, a moving bullion-filled boxcar. It can be the proceeds from a tightly guarded apartment tower, a diamond center, the Vatican, the Tower of London or Fort Knox. Targets that will have narrower markets but will still be in great demand are found in plutonium plants, industrial blueprint shops, embassies, armories, arsenals, pharmaceutical houses and exotic-seed nurseries.

The handling of the spoils must be taken into account in considering them as a target. Are trucks needed? Special packaging? Camouflage? Cool temperatures? Are they so hot that the heisters will hold on to them for a time? In essence, are the spoils transportable as well as marketable?

The mastermind. He is a man with a superior intellect who is amoral, sardonic and cool-headed. Like any aggressive person gone awry, the mastermind has a cruel streak and uses it to advantage. He is urbane for the occasion and can be crude for the studied effect: a consummate actor. There is an aura of bitterness that prompts the reader to wonder what he would have been like had he used his talents honestly. For dramatic effect, the mastermind is physically imposing in some way. It can be as simple as having steel-gray eyes or a six-foot, five-inch frame; whatever the trait, it is used as a weapon. The mastermind can be as randy as a goat or as celibate as an ascetic, but he is in control either way. In fact, *control* is a key word for this character in every aspect of life.

The mastermind does not have to be a man. I remember one very good heist novel, *The Exhibit* by Leslie Hollander, in which the mastermind was a well-placed New York society woman, with friends who were well-placed in the entertainment and advertising worlds. The book opens just before the King Tutankhamen tomb exhibit is to go on display at the Metropolitan Museum of Art. The woman covets these treasures and, with the help of her imaginative friends, orchestrates a complicated and ingenious heist of the treasures.

However you choose to portray this character, two traits will be constant:

   • *The mastermind is an excellent organizer.* As with so many creative people, the idea comes to this creative mind as a whole, and it sees that details drop into their proper places at each stage of the plan. Clever at improvisation, this character has the flexibility to choose from equally attractive options and to adjust to last-minute changes. He or she is, from beginning to end, patient and careful and triple checks every planned move and piece of equipment.
   • *The mastermind handles people expertly.* Having verified their backgrounds and qualifications, the mastermind probes cohorts for personality flaws. If someone proves weak and indecisive, he is, with all diplomacy, let go and is given payment for travel expenses. The mastermind, to the reader's initial surprise, will approve of other flaws—dumb, blind trust; mean streaks; deep bitterness and inordinate greed—and use them to advantage, knowing when to bestow accolades and when to bear down hard. Like a lot of bright sociopaths, he or she is a master psychologist who is a smooth manipulator of people for his or her own gains.

The cohorts. The mastermind chooses cohorts with backgrounds just as shady as his or her own—ex-cons, old Army buddies (dishonorably discharged), people known from other jobs. They are picked for their special skills that are tailor-made for this particular heist. The number of cohorts is determined by the kind of heist and how easily the author can handle a group. For instance, a bank job requires someone who is good with plastique, an electronics expert, a couple of brawny fellows for tunnel-digging and a wheel man. The mastermind may also need a front person to buy the equipment, though that is usually in the hands of each expert. In one book (*The Leavenworth Irregulars* by William D. Blankenship) it took only three men because they had one thing in common: They were ex-Army men who knew their way around Fort Leavenworth and the ins and outs of the payroll sector. In another book, it took ten men to pull off a heist in a diamond center (there were innumerable stores to rob). This author kept his cast straight by emphasizing the roles of the leader and his lieutenant, using them as a hub for the rest of the gang to revolve around and refer to.

Authors also supply off-beat names to help the reader keep the cast straight. One author gave his characters numbers instead of names. The mastermind was #1, his lieutenant was #2, and so on through #7. It was a simple way to keep the scorecard, and it created an eerie effect.

The cohorts often have ongoing backgrounds, as further identification, during the planning—a bookie, a shaky marriage, physical problems (real or imagined) and superstitions. All of them are totally different in physique and personality, which keeps their identities straight in the reader's mind and forces the author to create a good blend and a good balance of personalities.

The expense money. This is for buying equipment and paying bribes. It is also needed for transporting the thieves to and from the crime area and for supporting them during the trial runs. Authors do not waste many pages on *how* the expense money is obtained. In fact, some never say where it has come from, other than the mastermind's pocket. Others, in passing, will refer to the proceeds from a previous heist, or will mention that, say, a museum heist is being underwritten by an anonymous art collector. If, however, you are trying to fill pages or have a clever idea in mind, you might pull off a smaller heist to get the money for the big one.

The equipment. This can range from a simple lock pick to a bulldozer. I have already mentioned shovels, plastique, and electronics equipment for dismantling alarms and surveillance systems. You would, of course, also use the last for bugging phones and listening to the tumblers in a safe. There are tools to buy: crowbars, screwdrivers, jacks, jimmies, glass cutters and suction cups. There are ladders, ropes, blankets and dollies. Beards, wigs, stocking masks, gloves, theatrical makeup and uniforms. Cars and trucks to steal. But if there is enough money, everything is bought legitimately; one cohort in a stolen automobile caught running a red light could put a crimp in the operation. Plane tickets have to be bought in advance. Passports and other forged documents must be obtained. Everything is paid for in advance—in cash. That way, there are no records left behind and, besides, thieves do not trust other thieves.

Diagrams and schedules. Keep them simple; the action will be complicated enough as it is. If it is, say, an office layout, draw the desk and chair, the two occasional chairs with the magazine rack between them. Throw in the location of the potted fern's floor stand only so that the electronics expert will not knock it over in the dark. What magazines are in the rack or whether the chairs are naugahyde or wicker is irrelevant. If it is an elaborate layout, such as an Army base or warehouse, send a scout in ahead of time and have that person make sketches to show the rest of the gang—and get it done before the book opens. As with the expense money, do not burden yourself with details that would take away pages from the heist itself. Trial runs, though, can add nicely to the suspense, and serve as an opportunity to size up the characters. And here is where schedules get their shakedowns.

It is easy to keep schedules simple if the heist takes place within a short evening or the few hours before the dawn. It is necessary to keep them simple, as linchpins for a multitude of complicated actions. You can cram a lot of detail into a short time more successfully than you can spread out details over a period of days. The longer the time you take, either for planning or for the heist or for both, the busier you will end up having to be to maintain suspense. This is fine if you work in snafus, last-minute changes, the loss of a cohort and acts of God.

Whether or not you use diagrams in the book itself and whether or not you spell out schedules in neat columns on page 86, make them up for yourself before you begin writing a word. You have to know where you are going and, as important, where you have been.

The heist. If you have worked out all of the steps we have talked about so far, the heist should be a snap to write. Each cohort is deployed to the proper place at the right time. You know from previous observation that the guard will be on the third floor when you enter on the first and will be on the second floor when you slip by to go to the third. You have brought in your own packing cases and, once they are filled with the goods, you dolly them to the shipping room where the company itself will mail them to the addresses you have labeled them with. Then the criminals clean up the little messes they made in drilling and replace the broken pane of glass, gather up their tools and slip quietly into the night.

The operation has been well-planned and smoothly executed. The reader will be satisfied and may even wonder what is going to happen next, but the very smoothness of the heist will lull the reader into complacency and you stand a chance of losing your audience right there.

There has to be tension throughout the operation: keeping track of the guards, being careful not to trip alarms, having to work by dimmed flashlights, having to work *quietly*. There will be a fumbling of tools, whispered consultations, muffled curses when a finger is pinched. When the multimillion-dollar goods are seen for the first time, there will be a reaction of awe, which can paralyze the thieves for precious minutes. The real pros will be alert only to the dangers at hand, but there will be at least one cohort who bears the added tension of wondering *What if . . .?*, and while that person is grappling with a crowbar, visions of cellblocks will go through his head, endangering the cohort's usefulness.

If there is a pervading sense that something could go wrong at any stage, it will add to the tension. If something does go wrong, that heightens the tension even more. The mastermind will improvise to correct the blunder, which heightens the interest:

● A guard changes route after having heard an unexpected noise (blunder). The guard will have to be taken care of, without alerting the other guards.

● A different kind of alarm system has recently been installed in the new wing. It will take nerve-wracking minutes to figure it out.

● The cohort wondering *What if?* gets cold feet and time is lost persuading the waverer to continue or putting the person out of commission. (Flaws in the cohorts will have to be telegraphed to the reader before the heist.)

The getaway. The mastermind has timed the operation to a fine point. As the mastermind and the others have completed the job, a truck backs up to take the goods and sedans are there to spirit the criminals away. In the perfect heist, they leave silently and invisibly. A final piece of tension is inserted when a glove is unknowingly dropped or a footprint is left in a flower bed or a car will not start.

The disposal of the equipment. The truck and the cars are abandoned, sold or returned to the rental agency. License plates may be changed. Back at the thieves' headquarters, gloves, masks, ropes and the likes are burned. Clothes are changed. In a reverse process, passports and plane tickets are dispersed and out-of-pocket monies are reimbursed.

The dividing of the spoils. The nature of the haul determines how and when it is divided. If it is "clean" money, it is simple enough to put it into piles within an hour after the heist. If the haul has to be laundered or fenced, phone numbers are gathered and a tentative deadline for collection is agreed upon.

The dispersal of the gang. If this has been a perfect heist so far, each cohort takes a share of the booty (or leaves a phone number), pockets a travel ticket and/or documents, shakes hands all around and grabs a cab to the airport or bus depot. Sometimes, for the sake of the final mopping up, each person's means of departure is briefly spelled out with the goodbyes that are characteristic of the individual. A few are left to clean up their headquarters, with the mastermind cleaning up after *them.*

The final outcome. In heist novels, the characters are ingenious and daring, but they are seldom admirable human beings. They are, after all, crooks, and although the reader has been intrigued by their actions and has had fun watching them perform, the entertained reader now becomes the punitive judge. The reason might be as personal as not wanting six Manets to be hoarded for one person's clandestine pleasure, or it could be a more abstract sense of justice that must be satisfied. Whatever the reader's reason, you just cannot let these crooks run around loose and unpunished. The target is the seed of the novel, the execution is the sprouting and the resolution is the grim reaping. As you plant the seed, you must have the reaping in mind. (Sounds biblical, doesn't it?) Throughout the book you will have indications of what will become fatal flaws:

A falling out among thieves.

A person picked up for another crime plea-bargains information about the heist against a lighter sentence for the later crime. It is the cohort the mastermind had doubts about from the beginning.

The superstitious thief, in a lovely Freudian slip, leaves a thumbprinted good luck charm behind. (Irony plays a part in fatal flaws.)

A fence, after getting the goods, makes an anonymous phone call to the cops. The fence, in turn, is eventually caught.

Or—and this is something we have not discussed—an angry lover throws a wrench into the works. As in any suspense novel, sex as part of the heist is an option left to the author. If sex is thrown in gratuitously, it can produce a *Let's get on with it!* reaction from the reader who is bound up in the excitement of the planning. If it is used as a wedge between the cohorts or as a motive for a criminal's greed, sex can add to the tension and give dimension to the characters. The mastermind, for example, might be level-headed to the point of cold cruelness, but cannot keep his or her hands off of any member of the opposite sex within reaching distance. This fatal flaw causes dissension among several of the cohorts and eventually gums up the works. In any case, a lover or lovers can add to the balance of the cast of characters.

There is another form of punishment, one laid on the perpetrators by forces outside the law. In *The Leavenworth Irregulars*, which deals with the Army payroll, a tough old sergeant recognizes the heisters, figures out what is going to happen and lets it happen. Then, with his own men, he tracks down the ex-GIs and kills two of them in horrible ways in the process of getting their shares of the spoils and learning the whereabouts of the third man. The third man, whose wife is almost killed, comes to the sorry conclusion that the "successful" heist has proven to be a Pyrrhic victory, and dumps the sergeant *and the money* into an abandoned mine shaft. He acts as his own Greek chorus. He has punished himself.

There is yet a third outcome: The heisters get away scot-free and at book's end they are lolling on the Riviera, planning their next heist. This kind of outcome always delights me. It touches on the latent larceny in my heart and, I would venture to guess, in the hearts of several million other readers. It bestows on the armchair thief a vicarious pleasure in beating the system.

The caper is a lighthearted heist, and its values are mirror images of the heist. The author uses the same blueprint with the values reversed. There can be a foolish goal (target), seriously carried out; a weighty goal, frivolously carried out. Either way, there is a mad logic to the plot, even with its bizarre complications.

Four John Q. Citizens (in *Two for the Price of One* by Tony Kenrick) are driving through the Borough of Queens, New York, when their Edsel hits a pothole and the axle breaks. They trudge to the police station to make a complaint. The sergeant tells them to contact the Department of Transportation. There they are shunted off to the Highway Operations Bureau, which directs them to the Bridges Division, Emergency Only, which in turn sends them clear over to the west side of

Manhattan to the Towaway Parking Lot. When they explain that their car is still parked on Kissena Boulevard in Queens, the officer asks them what the make and model is. They tell him it is an Edsel and he suggests that they contact the Antique Car Association of Connecticut. In a final legal move of redress, they call the mayor's office. He is in Buffalo, addressing a convention on highway safety. In a paroxysm of paranoia (which they are prone to naturally), followed by a series of Byzantine moves, the four John Q.'s "appropriate" a U.S. destroyer anchored in Buttermilk Channel and train its guns on lower Manhattan. Once again, they phone the mayor's office (collect) with an ultimatum: *$112.83 for a new axle or else* . . . The city—finally—takes notice and the plot spirals down into egg-on-the-face apologies but no redress. At book's end, the four are on their way to Weehawken, New Jersey, where they are going to look at a Buick Roadmaster "in mint condition."

The four John Q.'s committed piracy, a very serious federal offense. And for what? A lousy axle. But the axle was important to these Edsel lovers. Little things are not necessarily unimportant things. The underlying theme of the book is that our lives are composed in part of little frustrations made larger by others not caring, and that civil authority is the most uncaring of all. The author used exaggeration to emphasize his theme, and humor to make the exaggeration acceptable.

In another caper (*Deal Me Out* by J. S. Blazer), roles and functions were reversed: The mastermind was not a conniving, cold-blooded man of the world but a twenty-seven-year-old kid, who just happened to deal in the "lighter" drugs. His target, a ton of hashish, was located not in a dank warehouse in the bowels of the city but at a pleasant dockside in Inverness, Scotland. He did not hot-wire a truck to carry the booty away, but rather had a friend buy a trimaran near Glasgow to transport the hash back to Long Island Sound. The loading did not take place in the dead of night; in a scenario too complicated to go into here, the young men were helped in broad daylight by the mayor of Inverness and the chief inspector of the constabulary, who thought the "bricks" were ballast. Sailing back home (and, incidentally, winning a trans-Atlantic race), they were double-crossed by the buyer. In a series of manic leapfrogs and reversals, the hash changed hands several times before it ended up in the East River. The young man got away, not in a car speeding through the night but by floating down the river to a cross street near his apartment.

In this caper, the young dealers were unwittingly helped by authority and betrayed by their own kind, a sort of double reverse. This author distorted reality in order to comment on life's ironies. He, too, used good-natured exaggeration and an outlandish plot to keep his message, in the guise of entertainment, subliminal.

A third author, (Jay Cronley, *Cheap Shot*), was more modest in his scope but no less devastating in his view of How Things Are. The plot concerns a bunch of real kooks who are intent on robbing a museum. Instead of messing around with the alarm system (which is a silent one anyway), they go to the source: the police precinct. There they round up the couple of dozen cops on duty and lock them in one of their two vans (the other is for the haul). Now the museum's alarm can ring at the precinct house until hell freezes over. Instead, as in any good caper, all hell breaks loose; the crooks forget which van is which. The scenes switch back and forth between the museum and the van containing the police. The ineptness on both sides results in a Mexican standoff. And that seems to be this author's comment.

Another museum heist—a caper, really—is Eric Ambler's *The Light of Day*, which was made into a funny movie, *Topkapi*.

Whether caper protagonists are taking on a city, the Atlantic Ocean or a precinct, they think big. The plots match their thinking: outlandish, clever, and comic. Capers deal with crime and, to some extent, punishment. No one gets hurt, except the really bad guys, and nothing much happens to them. Nor do the spoils necessarily go to the victors. The authors are trying to make points, not fortunes. Society (read: authority) is portrayed as dumb and insensitive and is the real villain of the piece. But the caper author, instead of mowing 'em down, thumbs a nose at 'em. Capers are essentially farces, with their broad comedy, improbable plots and overdrawn characters, and are welcome antidotes to the grim happenings in most mystery fiction.

For a kidnapping plot, the heist blueprint works up to a point, and then it is modified; after all, the target is a human being, and elements come into the planning that would not present problems in a heist. Here are the steps and the changes:

1. The target
2. The mastermind
3. The cohorts
4. Expenses
5. Equipment
6. Diagrams and schedules

7. The kidnapping
8. The contact
9. The exchange
10. The getaway after the exchange
11. The dividing of the spoils
12. The dispersal of the gang
13. The final outcome

If the target—the kidnap victim—is a child, its welfare dictates added precautions, both physical and psychological. If it is an adult, the kidnappers must deal with an antagonistic and sometimes formidable adversary. Whoever the victim is, he or she comes from a moneyed power base. Because kidnapping is a federal offense, the FBI, along with the city and state law enforcement agencies, comes in, tripling the odds against the culprits. The ransom, therefore, is high—in the seven-figure range.

Of course, the mastermind is a good organizer and a careful planner and always thinks that he or she has the foolproof system. Besides greed, there may be the added motive of revenge, with no intention of freeing the victim once the money is paid. Along with the suspense of working out the exchange is the added suspense of the victim's ultimate fate.

The cohorts are few: the abductor, two drivers, the go-between, and if the victim is a child, there is often a woman in the group who takes care of the child.

Expenses and equipment are minimal: a hide-out rented for a month, food, magazines, a Scrabble set, a television, a car—maybe two—and a telephone, and that can be a pay phone down the road. Masks might be worn in the presence of the victim.

If the victim is kidnapped from home, diagrams of the house and grounds are necessary. The whereabouts of the rest of the family and servants must be pinpointed. If the victim is to be taken from an airport terminal, nabbed while walking to the bus or forced off the road, a schedule of the person's activities is essential.

The actual kidnapping plan can be a simple one. If it is a child, the abductor crawls through an open window, wraps the child in a muffling blanket and sneaks back out the window. A more complicated transaction is needed when abducting a bewildered or angry adult from a public place. Calling the victim away from a table in a restaurant to take a phony phone call, or edging up on both sides of the victim at a reception, means taking into account onlookers and keeping the fine edge of surprise as a leverage in the abduction.

The contact may be a phone call, with the victim allowed to say a few words, or a mailed note accompanying a package with a piece of clothing or jewelry. More often, it is just a note or a call; the victim's absence is proof enough. Later on, proof might be forthcoming.

The exchange involves more diagrams and schedules. Because this is the trickiest part, the plans are meticulously worked out, and are a surprise to the reader. Seldom are the money and the victim exchanged in the same locality. The money is stuck in the fork of a tree on a lonesome road, or in a trash can in a playground—wherever good surveillance and an unobtrusive getaway are feasible. It is picked up, while the blindfolded victim is let out of the other car miles away.

The dividing of the spoils presents a different kind of logistics. Suppose the ransom is one million dollars in easily passed $100 bills. And say that the loot is to be divided five ways, to give them each $200,000. That means five stacks of two thousand $100 bills each. That is ten thousand bills; bulky, to say the least. So the kidnappers ask for $1,000 bills instead. That will mean five stacks of two hundred bills each; easier to handle but harder to cash. Kidnappings can inadvertently include a certain wry humor.

The dispersal of the kidnapping gang is similar to that of the heist gang. After the division of the spoils, the hideout is cleaned up and the gang members go off to wherever the author has decided to send them.

The satisfying outcome is to have the culprits and the money returned. This is especially true if the victim is a sympathetic character and the villains are not. The various law enforcement agencies have been working throughout the story and gathering information: through a tire print, a phone call traced, a hint dropped by the victim during an allowed phone conversation, a beeper hidden in the handle of the money suitcase, a cleverly planned reconnaissance around the money drop, a remembered remark made before the kidnapping. Or, as with the heist, a falling out among the kidnappers.

In the hundreds of mysteries I have read over the years, as an editor and as an aficionada, one of the rarest breeds I have run across is the kidnap plot. As an editor, I ran into *one*, and that was more of a caper than a serious crime novel. It was *Stealing Lillian* by Tony Kenrick, and it was concerned with the kidnapping of a nine-year-old girl who turned out to be such a little hellion that at book's end the kidnappers were negotiating to pay the parents to take her back. O. Henry used this "unwanted-by-either-party" theme in his short story *The Ransom of Red Chief*. His kidnappers also mistakenly thought that the child's parents were strong advocates of what he called "philoprogenitiveness."

I am not sure why this subgenre appears so infrequently. In terms of stirring empathy in the reader, it is a form that can be a field day for the mystery writer, for it touches responsive chords in all of us: memories of being lost in the woods; of an aging parent, forgetful, riding past the train station where we are waiting; of a childhood incident of accidentally being locked in—or out. These are echoes of "lostness" because of unwanted captivity. The kidnapping plot, by putting the victim in *the reader's* shoes, gives the reader a stake in the outcome. And until the last chapter, the skillful author makes sure that the outcome is uncertain.

There is, though, a practical reason for the dearth of kidnapping novels. If you are willing to grant that a good many plots are triggered by real life, then of recent years there has been an overabundance of kidnappings, few of which touch us personally. Throughout the Middle East and in South America, kidnappings take place every three weeks, it seems, and they are so inextricably tied in with manic, brutal politics that they strike no personal chord in us. With rare exception they would not inspire an author to shift that kind of scene, with its nihilistic turbulence, to this country. We are not comfortable with their alien values.

This may sound like a strange thing to say, considering that in the twenties we had our own turbulent times—which included kidnappings—and our own little generalissimos like "Dutch" Schultz and "Legs" Diamond. Dutch and Legs were *our* folk heroes, and it was our American brand of violence that, with a safe passage of time, became romanticized. I am sure that kidnap novels followed. But that was sixty-odd years ago and the kidnap novel seems to have lost favor with mystery writers and has been supplanted by newer genres. I regret this, because it is a classic life-or-death predicament that can be so effectively exploited in mystery novel form.

The field is not crowded. I can think offhand of only three other authors who have used this theme in contemporary settings: Ed McBain *(Every Crook and Nanny)*, Ross MacDonald *(The Moving Target)* and Mary Higgins Clark *(Where Are the Children?* and *A Stranger Is Watching)*.

ROMANTIC SUSPENSE

If Edgar Allan Poe is considered the procreator of the mystery story, then certainly Charlotte Brontë is the procreator of romantic suspense, for *Jane Eyre*, published in 1847, has the basic elements we still find in this genre: a plucky, resourceful heroine with a profession (the governess); an attractive, albeit tortured, hero (Mr. Rochester); a mystery (the mad Mrs. Rochester confined in the tower); and a fitting background (the harsh Yorkshire moors) which complemented their austere lives.

With such an auspicious beginning, the genre has thrived for well over 140 years; the elements Ms. Brontë used still stand in good stead for the writer of modern romantic suspense. But our backgrounds are more complex and our heroines react to them and in them in a more sophisticated manner; we are, after all, exponents of our times, as she was of hers.

Today's market, it seems to me, is broken down into two fields: romantic suspense written to strict formula, and romantic suspense which is freer in form, less strictured.

Let us take the formula kind first. It is primarily paperback houses that publish the formula novels, and they do so en masse: seven or eight titles every month from each publisher.

Each house has its preferences and its guidelines. Some houses want a heroine whose story is limited to her personal world: She is being stalked by unknown villains for secrets she does not know she possesses, or she is harassed by wealthy socialite in-laws who are guarding a family skeleton, unbeknownst to their son who married this upstart.

Other houses want a broader aspect. They like the heroine to be involved in the worlds of finance, medicine, law and other professions, and they emphasize the need for solid research in these fields. The heroine inevitably becomes the scapegoat in shady big-business deals: She is a chemist who has discovered a new and vital perfume and must uncover chicanery in her company as well as combat competition in the market, all the while trying to stay alive. Or she is a computer expert who discovers gross mishandling of a multimillion-dollar company's inventory, and this knowledge puts her in jeopardy, even though this was the purpose in hiring her.

Her position in these professions always places her in danger, and she fluctuates between innocent bewilderment and brave actions. Her naïveté leads her into dangerous situations that a more worldly-wise woman would avoid. This does not seem to bother readers, for they are eager to identify with the heroine's vulnerability and to experience triumph when she takes measures to cover her flanks, as it were.

The hero, through lack of understanding, sometimes does something stupid which also puts the heroine in danger—a bittersweet situation. Because the story is always told from the heroine's point of view, she often suffers without knowing the source of her suffering. When the misunderstanding finally gets straightened out, he is so contrite that he is immediately forgiven, for along with her pluck the heroine has an innately warm heart.

The variations on theme are endless: kidnapping, rare disease, rape, mistaken identity, insanity—every human condition is acceptable if it is handled convincingly. Backgrounds vary, too: big cities, farms, island resorts, Wall Street, Egypt, football, motorcycling, theater, art galleries, ad infinitum—any place or background that the author can write about with authority.

Physical appearances are extremely important in this genre. The heroine is always attractive (though not always beautiful), and takes pains to look her best and to dress as well as she can afford to. The hero and primary villain are ruggedly handsome and take pride in their clothes, their foreign cars and their well-appointed apartments. They live well and exude success: The heroine sets her sights high.

When the heroine and hero (or hero-turned-villain) meet for the first time, there is an instant shock of sexual attraction, and many of the heroine's attitudes and subsequent actions are based as much on getting her man as in getting out of danger; both goals share equal billing.

Besides providing lovingly portrayed physical descriptions and carefully built-up backgrounds of the heroine having been orphaned or divorced, the author puts the heroine through a range of emotions that indicate her sensitivity to others, based on her own sufferings and especially her own needs. It is in this realm that the romantic suspense writer most strongly elicits identification from the reader, for the reader is able to project wish-fulfilling fantasies into the portrayal of the heroine. As one romantic suspense writer told me, "The reader is the woman who, at three in the afternoon, knows that Mr. Right isn't going to come through her door at six." The ever-striving heroine, offering hope, lets the reader daydream and gloss over a less-than-ideal reality.

Romantic suspense novels also add spice to the reader's life. What could be a more heady combination than the erotic and the wicked? As a TV ad for one of the paperback houses announced, "They are better to read because they are too risky to live."

The romantic suspense author, aware of her market, creates a heroine who actually courts danger. Knowing that "something evil" is in her apartment house basement or knowing there is something "strange" about the man she has too hastily married, she nonetheless strides forward into the situation, bravely and mindlessly (and, structurally speaking, without proper motivation). Ergo, she is bound (and perhaps determined) to suffer fear and intimidation at the hands of the evil one. She does so ostensibly to deal with the danger in order to free herself of it. Catharsis is a noble goal but in romantic suspense it is based on a faulty premise: as in the case of so many sexual hangups, the heroine is programmed to equate surrender with annihilation. So ultimately it is not her good judgment and ingenuity that provide the catharsis but the appearance on the scene of Mr. Right, who has the requisite muscle power and is a safe bet in bed. The legacy of the Victorian cop-out still thrives in the late twentieth century.

There are a few critical voices in the field exhorting romantic suspense writers to quit using the easy stereotypes and to create more fully rounded, truly independent heroines. After all, these voices point out, if a woman is capable of holding down a responsible job in a professional field, meanwhile coping with extraordinary dangers, she deserves to be portrayed as something more than a good-looking clothes-horse on the make.

Writers might counter by saying, "The public likes what we write, so why should we change?" They are right. Romantic suspense is *big* business in the publishing world, and why rock the boat if the formula is paying off?

Your talent and your taste will tell you if you are going to be happy within the present confines of the genre, or if you want to break out of the mold and bring new life to it.

Guidelines for formula writing never remain static. If you like reading a particular author and would like to emulate that person's writing, keep in mind that eighteen months have passed from the time the author's manuscript was accepted to when you saw it in your bookstore. During that time, the publisher might have gotten a dozen manuscripts with a Texas background and half a dozen heroines holding Ph.D.'s in biology, and your biologist from Texas would lose out, regardless of how well you wrote. It is an ever-changing market. For that reason, a good many houses put out guideline information sheets, letting you know what their current preferences are. If you like a publisher's line, write and ask for the house's guidelines. Among the things you need to know are:

1. Will the publisher accept unsolicited manuscripts—that is, directly from you—or only manuscripts sent through agents?

2. Will they accept partial manuscripts with a detailed outline of the remainder?

3. Will they accept a multiple submission? If you intend sending copies to more than one publisher at a time, each publisher should know this.

4. What are the house's character requirements (physical appearance, age, marital status, national origin, profession)?

5. What are its plot specifications: point of view, conflicts, taboos, sex: the proportion of romance to suspense?*

6. What word length does the house prefer?

7. How long will it take the house to reach a decision? (You may not get an answer to this.)

8. How much does the house pay in advances? Most houses will not commit themselves unless they offer you a contract; some will give you a ballpark figure.

Their guideline sheets will give you a lot of detailed information. If you have a manuscript already written, then it helps in your cover letter to say that you write "in the style of" an author whom they publish. This will give *them* a guideline.

If you enjoy reading romantic suspense and would feel comfortable writing to a formula, and if you have a good set of characters in mind, along with an interesting setting and a plot idea that fits some publisher's formula, then this is the field you should write in.

There are so many paperback titles on the market, each in a publisher's line, that it would be better to explore a line you like rather than have me suggest individual authors to you, especially since many of them use several pseudonyms.

---

*A book review in *The Romantic Times* keynoted this proportion: " . . . for the woman who hungers for suspense but cannot live without love."

The less-strictured field of romantic suspense will more often than not be published as hardcover first, with a possible paperback reprint sale. It shares some of the elements of the formula novel: The protagonist is an attractive woman who encounters threats and even physical danger, though not as soon as in the first category. If she has a family, the ties are strong. She, too, will have a profession, or will at least be self-supporting. Settings here are also realistic, but unlike the formula novel, which sticks to the present with an eye toward the future, the hardcover novel will also deal with the past when it is called for. This is because the heroine and her setting are more slowly built up, which gives her more dimension.

And here is where the paperback and the hardcover part company. Whereas the heroine in the paperback is man-oriented, the hardcover heroine is problem-oriented. She is not self-centered, but strives for self-awareness. She is far from being an introvert, but she *is* a thinker. Consequently, she is a more realized character than the other kind of heroine.

This fuller portrayal shows in her relations with others. Rather than putting herself in a one-dimensional adversarial role—she against the world—she takes realistic stock of those she comes into contact with, and reacts appropriately. She is kind and uncondescending toward those on a lower scale—servants and service people—but at the same time she is no pushover for the social climber. Her "people values" operate on one-to-one and one-by-one encounters, which in turn lends credibility to the other characters (who are seen through her eyes).

This evenhandedness applies to the man (or men) in her life, as well. Sex, like other aspects of her makeup, is given its due recognition, but is usually kept on the back burner until she has sorted out her feelings. She is cautious about engaging in sex if it looks as though it would interfere with solving the problems the plot has produced. If she finds herself drawn to a man, she will note his looks, his intelligence, his manner of speaking and his grooming, as well as his sexual attractiveness. She will also be mindful of his humor, his kindness and his lack of affectation—the very facets that she likes in herself, or that the reader sees in her, which contribute toward making a whole person. Once she is hooked, though, she can be blind to the man's faults, which makes her very human, indeed, and which can cause her all sorts of psychological hang-ups and provide ammunition for the plot—especially if he turns out to be the villain.

She, like the other kind of heroine, is a romantic. That is, she appeals to our sense of adventure because of the dangerous situations she is placed in. But she is a realist in dealing with her ordeals because the author imbues her with effective means of coping with her problems independently. She does not pout and stamp her pretty little foot and demand that some hunk of a male intervene on her behalf. She does call upon some of the men in her life to help her, but the initiative lies with her and the men are part of a plan, not a first resort. This is not to say that she is in control from page one; if she were, there would be no conflict and, therefore, no romantic appeal.

This heroine pays careful attention to her surroundings. If a scene takes place in a room, she will be aware of the furnishings; in a garden, the kinds of flowers, herbs and trees. She will weave her descriptions into the scene so that you will *be* in that room or garden, for she has a discrete eye for beauty besides that which she sees in her mirror.

The author of this less-strictured novel is not beset with as many "ideal" limitations of plot and character as the formula writer. The author knows, of course, that imposed plot and character rules are comfortable to write to, but is also aware of their constricting nature. And so the heroine is not always beautiful or even, at first glance, attractive to men. (She grows on them.) She does not always get her man. Her end triumph, while fairly won, may have been won at too high a cost and she ends up wiser rather than victorious.

The bottom line for this kind of heroine, in my opinion, is that she will appeal to men as well as women readers. Men and women will be interested in reading about the heroine if she is a rounded person in her own right, with a firm sense of her own value and clear values by which she judges the world. One novel that I liked—*Vendetta Con Brio* by Beth de Bilio—had a male narrator for half the book, in fact. (Four other romantic suspense writers I like are Daphne Du Maurier, Mary Higgins Clark, Mary Stewart and Jessica Mann. I am sure you must have your favorites, too.)

Now, earlier in this chapter I mentioned that characters are subservient to plot in the mystery story. From my readings in the romantic suspense genre, there seems to be no danger of the heroine's persona upstaging her actions. In the very best romantic suspense, the reader's concern about the outcome is in proportion to the understanding the author calls upon the reader to have for the main character. In the best romantic suspense, the depth of the heroine and the events that make up the story complement each other.

* * *

The mystery genre and its subgenres are well-established now. The ways they have been handled—characters, plots, background, theme—have been used time and again. So what makes some mysteries stand out more than others? First of all, there are some writers who naturally have more talent than others and sell year after year because of their quality. But second—and here every writer can participate—a mystery that really makes a splash on the market is one that contains originality. That writer has risked using a timeworn idea in a way that it has never been used before: a unique main character, a plot inversion, a never-thought-of background or a twist on the theme. Often that originality springs from an author's own experience: growing up next door to a police precinct, having a friend who was kidnapped, going through a long court battle or suffering personally from a criminal action. This author is able to bring actual experience to the field with an insight shared by very few. Originality means freshness. Along with choosing a genre "world" that you find interesting and comfortable to write about, keep in mind that you know something about this world that is unique.

CHAPTER 2

THE REALM OF IDEAS

SINISTER INTENTIONS

HERE IS YOUR CHANCE to become a Dr. Frankenstein.

Most of the world, to keep its sanity, tries to look at the brighter side of life. You look for the gloomy side. You welcome danger, conflict and murder. You deliberately arouse feelings of anxiety in your readers; you baffle them, trick them and scare them. If you inflict these nasty things on them in a telling way, they will come back for more.

But first we must turn you into Frankenstein. Unfortunately, you will not have a sinister laboratory in the Swiss Alps in which to perform your hellish deeds. You will have to settle for the evils that surround your everyday life. You must learn to look for them.

You must develop a jaundiced view of other human beings, and look for the worst in them. We all tend to identify people, at the outset, by particular traits. Only later, as we get to know them, do we put the parts together to understand the whole person. For your purposes, it is not necessary to plumb the depths of an individual to spark the idea for a character.

The odd quirk can trigger an idea for a victim: the woman who refuses to lock her door at night ("People are so sweet.") can end up getting murdered in your book. An aggressive sort can be a victim, too. How many times have you watched someone muscle into a movie queue and thought, *I could break his neck*? He is a petty tyrant who *will* have his way. Your mind's eye sees him at home where he shouts at his wife and cuffs the kids, and ends up as a statistic under: *MURDER (domestic)*.

What about the villains? How do you spot them? I would not advise weekly trips to the dangerous parts of town. I do not even think they are necessary. With your newly acquired jaundiced eye, you can find mean people anywhere.

If you know an accountant whom you happen not to like, you pay attention to the undue pressures forced upon him and *know* that he is not above embezzling. If you dislike him very much, you can imagine him committing murder to cover his embezzlement. And what about the authoritarian nurse who poked you with needles, unexpectedly and painfully? You can see her filling a hypodermic vial with something lethal and injecting it into the vein of a rich patient.

What I am trying to stress here is that people who trigger reactions in you of pity, contempt or fear are worth filing away in your mind, along with their identifying traits.

Places can evoke dire trains of thought, too. Not the gothic gloom of a cobwebbed castle—that is too easy and will not stand up to five minutes' scrutiny. In fact, any place that you note with lighthearted glee, "What a swell place for murder!" will most likely not stick in your mind for long.

What you should note are places that, like people, bring out uncomfortable emotions in you. One of the interesting facets of writers is their need to exorcise bad feelings about places. When they successfully face these place conflicts, they get a kind of power from doing so and use it as a springboard for settings. One author, Dean Koontz, in his suspense novel *Whispers* set a scene in a roach-infested cellar. It was chilling to read. I commented to him, "You must really be on top of these things to be able to write about them." He answered, "No, I hate roaches and I hate cellars."

Have you watched a construction worker thread his way along an I-beam, ten stories up? A switchman standing rigidly between two moving trains? Were you not frightened to think of putting yourself in their places?

Other hazardous sites you might think about: theater balconies, leaky boats, labyrinths that run under building complexes. Empty rooms with rotted floorboards. Parks at night.

You can inject your own gloom into less grim surroundings: carnivals, fashion shows, playgrounds. Introducing discordance into their carefree atmospheres produces effective jolts.

Incidents that you experience or read about provide good sources for ideas. For instance; a telecast about a family that has been wiped out, butchered by a disgruntled in-law, down the block from you. Their proximity, their similar lifestyle and economic level, maybe having the same number of kids in the family, bring home to you your own family's vulnerability. How would you react to the same danger? In a mystery novel, how would you handle the danger successfully?

Or you are riding on a bus with a gang of sullen teenagers who, you feel, would create mayhem given the slightest provocation. In actuality, you sit there quietly and count the minutes until your stop. In your head, though, you imagine them taking over while the passenger sitting next to you shows the beginnings of a heart attack. You cannot whip out your badge and gun and shout, "Police! Stop!" because that is liable to help the passenger on his fatal way. What do you do?

These are clear-cut confrontations. I found a more oblique kind of trigger in an inch-and-a-half-long item in *The New York Times* some years ago. A man was found dead on the links of the University of Washington's golf course, the victim of a stray, high-speed golf shot. He had not died immediately. The police asked other golfers who had been in the vicinity if they had heard the victim's cries. One golfer said he had, and added, "I thought it was a peacock calling." What an evocation of helplessness—and irony!

You can be intrigued by a chance remark. A friend and I were sitting in a bar when three men came in and sat in the booth next to us. We paid no attention to them until we overheard one of them say, "We made it over the wall!" (Laughs all around.) "Let's get Jim over tomorrow." They went on to discuss the World Series. Escaped criminals planning to spring another convict! We sauntered up to the bar, ostensibly to get another round, and laid the scene on the bartender. He tensed, looked slowly toward the three men, then smiled. "Oh, them. They come from over there." He pointed to City and County Hospital across the street. "They sneak outta the TB ward." A happy ending (sort of) that would have made a good comic scene.

Another remark I overheard, this time in a restaurant, spoke volumes: There was a momentary lull in the crockery din and a woman could be heard saying to her husband, "I've changed my mind. You're not paranoid. You're stupid." The husband's face took on a wooden look and he said nothing, but my head could see into his head: *I'm going to double the amount on the insurance policy I took out on her.*

People, places, television, newspapers, personal encounters— these are the trigger mechanisms that translate reality into fantasy.

Another source for fantasy: other mystery writers' novels. You have been reading them for entertainment anyway, and as your desire to write one grows, you begin to read for, among other things, comparison. Quite a few mystery writers have launched their careers by thinking, *I can do better than that,* and did (or did not, but got published for their efforts).

Another approach is to be sparked by another mystery writer's theme but to see it with a different slant. Say that you have just finished reading a mystery in which two young lovers have been accused of murdering the woman's much older husband. The husband was a pillar of society, a philanthropist and an all-around good man. The town's consensus is that the young lovers were too naive and gentle to have committed the murder, even though the woman stood to gain from her dead husband's considerable estate. In their minds, the townspeople find the couple guilty of adultery but, in all fairness, not guilty of murder. Sure enough, the town's newspaper publisher, another pillar of society, acting on a long-time grudge, had done it.

Suppose at book's end you had found everything a little too pat: the innocence of the lovers, the goodness of the victim, the fairmindedness of the townspeople. Sure, it was touch and go for the couple for a little while, but you did not seriously think they were guilty.

In recasting the story, you want more fire to it: Behind the philanthropist's front was a bully, the lovers are not that naive, and the townspeople are not that gullible. The newspaper publisher—or someone like him—is still the culprit. But your viewpoint is that there is a strong streak of self-interest in everyone and that by showing it, you tell the story in a more dynamic way.

To pick up on another writer's theme is perfectly legitimate. Once the theme has been run through your set of mental baffles, it will be uniquely your book. There is no such thing as copyrighting ideas. Just be damned sure that everything but the theme comes out of *you.*

The ultimate source of fantasy is dreams. Their uninhibited actions seem so *right* and the feelings in them are so poignant that nothing in waking life can touch them. Authors have told me that they have gotten emotionally charged ideas from dreams that, when they awoke, put them in the mood for a character or a scene. I have always been interested to know when authors get their ideas from dreams, and some authors have been generous enough to share their dreams with me, and to explain how, on waking, they were able to translate a dream into a viable piece of writing. (They had stayed awake long enough to write their dreams down.) Even though the dreams made no sense at the time, there was a feeling behind the images they wanted to capture. It had taken them some while of thinking and rethinking before the crux of their dreams surfaced.

On one occasion an author told me that she had been able to break her writer's block after a dream. She had been having personal problems that took up unnecessary amounts of emotional energy; at the day's end she had nothing left to give to her writing. She realized that her problems did not merit the concern she was giving them but she felt guilty nonetheless, and this blocked her creative channels. Then one night she dreamed she was in the loveliest garden she had ever seen, and it was *hers*. The dream, joyfully, seemed to go on forever. The next morning, her first waking thought was, *Why should I be denied my own Eden?*, and she was able to throw off the spurious guilt and begin writing again.

Another author, who was a small-boat sailor and was familiar with the Florida Keys, described his dream this way:

> I am standing alone at the ocean's edge, ankle-deep in water. There is a wind that I can hear but can't feel. The water is so wide and far-reaching that there is no horizon.

As he himself recognized, the unmistakable feeling was one of *alienation*, and it explained why he opened his book in this way: The son of a major drug dealer is shanghaied to a distant shoal by another major drug dealer as a hostage in a gang war. The son watches the power craft zoom off to the far-distant shoreline and, cut off from the rest of the world, he is sure he has been left to die. (The second chapter starts the action with the abductor making a call to the son's father.)

Another author shared her key dream with me on a note of triumph:

> My daughter is wearing a crummy old sweatshirt, like the kind I wore when I was her age. She hands me a plate (of something?) which dissolves in my cupped hands.

Frustration—plus a "crummy" situation—underlay her dream, which had tapped into a real-life experience. The author's daughter had been "borrowed" at an early age by an unstable nursemaid. The nursemaid called every three or four hours to assure the mother that the child was all right. The author still remembers the frustration she felt every time the phone went dead. The police located the nursemaid (with the daughter) a day later, and it was then that the author began having this dream. When she brought the manuscript in to me, she had finally laid the ghost to rest by incorporating her experience in her mystery novel.

On the lighter side, I made note of another dream because it reflected a playful one-upmanship which fit in with the author's "waking" personality and, so, amused me:

I will accept the million dollars after I have gone to the john.

The book he got out of the dream featured a con man conning an even bigger crook by going him one better every step of the way. What *gratification!* It was a humorous story and *I* felt gratified by the con man's successful shenanigans when I read the manuscript.

Alienation, frustration and gratification are only three of the myriad emotions that are part of your makeup. As you have seen, they can be transferred to good and evil characters, prompting them to defensive and offensive actions. Apprehension, helplessness, fear, joy, jealousy, anguish, revenge, envy and sexual excitement, to name others—they all appear in your dreams. The images may be colorful and disguised, but the emotion is something you *feel* and needs no translation.

Remember that your feelings will be injected into every character you create, even though you may not be aware of it while you are writing. This should come as no surprise; everything you put on paper is coming out of your head—including evil. As a person, you will never turn evil thoughts into reprehensible actions, but the Dr. Frankenstein in you will—on paper.

The unconscious is a rich source for images and feelings. Think of it as your never-depleted bank account, one you can draw on for as long as you continue to write. As you have already discovered for yourself, writers are constantly on the alert for the meaningful image that serves as a springboard for book material. There is never a time clock regulating their minds. A vivid image at two in the morning is as valuable to them as a daytime insight.

NURTURING THE IDEA

At two in the afternoon, you can have similarly disjointed images, but at this hour of the day they are called "ideas." They, too, can come with dramatic impact and emotional forcefulness. They may be just as fleeting, and they can be harder to hold on to because of the distracting flak of waking-life noises. Be receptive to them, even the crazy ones. Oddly enough, the sillier they seem, the more valuable they can be; it is the oddities that catch the imagination and set it moving. Do not expunge them on the basis of logic. The improbable is a challenge to logic.

Whether an idea is crazy or sane, hold on to it and work it around in your head. Does it reverberate, bringing its own associations? Does thinking of a girl running down a dark lane bring to mind a mugger/ rapist? Does watching a bank teller riffle swiftly through a stack of twenties make you think that he would be a good card mechanic? These are starts, solid images.

But what if the idea is more tenuous? What if a picket fence comes into your mind? Hardly the germ of an edge-of-the-seat mystery novel. Actually, a picket fence did come into the mind of one author. She was less than entranced with the idea, but she let it play for a bit:

A small boy walks by with a slingshot and plays a tattoo along the pickets until he gets to the end of the fence and finds . . .

She came up with an aggie, a toad and, yes, even the end of the fence. And that seemed to be the end of the idea. The thought occurred to her that she was trying to write a mystery novel, not setting down her grandfather's memoirs. By this time the picket-fence compulsion, as she called it, had taken hold. She liked the fence idea, and she wanted to play it out. What she did was to run the scene backwards and then let the boy begin again. This time she added a summer's day and the buzzing of insects, shoring up her bucolic scene and extending the feeling of peacefulness. Then, almost leisurely, she followed one of the buzzing insects into an adjoining field, where a hacked-up body lay across the furrows.

This author did two important things: She played out her idea, and she kept in mind that it had to fit within the frame of a mystery novel. As it turned out, she tricked the reader into a false sense of security, then produced a shock which did create an edge-of-the-seat situation.

Play out your ideas. Let your mind off the leash of what you think is and is not "useful." By the law of averages, it will not always produce a profitable idea, but you can never tell when one will spark, and in the meantime you will get used to going to the well.

There will be moments when you have too many ideas, believe it or not. Say you are working on a scene, developing it within a certain time and spacial area. Another idea comes winging in from an entirely different but equally important area. What happens? Let me give you an example:

> A professional thief has been hired to steal blueprints from the office of the president of a major industry. The thief has been given a key to the inner sanctum, but getting into the plant itself will be up to him.

You are industriously working out a way for him to get past the guard at the gate, circumventing the alarm system and locating the office. It is tricky business, making his entry difficult and fraught with danger. You are poring over the diagram you have drawn of the grounds, and thinking about the weather that night, the thief's crepe-soled shoes and the time element, and trying to lay out the sequences of the scene. You are hard at work juggling a lot of thoughts.

Suddenly, out of nowhere, a new idea strikes you:

> The key doesn't fit. Was it deliberately switched? Is this really a setup to make the thief a fall guy in a larger context? Is the guard deliberately ignoring the break-in? Or was the thief given the wrong key by mistake and, if so, how will he handle this unexpected barrier?

These are intriguing notions and you want to get them down while they are fresh in your mind. But you are still very much involved in the first scene and you do not want to break the momentum.

If you cannot decide which idea deserves your attention, God help you; you are liable to lose both of them. The ideal solution, of course, is to put a pencil in each hand and keep writing. Lacking this ambidexterity, how do you manage?

There are two ways I can think of, neither of them totally satisfactory, but either is better than watching both ideas go down the tubes:

> 1. The new idea may strike you as more fruitful than the one you are working on, so drop the first idea for the time being. This is safe if you have already written a lot of it.
> 2. Or, if the first idea is still nebulous, put it on hold for only as long as it takes to write a few associative words describing the new idea:

key won't fit/switch before crime?/mistake?

Intriguing as it is, resist the temptation to expand the new idea right then. If it is worth developing, it will hold its shape until you can get to it.

NAILING THE IDEA DOWN

You have heard the admonishment "Harness your imagination." Well, you cannot. You can surround it, work in and out of it, on top of and below it. Trying to harness it, though, puts you in an impossible bind, like that of Caligula's soldiers who were ordered to throw rocks at the waves to subdue the sea. You can only tease, cajole, encourage or ignore it in attempts to start it going. Eventually, it will spring out unexpectedly, depositing a layer on your consciousness. (In the meantime, write down *anything* that comes into your head.)

It may come out with a phrase that has no immediate use but does have potential quality to it:

She banged on the bars of her cell. . . . The rictus of death . . .

Write it down. The imagination delights in the ephemeral; it could not care less about a rounded whole, for logic is not one of its strong points. Write it down, for memory is not one of *your* strong points.

An idea can be a flash of a scene:

He is picking his way through the debris of the ransacked house, looking for evidence that will nail the suspect.

Or a brief insight for a character:

Invariably she pats her hair just before she is going to tell a lie.

File it away for a time when you can wrap it in a fuller thought.

If a larger idea comes to your mind, by all means write that down. Take the time to expand it to its fullest worth, for it will not come that way again in that particular form. Memory is of no concern to the prodigal imagination.

Suppose now that you are sitting down and writing out some of your ideas. You are working along, comfortably set on where you are going, and suddenly you think of an impressive line. It is such a good line that you want to rework everything else around it. If you start to do so, chances are everything else around it will get thrown out of kilter. Write the line down and store it for some future use and go on with what you were writing. It is wiser to honor the train of thought in hand than to be distracted by a thought in flight.

Here is an example of how one author almost trapped himself this way. He started out fine on chapter 3:

> It was more than twenty blocks to the motel, but he couldn't chance taking a bus; his face was too well known by now. He started east toward the edge of town. His leg hurt, he was hot and the .38 pushed down behind his belt chafed at his back. The next six hours were crucial and he had to come up with a plan by the time he reached the motel. They would be waiting for him there.
>
> As he limped along on the hot sidewalk, he thought of Marilyn. She would be waiting for him, too, on the other side of town. She would have to wait.

The author allowed his hero some breathing space here while he reminisced about the night before (with Marilyn) for several pages, and found himself typing the line *As darker grows the night*. He recognized it as a line of poetry he had learned as a kid and found himself anxious to incorporate it into his story. He began again, revising:

> As the night grew darker, the man limped toward the edge of town. . . .

The author fiddled around, rewriting the two paragraphs; then he realized that changing day into night meant changing the time schedules of the previous two chapters. And what the hell was his character reminiscing for, anyway? He was being hunted, he was in pain and he had to do some serious thinking in the next twenty blocks. This was no time for a breather! It was hard for the author to let go of that line, but the line was not worth recasting the plot for. He tucked it away as a possible title.

This lapse into a flight of fantasy—*As darker grows the night*—occurred because the author had allowed himself an earlier lapse—Marilyn; had he not brought himself up sharply, he might have used the twenty blocks in plot-stopping daydreams.

Here is another kind of out-of-kilter dilemma: You are skating along nicely on a sequence. You have developed an idea in Scene A, but when you expand it in Scene B, the idea peters out. Instead of reworking Scene B to death, go back to Scene A and rework the idea to give B a stronger base. Even a clinker can be saved. Here is an example:

SCENE A   After a tense two hours of sawing his bindings against a jagged rock set in the foundation of the chalet's cellar, the prisoner makes his quiet, if shaky, way up to the living quarters and tiptoes past the drunken (sleeping) smuggler left by the others to guard the prisoner. The prisoner's status has now changed to that of a fugitive, and he makes the most of it. He grabs a rope from the porch of the chalet and runs, crouching, to the edge of the cliff. He ties the rope to a tree and begins rappelling down the mountain's slick face.

SCENE B   Halfway down, his rope runs out and he still has fifty feet to go before he reaches the valley floor. He is forced to work with hand- and footholds.

This is impossible, given the slick face described in Scene A, but he must be gotten off the mountain's face. Reworking Scene B, you could try these:

1. The fugitive laboriously climbs up the rope to the top.

This puts him back to square one.

2. He dangles for a while, then God sends him a helicopter.

This is unlikely. Go back and rethink Scene A:

Along with the rope, the fugitive steals a pair of crampons.

The dilemmas you encounter might be more complex, but the rule itself is simple: If you have worked into an illogical situation, check the steps that brought you to it.

So far I have discussed single-episode ideas: An idea comes to you, and you use it, discard it or store it away. But that is only the beginning. The stored-away idea can become part of a sequential process. You do not have to put the idea on a shelf and wait until you can find a single use for it. Your mind will create a channel to the shelf, so that other ideas will be placed on the shelf, too. You will recognize some of them as compatible right off:

First idea: A plane makes an emergency landing in a mountain pass.

Several days later: You are driving through the White Mountains or the Sierra Nevadas; when you look down, you realize the plane's wings would have been sheared off by the giant firs.

Your earlier thoughts of getting the plane out of the pass have been widened to getting the people out of the pass instead. It expands the possibilities for your plot.

Or take that woman who pats her hair before telling a lie. Without consciously looking for it, you notice when you pass her beauty parlor. You might even run into her at the drugstore, where she is buying a henna rinse. Now you see the patting gesture as standing for vanity as well as lying. *Ah,* you think, *here is a crack in her facade*—and you have a second facet of her personality to work with.

What about incompatible ideas? They, too, have a "shelf life." Sometimes you will find yourself stretching to make them compatible, usually when you are desperate for a plot idea. Let them ride, especially if they come close together; the only thing that binds them at the moment is their proximity, and desperation is not the most productive motive for writing. If you can keep a "relaxed ear" canted toward them, they can germinate themselves—that is, tie in with other ideas.

Storing up ideas on your shelf is not an onerous task. Most writers collect bits and pieces of useless information for the sheer fun of it, although an underground part of their minds keeps tabs on the possible usefulness of this flotsam. For instance:

You find an old brass bud vase at a summer flea market, but it has a triangular dent in it, so you don't buy it. That winter you take a trip to Morocco, and in the casbah in Tangier you sort through a pile of native-made rugs until you find one that will look nice in the front hall. Shortly thereafter, you eat something from the marketplace and get a bug that cancels out the rest of the trip.

Sometime in April you are laid up with the flu and remember the unpleasantness of the tail end of the Tangier visit. Your mind wanders back to the casbah and the rug stall and you remember that the stall next to it was displaying brass vases. By an associative leap, you remember the flea market vase with the peculiar dent and the woman who wanted to sell it to you. Dark-complexioned, wasn't she? Wore many bracelets? Did she, you wonder, bring the vase from North Africa, and if so, what was she doing at a flea market in the United States?

You have come full circle from last summer to this spring, touching on the commonplace and the exotic, and you have welded them together.

I used the word *underground* just now. You could as easily call it the *subconscious* or even the *unconscious*. You have seen where it works for dreams. It also works in your waking life, and it works independently of your conscious mind, sometimes uncomfortably so. You have been aware of this happening when a shameful thought surfaces and you quash it immediately, disavowing it. Or if an idea seems ludicrous, your conscious mind—the guardian of logic—writes it off. The two— or three, if you prefer—parts of your mind work in tandem to produce your thinking, whether you like it or not. Treat them as soul mates (or cell mates, Dr. Frankenstein). The more parts of your mind you nail down, the more productively they will work for you.

I also mentioned, in the example above, that the thinker had be- gun associating these widely spaced ideas while in bed with the flu. The reactions of your body are good sources: illness, insomnia, physi- cal handicaps, hypertension, pain, sexuality, drunkenness and mari- juana highs. If you have experienced any of these—and I am sure you have—you will be able to describe hangovers or how it felt to be in a car crash or the tension and subsequent actions induced by sleeplessness.

Take sleeplessness, for instance. Too many authors describe a character's insomnia with a phrase such as "he paced back and forth," and let it go at that. What about the rotten (or surprisingly good) late late shows you have sat through, the dawns you have seen? The deple- ted refrigerator? The added tension of waiting for a call that could an- nounce life or death? The growing fatigue that leaves you with a sick feeling? The impotence of being suspended in time?

As I said earlier about emotions that come out of dreams, insomnia can prompt a character to action. Or prompt *you* to action: a plot idea from one of the late lates! And, too, on those nights when you cannot sleep, you could be writing, which would do away with any sense of being "suspended in time." Put the time to work, to your advantage:

a fateful decision that comes out of fatigue and frustration

a predawn action on the street seen from your window

Writing is the result of cerebral activity, but a good writer knows when to bypass the brain and go directly to the gut.

Here is one phenomenon in the realm of ideas that has brought me tearful letters and frantic phone calls. The message goes like this:

"I got the whole chapter done. Then I reread it and, God, it's a lot of crap!"

I advise the author to send it on to me, and when I read it, I find it deserves no such opprobrium. It is often quite good, far better than the author thought it was.

Other than being stranded on an arctic tundra without a pencil and pad, I can think of no greater hazard for the beginning mystery writer than experiencing what I call "the fading ink phenomenon." Say you have written down an idea, or several, perhaps even pages. Going back over it, the writing does not have the same impact that it did in the throes of your imagination. It cannot begin to represent the magnitude of the emotion that went on in your head. On paper, it looks pallid, flat—just so many black symbols. You have lost the "magic" in the transition from head to paper. The thought has "died," in the way a pebble loses its colors when you pluck it from the surf, out of its aqueous prism.

You are not alone. All writers worthy of the name have been discouraged by this reverse sea change. Do what they have done: Walk away from it. Intuition, backed by experience, has taught them that the *art* of writing is only approximate. There is a great distance between the genesis of a thought and what can be realistically expected from its execution to paper. As they have learned, you need time to absorb this, to be able to come to grips with the ideal that melts down into reality.

After you have walked away, pick up a mystery by an author whom you admire. Those same twenty-six black symbols—for all that they represent less than the ideal—have the power to move you. They have coalesced into articles of faith in the *craft* of writing. When you can accept these articles—that you have truly injected your own power into those symbols that seemed so powerless moments ago—then you and the experienced author share something valuable: The Secret of the Illimitable Gap and the Weight of the Imperfect Span. Your audience will never be aware of the hiatus, nor know the difference between the ethereal highlights you experienced and the earth tones you settled for.

Nurturing an idea and nailing it down often go hand in hand. When you are confident that, after the first idea, there are more where that came from, the more ideas you let out the happier they will be. Unlike anaerobic organisms, ideas flourish in the air. Of course, they will not flourish in hot air. Bombastic prose used to inflate a minuscule idea is self-defeating. You will write your share of it, but eventually—or soon, I hope—you will become aware that you cannot lay eggs without passing wind.

That is okay; do not worry about it, for a writer's second greatest gift is ego, and mystery writers are no exception:

What I write is good because I wrote it.

And from the beginning, please, believe it.

If you are satisfied with what you have written, try it out on your family. Try it out on your friends. Form a group with other beginning mystery writers. Rap sessions with other mystery writers can be extremely helpful. You may, along with the Presbyterians, consider yourself among the Sweet Elect ("and the rest can go to hell"), but writing can be a lonely pursuit, and peer communication can offset the loneliness. Watch out, though, for disguised jealousy or overabundance of praise. Self-interest is paramount in these sessions.

Understandably, you want feedback, preferably of a laudatory kind, which you are pretty sure to get from a targeted audience. A few criticisms will be deferentially offered, none of them threat-size, and you will take them or you will drop them. You will, though, have learned an important nail-down lesson: Ideas solidify in communicating them. As you are reading to family or friends or peers, you hear your words as if you were silently reading someone else's. The tonal sound—alien to the written word—distances you from the words; you become part of the audience. Fortunately for your career, and because you are a writer, another part of you is sitting in the balcony, judging the effects. If your audience is enthralled, that is wonderful. It means that the idea is intriguing and that you phrased it well. If your audience gets glassy-eyed, that is disconcerting. It means that the idea was not very good or that you wrapped it in muggy prose or sloppy grammar. Some ideas do turn out to be anaerobic and will die in the airing. Down deep, you will know it, but if it still hurts to let them go, bear in mind that they are clogging your conduits, keeping other ideas from flowing through.

There are other ideas in you. By the law of averages, some of them will be clinkers, but you will not know for sure until you work them around, try worrying them into shape and finally, with relief, toss them out like obstinate delinquents.

You and your ego will do a lot of fencing in the writing years ahead. There will come a time when you graduate from writing for an on-tap audience of well-meaning listeners to writing for an audience of one—yourself. The tonal sounds will be in your head. Only secondarily will an audience figure into your writing process, though it may continue to be part of it.

There is a second approach to writing, a second kind of writer. If from the start you do not have an audience, perhaps because of unsympathetic surroundings, you will have to develop the tonal sounds on your own. If you are the more cautious type, you may want to start here anyway. Inspiration does not automatically supply you with a full-blown ego. You may be the kind of writer who has to do ego-building at the same time that you are storybuilding. You do a lot of Dutch-uncling: *Is this right? No, it doesn't sound right. How about this? Mmmm, not sure of that either.* You do as much worrying as writing. Remember: As you are testing your ideas, you are also building a self-image as a writer. You take fewer risks, but in the long run you may end up laying fewer eggs.

There is a third kind of writer, one who actually prefers to bear the entire weight and responsibility of ego and output. You are the more private one who, by your nature, prefers to nurture your ideas alone until you have a finished manuscript to show to the world. You know that what you have accomplished is not necessarily perfect, but it is a completed project, a genuine whole. It is your means of taking measure of yourself, and you probably work this way in other areas of your life.

These three kinds of writers share some of each other's attributes, and the technical aspects will be the same for all three. But whether you are comfortable being a public entertainer or a prudent deviser or a cloistered entrepreneur, you face the same twenty-six symbols, those articles of faith that are the foundation for the craft of writing. You will get into the habit of going to your well, and to the world, for ideas. You will, in fact, become an idea person, and you will capitalize on your talent by using the mechanics of your craft to develop the art of your mystery novels.

CHAPTER 3

SUSPENSEFUL PLOTTING

THE BACKBONE OF THE BOOK

IN DISCUSSING PLOT, I will mostly use the straight murder mystery as a matrix because of its classical form and its simplicity. But keep in mind that the subgenres have legitimate statuses in the modern mystery field, and if you analyze them, you will find that they all contain the elements of the classical form and are simply variations on it.

In the classical form, white-collar crimes, kidnappings, heists, etc., are often used as subordinate crimes leading to murder, or as motives for murder. As the primary crime in a mystery novel, I do not find them nearly as dramatic. A murderer has more to lose than, say, an embezzler: The stakes are higher, the criminal is more desperate and the drama is more intense. Once you have learned the bases of the classical form and want a change of pace or a change of theme, then you can experiment with the variations. But first off, let us explore the classical underpinnings.

In my years of reading manuscripts and talking with hopeful writers, one impression has made its mark very clearly: these writers have the notion that, because mysteries are fun to read, they are easy to write. Nothing could be further from the truth. So often, writers have chosen their crime, brought in suspects and sleuths, piled motive on motive, thrown in gimmicks, colorful backgrounds—the works—and the reader could not have cared less. What these writers did not take into account is the underlying thrust of the mystery: the inevitability of cause and effect.

In mysteries, the cause is desperation and the effect is disaster. It is the writer's task to convince the reader of the grimness of the situation and the importance of righting it. To do this, the writer has to direct all of his or her attention to the facts and impressions that deal directly with the crime and its solution. Too often, the motives are weak, the gimmicks are silly and the background overshadows the foreground. Too often, characters are introduced at random and are either nonentities from the start or fade away without having accomplished a purpose. Sometimes neophyte writers put in information they are proud of having and think it is fun to show off, but which is irrelevant to the thrust and so diminishes its power. In the glow of their self-indulgence, they rely too much on the reader's indulgence. Because of such digressions and irrelevancies, the logical connections between cause and effect are weakened and, therefore, the emotional impact of the story is weakened.

I think you will agree that cause followed by effect implies a connecting, logical span between them, a span composed of people, events and time. Cause—the reason for the story, the crime—is the idea for the book. Effect—how the story develops—is the plot. The plot forms the backbone of the book.

The plot becomes alive—turns into a story—when you introduce the characters who cause the events and, in turn, are affected by them. To put the events in their proper order and to set up a cast of characters to put the events in action, you need a structure. This means setting up your priorities—which elements are primary and which are secondary in importance. But first, you must know what elements to prioritize.

I will assume that you have mulled over your plot options and have come up with one you like. You have probably gotten the idea from any one—or several—of the triggers described in the preceding two chapters. You will most likely have decided on a murder mystery, so you need a victim and a murderer. You know that the victim is killed because he or she has thwarted the murderer in some fashion. This brings in motive. Out of the motive the solution will arise, so you need a sleuth as well.

To begin with then, you need six elements: three main characters, a crime, a motive and a solution.

Now set the scene for the crime—where the action will start. Where do you place your victim so that the murderer has access and opportunity? How is the murder done? How does the murderer leave the murder scene?

The time of the crime is important. It is the linchpin for alibis—and here is where you add other suspects, to flesh out your story and to create doubt in the reader's mind. The suspects need to be delineated individually: their traits, physical appearances and backgrounds. You need biographies of all the characters and you need to spell out their relationships to one another. You need clues that will point to the various suspects and that will eventually lead to the solution. The story is acted out against a backdrop—one of the "worlds" I talked about in chapter 1, or one of your own choosing. And, finally, you must decide who is going to tell the story—the author or one of the characters—for this determines your viewpoint, which will underscore your theme and determine the book's structure.

There are two ways of bringing all these elements together.

The first way seems to be the easier: You think up three main characters and give them a murder to deal with and the reason for it. Then you work out how the murder is to be done—and you are off and running. The advantage of using this approach is that you can do your thinking while you are mowing the lawn. There is no time lost; you are getting double value out of the fourth dimension: Your hands (and feet) are gainfully employed, leaving your mind free for the creative side of you. Shortly afterward, you go into your study (or that part of the dining room you have taken over) and type out your opening scene. The results are most likely quite good and you have every reason to be proud of what you have written. You have the victim skewered with the silver letter opener, the murderer has made a clean getaway and the distraught housekeeper is about to phone her nephew, who happens to be a private eye.

It is an attention-getting first chapter and you are inspired to get right into chapter two. The d.h. lets the n., who is the p.e., into the library. The n. fiddles around with the corpse, fiddles with his tie and then announces, "This man is dead! Brutally slain!" The d.h. wrings her hands and agrees. This disconcerts the n.-p.e. who thinks, *No argument? Where do I go from here?* Indeed, where does he go from here?

So back to the lawn mower. This means waiting two weeks until the grass accommodatingly grows to mowing height, or a little sooner if you can finagle a job at a golf course. . . .

Functioning on 99 percent inspiration and 1 percent perspiration may work for you, and if it does, I am not about to knock it. There *are* authors who work this way, stopping only long enough to jot down information they want to include in the next scene. They would feel stifled if they had to plot three scenes ahead, let alone an entire book. Somewhere just under the surface of their minds, the raw materials are stored, ready to be tapped as inspiration hits. They have their fits and false starts, but under the surface there is also a solid layer of intent that will put them back on track—if not right then, then when they do their rewriting. And most of them rewrite, thinking of their first draft as an elongated outline. For them, the "real work" begins after they have finished—filling in plot holes and rounding out characters that inspiration neglected.

The second way of handling your raw materials is to do the "real work" before you even begin the book. If you have a methodical bent of mind, if you can postpone emotion in favor of here-and-now logic, this second way will be a boon in the long run. It will save you time and work and minimize confusion. You do this by using a drawing board instead of a lawn mower.

Take all the elements I listed a few paragraphs back and jot them down, ignoring their relative importance or place in time. Do not even think about priorities or structure. You simply want to spread them out so that you can see them. *For the moment*, they are all equally important. The clearest, simplest way of spreading them out is with a radial graph—the first piece on your drawing board.

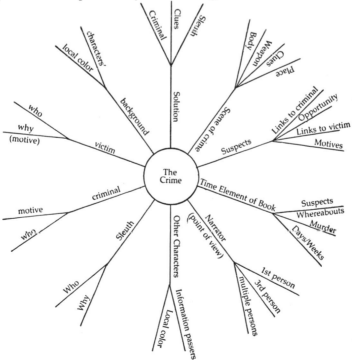

The inner circle, of course, will be the crime itself, the reason for the story. Each of the elements will be represented by an arm radiating from the circle. I would suggest that you label the first arm "Scene of the Crime"—where it all starts. Then add your main three characters—victim, murderer and sleuth—and then your suspects and other characters. And, finally, fill in the other arms according to your priorities or as they occur to you. You can give each arm smaller arms—offshoots—indicating further descriptions. You could add a third set of arms, or a fourth, if you want to do a lot of pinpointing at this stage. I would advise against it. Your radial graph would end up looking like a crazy spider web. The value of this graph is its simplicity and, remember, it is only the first step.

The next piece for the drawing board is another structure: the good, old-fashioned block outline. Here you can list all of the elements (the arms), one under another, and put down as much detail as you have thought of so far. This outline is not chiseled in stone; you may end up working your way through three or four outlines as other thoughts occur to you. A word of advice here: Try not to get bogged down in outlines. We will later get into two more structures, where you will have more elbow room and can flesh out the details more fully.

Let me show you an outline formulated by a beginning writer. I have chosen a specific example because it shows the transition from the theoretical radial graph to a working outline—the step where theory turns into practice.

As a story, there is nothing terribly original or offbeat about it, except for the bisexuality, but the author did throw in a couple of nice twists. I have chosen it primarily because it *is* simple and because of his careful spadework. He had no illusions about the book presenting itself to him in a blinding flash. "Every idea I had," he told me, "was hewn out of the living rock . . . me."

THE CRIME—MURDER
(Title?—to come)

Scene of Crime
    8 o'clock Monday night. Gun at close range. In victim's house. Made to look like robbery. Safe open.

Victim
    Victor Saybrook, 60, widowed, no children. Wealthy businessman, about to retire and get remarried. Disliked by many as hard-nosed.

Criminal

Tony Saybrook, 24, nephew, college dropout, into drugs, bisexual. Being blackmailed by male lover. Wants to get married. Charming, but a mess.

Sleuth

Tom Bergson, 40, head of security at Victor's plant. One of few people who liked Victor and loathes the charming Tony (sponge).

Suspects—Motives

Tony—inherits if Victor doesn't remarry. Likes uncle?
Ed Brannigan, 38, ex-con Victor sent to prison (why?).
Helen Willoughby, 50, Victor's possessive, embittered secretary.
Katie Mitchell, 25, Tony's swinging girlfriend. Loyal to Tony. Hated Victor?

Time Element

Suspects—where that night? Alibis?
Need to solve crime before Victor's will probated?

Other Characters

Damien Kelloway—Tony's boyfriend
Bergson's wife? girlfriend?
Victor's fiancée—necessary?
Desk clerk—Brannigan's hotel
Victor's domestic help—one of them finds body?

Motives—Spelled out

Tony likely suspect because he needs money for drug habit. Bergson learns that Katie keeps Tony supplied. *Out* as suspect for now.
Brannigan released from San Quentin week before murder. Establishes shaky alibi through desk clerk. Underworld connections for gun. Learned to pick locks and crack safes in prison? Drunken Helen tells Bergson of being thrown over by Victor for fiancée. (Woman scorned) MAYBE
Katie Mitchell. Bergson can't see how she would gain by Victor's death. OUT

Background

San Francisco Bay Area
    Pacific Heights—Victor's home
    Berkeley—Tony's pad (lives with Katie?)
    Richmond—Victor's plant
    The Tenderloin—Brannigan's seedy hotel
    Telegraph Hill—Bergson's apartment
    Other locations for other characters? Later

Solution—Lead-up

Bergson accepts invitation to post-funeral party at Katie's (why accept?). Everybody high on drugs. (Bergson pretends to be?) Meets Damien who is very spaced out, who tells Bergson that Tony is going to buy him (Damien) a Ferrari. Blackmail exposed! Some kind of interplay between Damien and Katie gives Bergson idea: convinces Tony that Damien and Katie are sleeping together. Tony, enraged, screams out to Damien, "After what I did for you!" Bergson leads him into confession.

Turns out that Damien and Katie had worked on Tony to kill his uncle and once he inherited they would milk him by further blackmail.

Explore: Who gets Victor's money? A twist in the will after all? Fiancée important/necessary? Brannigan and Helen get together? Then change her age to 33.

Narration

Bergson's viewpoint? Ties into everybody, stronger narrator? Author (me) tells story? Can know things Bergson doesn't know.

This was the author's first outline. Working from the radial graph, he set the crime scene and sketched in his characters, background, motives *and* solution. He also had a lot of question marks, and at the end of the outline had thought of a subplot (Brannigan and Helen).

What he did not include were:

Means (of getting gun)
Opportunity (being sure Victor was home; getting in)
Alibis
Bergson's stake in solving the crime other than liking Victor.
The fiancée's role. She had no identity, yet it appeared she might be pivotal in determining Victor's will (which would affect Tony) and supply a reason for Helen to commit a spite murder.

However, he had made a good start. With his beginning and end in mind and his cast of characters almost complete, he felt confident enough to block out a second outline, answering the queries and filling in other details.

He decided to include the fiancée:

Karen Austin, 30, management analyst. Employed by Victor. Bergson secretly in love with her.

Karen gave Bergson a reason for solving the crime and provided a second subplot (Bergson's interest). She held a higher position than Helen, which gave Helen more cause.

Brannigan had been justly convicted, but is straight now.

The author did not yet know who had discovered the body; he was not ready to start the book.

The questions of means and opportunities (which would include alibis) had to wait until the author knew his characters better, so he created biographies of them.

> *Victor:* Five-nine, stocky, gray-haired, son of a Philadelphia dock worker. Scholarship to Temple U., ditto MIT for a doctorate in engineering. Got into electronics on ground floor. Married above his station to Martha——?, Philadelphia Main Line family, about the time he started his own components firm. Fifteen years before, had moved to California where the electronic industry was taking hold. Childless, he and Martha took Tony under their wing to give him a better chance. Martha dead five years.

> *Tony:* Came from same south Philadelphia background. Father was alcoholic, also a dock worker. Mother split when Tony was baby. Tony has lack of centeredness, lack of goals, in and out of colleges. Resents Victor's success, compared to his father's. Handsome kid, trades on his charm. Attracted to Katie because she is so in control of herself, which gives him spurious sense of control of himself. At Katie's party that night.

> *Bergson:* Big build, blond, third-generation Swede. Raised in San Francisco. Hired as guard for new plant fifteen years ago. Rose in ranks as company grew. Valued employee and good friend of Victor. Divorced, no children. Doesn't get Karen at end, doesn't try. Figures his lack of education is a barrier.

The author did the same for the other characters:

> *Ed Brannigan:* Worked in Victor's plant as a guard. A gambler. Abetted thieves stealing from Victor's plant to offset his debts. Got in over his head, yet basically a nice guy. Coincidental that he gets out of prison a week before murder. Looking for a job in a different field. (A trade learned in prison?) On night of murder is in his hotel room, looking through want ads. Two exits from hotel, so desk clerk not sure if Brannigan is really in his room, as he claims, that night. As ex-con, cops and Bergson assume he has access to gun. In appearance, a feisty little Irishman.

Helen Willoughby: Has apartment on Clay Street, not far from Victor's home. Drinking that night by herself? No doorman, so could have left and returned unnoticed. Access to Victor's gun at plant. Pleasant-looking, good dresser, efficient on job. Lonely off job.

Katie Mitchell: Comes from wealthy San Rafael family which has given her up as bad apple. College dropout who stayed in Berkeley as drug dealer and great party giver. Met Tony at UC. Very pretty girl, lovely soft face hiding a brassy brain. Gave party that night attended by Tony and Damien. Could have gotten gun through her drug connections.

Damien Kelloway: Instructor at UC. Middle-class Midwesterner. Good-looking, suave, a wheeler-dealer on and off campus. Swings both ways. Met Tony through Katie.

Karen Austin: Bright, good-looking, ambitious. From Chicago, where Victor met her at electronics conference (job market for hopefuls). Very good at her job. Loved Victor and ideal business partner for him. She will find body, which gives her importance, even though Victor is dead, and ties her in with Bergson, whom she calls first. She will inherit Victor's stock shares in plant.

Writing out these short bios, the author answered some of the other questions in his outline:

Victor's will. Not only does Karen end up with controlling interest in the plant but, by default, will get Tony's shares as well. Victor has left Helen a sizeable chunk of stock, much to her surprise.

The fiancée—so nebulous the first time around—has become a major character, though never a suspect.

Brannigan and Helen will not only get together but will go into business together (the trade he learned in prison), using the inherited stock to start the business.

By now, the author felt he had enough information about the characters to be comfortable in maneuvering them in and out of the story. When he wrote the book, he added other attributes as circumstances warranted—mannerisms (guilty looks, surliness, devil-may-care attitude), clothes, drink preferences, voices and physical appearances (as part of the introductions). He used these attributes to let characters

*I suggested that he rethink these names. There were too many "Ks"—Katie, Kelloway and Karen.

make their points or to throw in stage business.

Then the author went on to background. He gave it substance. He checked routes and travel time. He scouted Pacific Heights to find a suitable mansion for Victor. He walked through the Tenderloin to spot Brannigan's hotel. He drove to Berkeley to absorb Tony's ambience. From Berkeley he drove to Richmond, which seemed too rundown for the plant, Saybrook Tectronics Inc., so he moved it to Silicon Valley near San Jose. He gave his people favorite bars and restaurants (which were some of *his* favorites) in North Beach and along Hyde Street. He made a note to include the fog and the two bridges and a restaurant in Sausalito (where Helen would have her drunken scene with Bergson).

When the author's characters began living in his head, and after he had his terrain mapped out, he had to decide who was going to tell the story and how. He had already picked Bergson as the sleuth. But did he want first-person narration? It would lend a sense of immediacy to the story, and a sense of active participation, if the reader could sit inside Bergson's head from beginning to end. But if he made the narration third-person, then he, the author, could follow Bergson around and get inside other characters' heads, too. This second choice would give him a bird's-eye view, and it offered an attractive omniscience.

It was important, even at this early stage, to choose, because the book's structure would depend on how the story was narrated.

The author put himself in Bergson's shoes. He remembered driving across the Bay Bridge (*Mercedes convertible for Bergson? Yes!*), the tape deck on, the wind blowing his hair, his sense of purpose. Bergson, too, would have a sense of purpose (especially since the cops were not doing much about what they considered a run-of-the-mill murder in the course of a robbery). The author thought of Bergson's physique— tall, broad and blond. Impressive-looking. He certainly could not have Bergson stand in front of a mirror and describe himself to the reader. He thought of Bergson, so sure on his job, and so shuffle-footed around Karen. His loyalty to Victor. His healthy contempt for Tony's too-easy life of self-destruction. Bergson had so many positive and strong traits he himself was not aware of that only an outsider would be able to do justice to him. By the same reckoning, the author thought, Bergson might not be articulate enough to tell the story.

It was then that the author made his decision. He would tell Bergson's story for him.

The author was now ready to go on to a third structure: an outline of the contours of the book itself. Remembering the age-old rule that every story has a beginning, a middle and an end—an introduction, an elaboration and a conclusion—he drew lines for three columns on a sheet of paper and topped each column with a number denoting a division heading. He also added a fourth column marked "Wrap-up." He included the wrap-up because he knew that in order to surprise the reader at the end, he could not tell everything that Bergson had discovered as he went along; it would have cut down on the suspense.

1.	2.	3.	Wrap-up
Intro. victim & criminal	Develop. of suspects & interrogations	Eliminate suspects	Explain links & clues kept from reader
Murder scene & clues	Laying down clues	Zero in on criminal	Resolve subplots
Intro. who finds body	Intro. of subplots: Love interests (2)	Confrontation & catching criminal	
Intro. sleuth	Flight by suspects		

Using this profile, the author had a pretty good idea of what should transpire in each third of the book and in the wrap-up. The thirds were only a rough estimate. For instance, division 2 would most likely be longer than divisions 1 and 3, and the wrap-up would be the shortest section of all. He had read and analyzed enough mysteries to know this. He did not include names, places or time schedules here. At the moment, he was intent on plot structure alone—the backbone of his book.

For a week afterward, he mulled over his characters as he tried fitting them into the divisions: what they were doing when and where. He told me later that his brain began to resemble a kaleidoscope, with his characters and events and locations just so many pieces of colored glass that changed form every three seconds. He felt he needed still another structure that would pin these pieces down and give them coherent shapes.

He came up with a fourth—and, he hoped, final—structure: He would break the divisions down into chapters (or, as he put it, "build the book up.") He did a rather extensive job of it; he wanted to pin down as much as he could before he began. It would be tough enough going, he said, "just writing the damned thing!" without having to worry about who was where and when from one division to the next. Once he had outlined his chapters (there turned out to be fifteen of them) and the wrap-up, he felt confident enough to begin writing.*

If these four outline forms seem to you like an inordinate amount of bookkeeping, keep in mind that once they are done, you have solved the problem of organizing your story by logical steps. You will be less likely to paint yourself into corners, and you will avoid two often-committed blunders: coincidences and irrelevancies.

An important use of outlines is that they tell you where you are going and, just as important, where you have been.

I suggested earlier, in talking about the block outline, that you not get bogged down by it. This applies to any outline, which is essentially only a guide. As you build chapter on chapter, you will find the book coming alive under your typewriter keys. Let it have free rein, because when you feel it coming alive, you will need your outlines only as reference points. A rigid adherence to an outline by then would only constrict your imagination and cramp your style.

So far, I have referred to the plot as "the backbone of the book." Still thinking structurally, now try to imagine the book as an armature—the stiff pieces of wire that a sculptor bends and twists to make the stick figure that becomes the foundation for the clay that follows. With the four outlines under your belt, you have, in essence, created an armature. You have your basic structure.

You have your crime, your motive and your solution. You have given your characters biographies. You have laid out your background and have determined your time span. You know who is going to tell the story. Now you want to put clay on your armature. It is time to begin the book.

*If you are curious to know how he "built up" the book, see his chapter and wrap-up outlines in the Appendix.

CHAPTER 4

THE OPENING GAMBIT

THE VICTIM

IN THIS FIRST THIRD of the book, appealing to a reader's emotion is as important as appealing to a reader's logic. In the mystery novel, the primary emotion is suspense, and it should start on page one. The reader should be intrigued by your opening scene, either by a murder just happening or by a murder that is going to happen shortly. If the murder happens immediately, the shock value lays the ground for suspense. If the murder is yet to come, the anticipation generates suspense. You can build excitement, especially if there is doubt about the outcome. Say the victim escapes, then is caught again and battles fiercely before succumbing to the murderous onslaught. If you draw the scene out for all it is worth, the reader is caught up in the struggle and cares about the fate of the victim to the point of identifying with him or her.

That first emotional impact will determine the reader's involvement in the rest of the story, so be sure the reader has a ringside seat. Murder committed off stage is no murder at all to the mystery aficionado. To be done, it must be seen to be done.

How you set the groundwork for suspense in the opening gambit can very well set the tone for the rest of the book.

The opening line should hook the reader, as well as give some information:

He stood with the gun pointed at the rigid form of Miss Dalway, looked into her startled eyes, then fired four shots into her body.

You have begun with a murder, and you have already introduced two characters.

I watched helplessly as he ran into the oncoming traffic.

Here, you have immediately established your first-person narrator and have also set up a piece of the action.

The moonlight honed the trees into black skeletons.

In this first line, you have set a sinister tone for the book.
  The opening line—or opening paragraph—should state a startling action or describe a memorable character or a mood, and it should be done as economically as possible to be an effective hook.
  A strong opening can also serve as a launching pad. Take that first example, where Miss Dalway is murdered. Would it not seem logical that the first action the murderer would take would be to make sure she was dead, then to cover his tracks and leave Miss Dalway's apartment as quickly and as silently as possible? The cracking open of the door, the peering into the hall, the leading away from the murder scene to the outside world give you the transition you need to start the story on its way.
  With the second example, you have a choice of going two ways. You could allude to the scene leading up to the person's rush into the street:

I saw that I had pushed him too far. Why hadn't I . . .?

That gives you an opening for a flashback* leading up to that moment. Or you could have the narrator come to his or her senses and chase the fugitive:

I shook off my surprise and sprinted after him. . . .

That sends the story forward, and you are off and running, too.
  In the third example, where the trees take on a macabre form, you

---

*Actually, I would not recommend flashbacks for your first book. They add a dimension to time, true, but they also involve two sets of emotional thrusts which are tricky for the beginner.

could carry on for several paragraphs, bringing in the rugged cliffs, the dark meadows, but always moving toward the old house where the action begins. (Be careful with your word choices in creating a mood. Too many adjectives—"starkly etched," "moaning wind," "terror-filled atmosphere"—will not build up a mood but, rather, will drown it in excess.)

You will not establish your entire opening scene in one line or one paragraph, of course. After the initial eye-catcher, it will take you two or three pages, perhaps the whole chapter, to set down the scene. But if your first few lines start an action going or introduce a main character or set a mood, the following pages will be easier to get into.

To keep the momentum going, it is a good idea to pack a lot of information into these first pages. You have whetted the reader's appetite; now offer the reader something to chew on.

Introduce the scene of the crime early. Start the action going right away. If you have a murder within the first few pages, be prepared to manufacture a buoyancy, enough activity to carry through until the next action—the investigation—because if the victim appears early, sprawled in blood, you have just given the reader one of the two highest points of the book. (The other is the solution.) So if there is an early introduction of the murder, emotionally you have already shot half your wad and there will not be another time the reader is as enthralled until the solution. To borrow a phrase from show business, murder is a hard act to follow.

How do you maintain the buoyancy? Introduce a strong character, one who will be interesting to the reader and who will play a vital role in the story. It could be the one who discovers the body, or the sleuth. Or you can shift to a scene that is far from the grim murder scene, in both miles and tone, far from the blood and gore we have just witnessed, a scene that is replete with normalcy and calm. It could be the victim's wife working in her garden, tending to her azaleas and thinking about their upcoming vacation, just prior to a visit from the police. A diametrically opposed set of emotions, one following closely on the other, has a dramatic impact that certainly qualifies as buoyancy.

It might be easier for you to get into the book if you work up to the murder. As I suggested earlier, you can show the murder *about* to happen, and put the reader in the victim's shoes or in the murderer's mind. Another way is to open the scene in which the murder is being planned. It could be an assassination group working out strategic details around a coffee table. It could be the murderer buying the gun. Or a fierce quarrel between the murderer and the victim, the one hotly making accusations and the other just as hotly denying them. To attract the reader's attention, *criminal intent* is as legitimate as the crime itself.

If you write with suspense in mind from the start, you will accomplish two functions: You will hook your reader right off, and you will more easily be able to maintain a suspenseful tone throughout the book; the opening suspense can serve as a reference later on. For instance, if you get bogged down in the middle game, reread your opening pages. They can put you in the mood for getting back on the suspense track.

Introduce your three important characters early. As I have already said, it is the characters who bring the plot to life. If your crime is right up front, your victim, murderer and sleuth will be, too.

Once the narrator is satisfied that the victim is dead, describe the body—its position, signs of struggle, clothes, jewelry, and if the victim is a stranger to the narrator, the victim's sex and body characteristics. Include as many traits as you think necessary to show that this was once a human being. Too often I have read murder scenes in which the victim seemed to be just a mound of inanimate tissue. It put me off, and I lost interest right there. However, watch out for "a look of horror" in the victim's eyes; there will not be any kind of "living" look. Nor will there be, so soon after death, any kind of rictus—grinning or grimacing—indicating a last scream. These kinds of physical anomalies are best left to nineteenth-century gothic writers, who used them successfully on less sophisticated audiences.

Give some background on the victim without cutting into the drama of the scene. You could comment on looking at the body with a short introduction describing the victim before the murder.

> In life, he had been known for his shady business deals. A handsome, robust man, he had also been known for his popularity with women. In death, he looked neither robust nor popular. He had gone into one last deal, and it had caught up with him.

It does not have to be much, just enough to establish the fact that this was once a living person. As the story unfolds, the investigator will uncover the victim's past, in the search for motive and murderer.

Even though only you know who the murderer is, the culprit must be firmly planted in your mind, for there might be dialogue between the murderer and the victim, or the method of murder may be peculiar to the murderer. You can also give other hints about the identity of the culprit. If a knife was used, the murderer might clean the blade on a piece of the victim's clothing, showing a compulsive neatness as well as a brutal insolence; might grind a glass underfoot or put a record on the turntable as a "calling card." In the same fashion, the way the murderer searches for something after the slaying tells the reader something.

You have already worked out who the sleuth is and what relationship he or she has to the victim—in other words, why this particular person has been chosen to do the detecting. If you are using third-person narration, a description of the sleuth and the sleuth's qualifications are in order. A first-person narrator will have to let the reader know by degrees, for it would be awkward to have the sleuth give the reader an autobiography up front; it would introduce an intrusive self-consciousness.

The sleuth will first of all become familiar with the scene of the crime—the layout, the method and the means. How was the victim killed? Knife? Gun? Garrote? Was the place of the murder easily accessible? A busy street? An apartment? A lone cabin in the woods? These factors are so obvious that readers do not think of them as clues, but they are.

In the opening gambit, you will probably bring in other characters who will be important because of their relationship to the victim, and who will appear throughout the book: spouse, friends, business colleagues, acquaintances, even strangers. Keep the number down, though, because you will have plenty going on already, and try to space their arrivals in intervals so that the reader does not need a scorecard to keep track of them. Let them have their first moments on scene so they can be impressed on the reader's memory.

Other characters, if your scene needs them, will not be memorable: the building superintendent, the cops, ambulance attendants and nosy neighbors. They will volunteer information (useful and useless) and serve as background "noise."

Your sleuth should follow on the heels of these other characters, if not sooner. Through the sleuth's eyes you will describe the murder scene panoramically for the first time. And this is a good place for your first clues to be laid. In fact, anywhere from page one on up to now is a good place. The reader has been so taken with the murder and the ensuing fuss that no attention will be paid to the clues you slip in. As I have mentioned, the location of the murder scene can be a clue in itself.

If you have the reader caught up in the circumstances of the crime and in the ambience surrounding the crime, and then casually throw in the fact that there are two sets of footprints leading away from the body, the reader is not going to remember that important detail.

If you are telling the story through the eyes of the sleuth—either in the first or the third person—chances are that clues will not be introduced until the sleuth is on scene. It is the sleuth who is going to solve the case and so it is to the sleuth that all details must eventually become apparent.

I have talked about the most important elements that go into the first third of the book, and now I would like to give you a sense of the tone of this section.

Your opening chapters will be concerned with laying out the facts of the case. There will not be any cliff-hangers or sudden surprises. You are setting out to invest the reader with information, not fear. Fear will come later. What you want to do now is to arouse the reader's curiosity:

a) Who is killed?
b) Who is affected by the crime?
c) Who wants to solve it and why?

The chapters comprising a) and b) contain basic information that also contains the solution, and so some of your information will be camouflaged, to misdirect the reader, by emphasizing the grimness of the crime, the exoticness of the setting (if it is exotic) and the activities of the police and their technicians who have been called in. These are eye-catchers that are really eye-diverters. Another invaluable eye-diverter, because it adds feeling, is the reactions of the characters on scene. Make the reader respond sympathetically, play on the emotions, and you will cancel out the reader's thought processes that could lead to picking up clues.

Let your characters show shock. The equilibrium of their lives has been shattered, and suffusing these opening chapters is a sense of *solemnity* in the presence of a wrongful death. Their world has gone awry, thanks to you, the author, and now you must set about righting it. You do that by introducing c) the people who care the most. Besides those who are close to the victim, there will be the sleuth who steps into the picture, or a pair of sensitive police detectives. Whomever you choose, the sleuth(s) takes over and injects a steadying influence into the emotional maelstrom. With the introduction of c) you have made your first link between cause and effect by imposing a new set of circumstances on the old which moves the plot forward and lets you segue into the middle game.

.

CHAPTER 5

THE MIDDLE GAME

THE SLEUTH

THE MIDDLE GAME picks up and develops the events of the opening gambit and must eventually edge toward the end game, besides carrying its own storytelling weight.

This section is a tricky one, for there are many components that go into it. If the plot is the backbone of the book, the middle game contains the supporting vertebrae. Most of your complications will be centered in this section, and that is why it is essential to have your chapters well blocked out beforehand. You might also want to refer to the diagram in which you blocked out the book into thirds and a wrap-up.

I think you will end up needing both sets of references. Use the chapter-by-chapter layout so that you will know where you are at every step. (See Appendix.) Refer occasionally to the four-part diagram on page 68 to give yourself a sense of the overall pace of the book as you go along.

What do I mean by *pace?* Keeping the story moving. Keeping it charged with action and emotion. Unfolding one event so that it leads into another.

Momentum is another good word for *pace.* Walking is a good example of the kind of momentum you need. You put your right foot forward. Then, to keep from falling, you bring the left foot forward, which puts you forward again, so the right foot moves forward to save the situation. This happens over and over as long as you are walking. It is the same when you unfold one event after another—an action, an emotional reaction or—perhaps most effective of all—a crisis.

You could, I think, refer to the events in a mystery novel as a series of crises. You have a big crisis in the murder, and another big crisis when you reach the identification and apprehension of the murderer. In between, you have a series of smaller crises. You could call these crises "peaks of interest," and, if you have enough of them, and if they blend in well together, you will have achieved a good pace.

How do you achieve these peaks of interest? It is one thing to confront the reader with a corpse and produce shudders of "There but for the grace of God go I," and later to confront the villain with an airtight case that will lead to eternal incarceration; these are obvious peaks. But what about the less dramatic events, the vertebrae that connect the story? What are these small crises and how do you bring them about?

You have set up an intriguing situation in the opening gambit, and the reader wants to know why it happened. Begin your investigation on the heels of the murder, with the sleuth looking into the victim's background for a *motive*. If the victim was a little old flower lady who did not have an enemy in the world, then you had better replot your book. If the victim proves to have been a dyed-in-the-wool SOB, leaving a swathe of destruction wherever . . . then your sleuth will be overwhelmed with motives, and you and the reader will *again* need a scorecard to keep track of the suspects. Keeping in mind that there will be one motive per suspect, plan on using only the number of suspects you can handle comfortably.

The sleuth, being a student of human nature, is aware of the kinds of attitudes that prompt people to murder, and knows that the common denominator for all motives is self-interest.

> • Greed is by far the most common of our human failings: to collect insurance, to gain an inheritance or to cut someone out of an inheritance; to do someone out of property; to do away with business competition; to cover up illegal transactions.
> • Thwarted love runs a close second: getting rid of an unwanted spouse; getting rid of someone else's unwanted spouse; committing murder to protect a loved one, a quid pro quo of dubious morality.
> • Revenge is an action in retaliation for a deep hurt. A man's family has been wiped out, and he goes after the sadistic culprits; a long-held grudge grows as the years pass, and finally bursts; a psychopath rights imaginary wrongs.

Love, greed and pain are three classic motives of self-interest, elemental emotions that justify themselves in irrational ways. Whatever the motive, it will seem like a need as much as a desire, *and the murderer will see no difference between them.*

Very quickly, bring the sleuth into contact with the innocent and guilty alike. He or she will make no judgments at the beginning except for personal taste. There may be sympathy for the widow and contempt for her brother-in-law. Personal clashes, outside the line of duty, make the sleuth and the characters more interesting when they meet. The same can be said for affection or sexual attractions between them.

The sleuth, forming first impressions of the possible suspects and subtly or not so subtly delving into their motives, will be asking questions and digging into backgrounds that provide the *opportunity* for murder. Most of the suspects will have alibis on first meeting with a sleuth. Other alibis will come later (someone has been protecting someone, or a character committed a lesser crime at the time of the murder and was covering that up). Some of the alibis will be broken down and those people will become suspects a second time later on.

Opportunity is as important as motive, and suspects without opportunity will be ruled out even if they have strong motives. Say the author decides to include one of the victim's sons-in-law, who works in the Saudi Arabian oil fields as a rigger—a colorful character who is going to be fun to write about. But if he is attaching derrick cables at the fatal moment, the author can only introduce him at the funeral, so he is no one for the sleuth to fool around with and waste the reader's time. The son-in-law may have hated the old man with a passion—a good motive—but it was, to put it lightly, inconvenient for him to knock the old man off. The author reluctantly drops this colorful character.

In the mystery novel, murder is seldom a sudden, impulsive act; it is a planned operation. The murderer has to figure on catching the victim at an opportune time, and so will study the victim's work and play habits and develop a schedule from them and then decide on a time slot for the crime. With this kind of planning, the murderer, of course, is at the mercy of schedule changes and unexpected visitors. (These intrusions can add interesting complications.)

Another way to carry out the crime is to set the victim up, to arrange a meeting somewhere on safe ground. Using this method, the murderer is able to call the shots. By *safe ground* I mean a place where there are no chances for witnesses, which offers the best cover and which provides an easy avenue of escape. The challenge you will have with this method is getting the victim to appear in a place that the murderer has chosen.

There is a third choice, and I am not sure that I would recommend it: catching the victim on the fly. The murder has been decided upon and the murderer just happens to encounter the victim on safe ground and just happens to be carrying the murder weapon. This method is too perilously close to coincidence to satisfy anyone, unless you can work in the *irony of chance* to your advantage. But this can get you into philosophical realms that are best not explored in a first mystery novel.

If you have the motive and have set up the opportunity, you still have to figure out how the victim is done in, the *means* of murder. I have already mentioned a gun, knife and garrote as possible weapons. These would be easily enough obtained by a professional killer, especially a gun, but what about the novice, someone who is going to kill for the first time? How does that person lay hands on a weapon? Has the scheming wife persuaded her doomed husband to buy her a .25-caliber automatic to protect herself from "burglars" while he is on the road? Does the disgruntled lover strangle his wayward girlfriend with a nylon stocking because it is easily at hand? Does the knife wielder know enough anatomy to aim for the heart between the third and fourth ribs? You have to decide on the availability of the death instrument and the ease with which it can be used and gotten rid of (or foolishly kept).

The appearance of the death scene can be made a part of the means. The murderer might want to set the crime up to look like suicide—throwing the victim out of the window or placing the gun by the body. Or plan the crime scene so the evidence points toward another suspect as the murderer. Or leave no clues at all—a bona fide enigma that will intrigue the reader and call upon your ingenuity to arrange. Making the murder look like an accidental death will also call upon your ingenuity and can keep the reader guessing longer. The sleuth will not only have to figure out whodunit but, first, was it even murder? The victim's death might be made to seem like a hit-and-run, a "fall" in the shower with subsequent drowning, or contact with a section of frayed insulation.

CHALLENGES

With motive, opportunity and means as subjects of the search, the sleuth can begin the investigation. This means a lot of interviewing, a lot of tracking, a lot of probing. To keep the book from reading like a Dun & Bradstreet report, to keep the pace and the reader's interest up, you are going to have to throw in tensions and conflicts and little crises.

I have read murder mysteries in which the crime occurred in the penultimate chapter and was solved in the last one (in a quick wind-up). They were thin psychological studies leading to murder and belonged in a different part of the library. They were mostly domestic dramas, and anywhere along the line I felt that the couple could just as easily separate or the angry spouse could calm down. In reading them, I referred to the jacket copy more than once to ascertain that, yes, this was billed as a murder mystery. The only challenge the author offered me was: When in the hell was something going to happen? With books like this, I find myself doing a lot of skimming, and I never pick up that author's books again. I want to read what has been promised, and a murder mystery, to me, should have excitement, or the pretty-soon expectancy of it, throughout. I want those tensions, conflicts and little crises, and I am grateful to authors who provide them.

Here are some of the ways they do it:

• A murder has been committed and the sleuth is hard on the heels of the prime suspect. It looks as though the book is going to end in the middle. Then you bring in a second murder. It *may* be tied in with the first, but the prime suspect seemingly had no access to the second victim. Two murders. *Two* suspects? The sleuth's straight path has forked; which path should be followed?

• Multiple murders, especially if they are a part of a pattern, can produce a series of peaks of interest, as well as infuse the plot with an on-the-edge-of-the-chair expectancy—who is going to get it next? Multiple murders can serve as a cover-up device for the intended victim. A supposed sniper is taking pot shots at random and, along the way, "happens" to kill the real target. Multiple murders are also committed because of vendettas and by psychos. If your plot demands mass murder, that is, a number of murders, then keep the numbers vague. Experienced authors have told me that after the first two or three murders, they will refer to further mayhem rather than detailing the acts. Otherwise, tedium sets in and the story loses its edge.

• Next to an actual murder, the threat of murder can be even more than a peak of interest; it can act as a sustained plateau of suspense. To keep the level of interest up—after all, once you reach the top of a plateau, it *is* flat—peaks should arise from the plateau. You can have a Damoclean sword hovering over the victim, but this can lose its menace unless it sways ominously every so often: The victim has taken self-protective measures, only to have the intimidator break through the protective barrier; through an error of judgment, the victim walks into a trap set by the culprit; the victim is double-crossed. The idea is to create situations where security proves to be an illusion.

• If your plateau is the backbone of the book, where threat prevails throughout, you had better rescue your victim at the end. No reader should have to go through two hundred or more pages of agonizing tension without an ultimate release.

• Physical hazards are devices for creating ongoing suspense, especially when they happen to sympathetic characters. Often it is the sleuth who sticks his or her head out looking for information or following up on hunches. The danger lies in two areas:

1. from other characters—interviewing a psychotic Mafia don about an arch rival; and
2. from physical hazards—descending into a long-abandoned mine to locate a cache of papers stashed there years before.

• A character can be put into jeopardy by surprise: run down or almost run down by a car; threatened by a gun, or a landslide or other acts of God.

• The threat can be psychological, with one character having a neurotic hold over another and the other painfully bending to the will of the first under threat of something even worse happening. This has dramatic impact when both characters are concealing vital evidence and one of them does not want it revealed. This piques the interest of the sleuth, who goes to work on the weaker character.

While we are on the subject of psychological cruelty, let me say a word about sadism in the mystery novel; it is surely a salient peak of interest! I would venture to guess that mystery authors who deal at length with physical abuse have unresolved sadistic tendencies and sublimate them in their books. You could say the same for surgeons and soldiers who sublimate in their fashions. Mystery writers, though, do it with words, not deeds. Torture seems to be prevalent in books where the narrator is a macho type, though he is usually not the torturer. In fact, he will eventually put a fig leaf over these dark delights by reacting with horror and rescuing the victim, who is often a wrong-headed woman or a petty criminal—"expendable" types. But before the rescue, we are treated to the pulled fingernails and the lighted matches, sometimes in fulsome detail. I will grant you these details are fascinating in a sickening way and, for moralists, call attention to man's inhumanity to man. Some authors justify their excesses by pointing to "the streak of sadism in everybody." But sadism implies an action toward someone; that would be the author at work. A reader who goes along with these brutal actions is the passive (and compliant) recipient, so the author in effect is catering to the reader's masochism, if there is also "a streak of masochism in everybody." In real life, people confine this trait to skydiving and sessions with the IRS. In reading books, they will go farther afield, and the majority will hold still for some physical brutality; they are only reading about it, so there is a buffer zone of distance between them and the victim. For the more imaginative reader, you would do better to set the torture scene and let the reader imagine what is going to happen. This way, you can produce shudders without turning stomachs.

Challenges play an important role in creating peaks of interest, and are integral parts of the plot. For that matter, the mystery novel is based on challenge: Whodunit? To arrive at a satisfactory conclusion, the sleuth faces many smaller challenges on the way, and these fall into two categories: ferreting out information from suspects, and finding and interpreting clues.

FERRETING OUT INFORMATION

Your sleuth will ask a lot of questions of the characters to pin down their motives, means and opportunities. Some of them will have weak alibis and others will lie. Still others will have no apparent reasons to kill the victim. They will all, to some extent, present themselves as angels or brick walls. Few if any of the characters will cooperate to make the job easy. So the sleuth has to "read" them for weak spots in their alibis and chinks in their personalities. There will be at least one person the sleuth will initially misread, bringing about confusion and sometimes small calamities—cross purposes and blind spots—that need to be righted before the investigation can go on. Then the sleuth will have to rethink his or her reading of that person or go to others for additional information. It almost goes without saying, but not quite, that the sleuth will misread the murderer for most of the book.

I have already talked about giving your characters specific traits so they will be recognized as individuals; you did that when you worked up their biographies. Now think of those traits in terms of whether they whet the curiosity of the sleuth. One or some of them will manifest oddball behavior that catches the sleuth's interest, or perform an action that is out of character—another signal to the sleuth. Another character will appear to be so blah that the first impulse is to dismiss *that one* with a negligent wave of the hand. This could prove to be a mistake and the sleuth will later have second thoughts about this "angel."

How the characters react to the news of the murder will be noted by the observant sleuth: protesting too much or not caring at all; verbose or tight-lipped; genuine grief. These reactions will plant suspicion, or divert it, in the sleuth's mind.

Let your sleuth have hunches about people. This imparts a sense of daring, which is attractive. It shows the sleuth off as having intuition, which is complimentary. As I said earlier, emotion is as important as logic in the mystery novel, and your sleuth is a feeling human being working with and against other feeling human beings. The sleuth is not a computer, is not going to have all the facts at fingertip reach—certainly not until close to the end. Until then, to keep from creating stalemates, your sleuth is going to have to trust to intuition—hunches—sometimes. But hunches do not come from out of left field, though it seems as if they do. They are the result of calculations that are so lightning-fast that the conscious mind does not at the moment register the process, only the result. Acting on them is like taking a leap of faith, which the sleuth will then try determinedly to shore up with solid facts; at some point, the sleuth will sort out the thinking process and share it with the reader. Would it not be simpler to explain the process before acting on it? Yes, but then you would do away with a nice piece of suspense.

You can bring in an added fillip by pointing a finger at the wrong person. But do not let a character act suspiciously without justification. Build up a good case and raise the reader's hopes. When the sleuth realizes that he or she is on the wrong track, it is not enough to say, "Oops, I goofed!" That is like crossing a small footbridge that has no middle. The reader is willing to share a few crestfallen moments, but then get the sleuth on the scent of another suspect to start the action going again. With skill and luck, the quick switch will befuddle the reader. Use small surprises as stepping stones leading to the big one.

Another challenge for the sleuth is a suspect's disappearance. Has the suspect been murdered? Has the person fled, and if so, was it because of guilt or self-preservation? Or was it a kidnapping? There has to be a suspect around to accuse and the sleuth is going to have to find the person in order to point the accusing finger. Depending on your plot, the sleuth will end up taking the person off the suspect list or running the murderer to ground.

Among the most interesting predicaments for the sleuth is knowing who committed the murder but not being able to prove it. You could even use it as a premise of your book, but many varied situations would have to transpire between the hunted and the hunter to sustain the suspense—an unending series of small crises. If you feel you are not yet enough of a strategist to sustain an essentially one-dimensional structure, it is better to use this ploy toward the end of the book. This works if the murderer has been uncovered by elimination of the other suspects; only X would have had both the means and opportunity. And here the solution might lie with the so-called motiveless person when the sleuth unearths a family skeleton or some other factor that has been well hidden, and the motive was not apparent until near the end.

An edict of mystery writing in the twenties and thirties exhorted the author to have the sleuth suspect *everyone* at least once, so the number of peaks of interest would be limited only by the number of characters in the book. Even the little old flower lady would be suspected of stashing cocaine in her bouquets because her nose dribbled suspiciously. Mystery writing today is not approached as if it were Twenty Questions versus twenty characters. This kind of scattershot overkill does not intrigue today's sophisticated reader for one moment. The sleuth is no less busy nowadays, but the field of operations has expanded greatly from the time of prowling around the confines of the country manse. The activities have broadened to where backgrounds for the characters—psychological and physical—are more fully explored, and so fewer characters are needed in the search for the guilty.

LAYING CLUES

A suspect's behavior ties into the crime, whereas clues lead to the suspect.

Clues are pieces of evidence that lead to the solution of the crime. They are capable of being seen, heard, touched, smelled or tasted—in all ways, physical—and their properties are *recognizable* to the reader: cindered scraps of a will, a trampled flower bed. Clues of an everyday nature with everyday names are the fairest to the reader. If the sleuth smells trichloroethane on the victim's suede boots, you had better say instead that the sleuth noted that the victim's boots had been recently treated with a water repellant.

Clues take on spatial and temporal characteristics: who was where when. These kinds of clues are important for laying false alibis or for clearing a suspect.

Clues will arise out of their environment. They will be there because of what happened: the torn-off button or the smashed vase, indicating the kind of struggle that occurred before the murder. They will play a part in the motive: a crooked accountant with a set of phony books to be sought after.

Clues will stand out because they do *not* belong in the environment: a tie that clashes with a shirt, showing the murderer to be colorblind, an important factor if the murderer is seen running a red light unknowingly.

Clues can build from other clues and work in pairs or trios. In the case of the murderer's color-blindness, two indications were given, the second clue driving home the importance of the first.

Clues can be noted without stating they are clues. Say the sleuth describes a photograph on the victim's mantelpiece, showing the victim and X standing in front of the Colosseum. Then taking the picture out of its frame, the sleuth notes the photo lab date: February 198–. Later, when the sleuth is interrogating X, who swears he did not meet the victim until June of that year, the value of the photo date becomes evident to the sharp reader.

Along these lines, here is another way to plant a clue: The sleuth takes an inventory of the victim's purse, noting the cosmetics, keys, pen, date book, etc. Among those harmless items will be one which will figure into the later scheme of things. You could call this the ploy of protective coloring. What you have done is to give all of the objects the same value to the sleuth's camera eye, objects that will be sorted out later.

You can bury clues on a grander scale, wrapping an entire episode around them: a circus scene or the goings-on in an ad agency. You drop in the clues while entertaining the reader. To play fair, let the reader know that the sleuth has come looking for information. With this red alert, the reader will pay closer attention and be prepared to meet the challenge. However, if the circus antics or the agency operations are entertaining enough, the reader will mislead himself or herself by overlooking the clue(s).

Speaking of buried clues, do not forget one of the most famous ploys in mystery literature: the clue that is in plain sight. Poe was the first to make use of it in *The Purloined Letter*. It is still worth using today. It could be a diamond bracelet or a sixty-foot-tall statue. Its essential quality is that it is always there for anyone to see, and everybody takes it for granted.

Then there is the instance in which the value of the clue is known but you postpone an explanation of its value. Say the sleuth comes across a document and thinks, *Now I know why X was so anxious to get his hands on this*, without describing its contents. The reader knows that this will be explained eventually and it adds to the suspense and brings a surprise when it is explained.

Arcane clues should be left in the hands of experts: blood samples and skin and hair fragments; scrolls written in an ancient language. A sleuth who is not a biochemist or an archeologist will defer to the proper authorities, either buttonholing a professional or reading up on the subject. An author who also happens to be a super scientist can dazzle the reader with clues based on abstruse knowledge, but wonder and admiration go only so far; the reader has to be able to participate in discovering the meaning of clues and their applications if you are going to play fair. Remember the trichloroethane!

It adds to the suspense when you describe a clue and emphasize its importance but purposely do not say why it is important: "I read through the bundle of old letters. They were a real find, and another piece of the puzzle fell into place." As I said about hunches, be sure to tie this discovery to an explanation later—jogging the reader's memory if it is much later—to show the connection.

You can give clues by inference: actions seen out of the corner of the eye. The sleuth refers to a missing document and the suspect's hand involuntarily moves to a breast pocket.

And there are clues by analogy. The sleuth sees a crane at work and gets an insight into the way the body must have been shifted from one place to another.

A lack of clues can be intriguing. As you very carefully describe found clues, here you very carefully note the lack of them—a victim without a mark on the body, a person without a history, a lack of disarray at the scene of the crime. Your sleuth will eventually discover how the person died and will ferret out the person's background for clues. But for the opening of your book, a lack of clues presents what seems to be an insuperable challenge.

"Misdirection" is the name of the game for clueing, as you can see by the examples I have already given, and it plays its most important part when you introduce a clue that almost shrieks, "I am a clue!" It is a kind of evidence that is absolutely essential to the plot and there is no way to camouflage its role; the minute it is introduced, the reader recognizes it as a clue. What you do is to create a diversion quickly, leading the reader's attention away to another observation. If it is an object, the sleuth can downplay its importance or misinterpret its value. If it is a person, irrelevant attributes of the person can be described: wearing the wrong-colored clothes, not being on time. An unexpected action can be put in to send the reader's interest off in another direction. What you have done is led the reader into misleading himself or herself.

The utmost limit of misdirection, of course, is the red herring.* This is a false clue put in not to test but to confuse the reader by deliberately going off in a wrong direction. Like real clues, red herrings take on the semblance of legitimacy and are treated seriously until they are exposed. It is not wise to have many of them or to have the sleuth pursue them for long; otherwise, the reader will (rightly) feel cheated when these false identities are exposed. Red herrings are not that essential anyway. You can mislead the reader by using only legitimate clues, and still feel confident that the reader will supply the confusion.

Because clues are the underpinnings of the solution, what the sleuth observes will determine the way the investigation goes. If you are playing fair with the reader, everything the sleuth sees, the reader will also see, including details that have escaped the murderer. What provides the challenge to both sleuth and reader is the *significance* of the details, which the author may, at times, hold back. This happens when the sleuth does not see the significance immediately or is waiting to match the clue up with something else before telling the reader, and this must be made clear when that "something else" is brought into the picture.

As I have noted, you can put clues in using any device you choose, and explain them or not. What you count on for the final surprise—the

---

*Using a red herring to throw someone off the track dates back at least to the seventeenth century, according to *The Oxford English Dictionary*: "The trailing of a dead Cat or Fox (and in the case of necessity a Red Herring) three or four miles and then laying the dogs on the scent."

solution—is the reader's careless memory or an inability to understand the value of the evidence. Readers these days are a pretty shrewd lot and some of them will be right along with you, maybe even ahead of you, if you have been fair. If so, they will continue reading, even flipping back to pinpoint clues. The sharp reader will still enjoy the story, even after figuring out whodunit, to see how well you have worked out your plot. That is why it is important to have your clues solid and well spaced, and to leave no loose ends.

This brings to mind yet another chart you might consider making, to keep track of your clues and where you have placed them. This is as vital to the mystery writer as making a sponge count is to a surgeon during an operation. A chart of clue placement will prove invaluable when you are revising; it is easier than you realize to drop a clue or put in a new one without remembering to follow up. If the idea of still another chart makes you groan, then try this: Wherever you place a clue in your chapter outline, type it in caps or underline it in red.

How do you place your clues? Your first step is to think of them as necessary tools for the sleuth, indications of the direction to follow in interrogating suspects (what to ask) and examining scenes (what to look for). Clues are not only points of interest, they also supply some of the oil to keep the plot moving.

If you are unsure of what clues to insert or where, you might try working backward: Start with the solution. The murderer is caught (or found out). What final item was instrumental? A train schedule left behind in the haste of departure? Going back another step, what remark was dropped, alerting the sleuth to *someone* taking the Midnight Special? Another step backward: Why was the sleuth able to overhear the remark?

Or you can work forward, still keeping the solution in mind, by tracking the murderer's trail through the story. After the murder, the culprit resumes a normal life except for making more frequent visits to the doctor/bank/lover. Or the culprit arranges a trip. Track the plans the murderer has made as a result of the murder. Not all the actions will necessarily appear in the book, but if you know where the murderer is at all times, then you can lay the spoor as you go along, and this can be brought out by hindsight or by a confession in the wrap-up.

As you incorporate the clues in your chapter outline, they will seem to stick out like sore thumbs. But remember, you will disguise them as you write, using some form of misdirection that will camouflage them, and they will be obvious only to you.

I have used the term *follow-up* several times; that is, watch out for loose ends. But a mystery story is not like a crossword puzzle, where one set of squares is filled in and then you go on to another set. That would be a bore. Your sleuth is going to run into blind alleys following up on false information. This makes the job harder and more of a challenge. (It also fills up pages!)

Clues are not necessarily proofs of guilt. They have to be checked out, and some of them fizzle out. Say your sleuth has come up with a promising lead. It may not prove fruitful, but only you know that, so play it for all it is worth for the amount of space it deserves to keep the reader on tenterhooks. The sophisticated reader is well aware that the sleuth will encounter false clues; this is part of the fun, part of the suspense. But be sure you eventually expose it as a false clue.

If the lead does prove fruitful, do be careful not to have the sleuth say, "And then everything fell into place." If everything does, too often it will be pages later and the author has not made a logical bond between the occasion of the light bulb going on and the solution. As I have said, remind the reader of the first clue and show the connection.

If the sleuth says, "Everything fell into place" halfway through the book, watch out! At this stage in the story there has not been sufficient opportunity or time to set everything in place and the narrator is just juicing up the current to give the reader a meaningless jolt.

Another piece of specious suspense to watch out for is when the light bulb has once more gone on in the sleuth's head and he or she slinks off scene, muttering about something that has to be looked into because time is of the essence. In the next scene the sleuth is draped over a bar, mulling over half a dozen possibilities or recapping previously gathered information, and God only knows what happened to the essence of time. If the investigation does not follow on the heels of the clue, the reader is not sure whether the sleuth's mutterings were a promise or a threat; neither one has materialized. Turning a blind eye to logical connections damages an author's credibility, and leaves the reader up in the air.

In the chapter on the opening gambit, I said that clues could be successfully laid in the early scenes, where they are buried in the excitement of the discovery of the murder. Obviously there will be more in the middle game, and the cumulative effect of the preceding clues can be topped by one essential clue the sleuth needs to complete the puzzle. The plot will not depend entirely on this one clue—unless you are emulating the mystery writers of the twenties and thirties, heaven forfend! That is too much of a burden to lay on a writer. But in its own right the one clue will be pivotal; it will set the sleuth finally in the right direction, either by tying up all the other clues in a tidy bundle of evidence or opening up a path to the solution. Then, and only then, can you say, "Everything fell into place."

Telegraphing

A correlative of clues is *telegraphing*. This is a device in which you set up a situation for which there can be only one conclusion, and you give broad hints about what that conclusion will be. Suppose that toward the end of the book, your culprit overpowers the sleuth, escapes and steals the keys to the sleuth's car, and is getting away! Then you switch the scene to a road gang repairing a washed-out bridge. The gang is about ready to quit for the day because a storm is building. They prop a DANGER—DETOUR sign against a bridge truss and take off in their maintenance truck. The wind rises and blows the sign over on its face. Then a scene-switch back to the culprit, driving away from the house and speeding down the road toward the bridge. . . . Melodramatic but effective. Readers get a kick out of knowing that something dire is going to happen to the culprit soon and knowing how it is going to happen. There is anticipation, laced with a sense of revenge, that the culprit is about to get his or her just deserts.

Not so effective is when you lay down clues so obvious that you inadvertently give away too much, telegraphing conclusions before you are ready to disclose them. This happens to writers who underestimate their readers. They are so concerned about being too subtle that they smear the evidence around with a broad brush. They highlight clues by repeatedly referring to them, or in some way giving them too much attention. If the victim's cameo brooch keeps cropping up in X's possession, that clue will assume such weight that the story line sags long before the end.

Unintentional telegraphing occurs when you do not camouflage clues properly or when you overemphasize their importance. Either way, you are selling the reader short.

Coincidence

Another danger of underrating the reader lies in the use of coincidences. They are challenges only to the reader's common sense. I occasionally come across a mystery novel in which the sleuth will chance upon a clue that the author has shoved under the hero's nose, or the sleuth will accidentally run into someone who has information the author wants to get across. The author will cover this dishonesty by having the sleuth say, "I could hardly believe it myself," but expects the reader to believe it. No matter how fanciful your clues are, they must be credible, and they will not be if they come from out of left field.

The Greek and Roman dramatists used coincidences legitimately, god-ridden as their plays were. The philosophy behind their dramas was that no matter how much humans strove, the gods directed their destinies. These dramatists brought in messengers and stage machinery (like thunderbolts) to intervene in difficult situations to impress upon man how puny his state was. The device was called *deus ex machina*—god out of the machine.

Today, using improbable characters or artificial devices to untangle a plot line will not work. I gave an example of this in chapter 2 in describing the fugitive climbing down a cliff and literally coming to the end of his rope. The author had several options for saving the situation, the latter one being an unexpected (i.e., unprepared for) helicopter zooming in to the rescue. This was a *deus ex machina* the author might have used to get the hero out of an untenable position, to get him out of a corner the author had painted him into. But it was an author's convenience that would not wash and, if you remember, the solution was to alter the preceding scene to avoid this piece of illegal trafficking.

Now, there are times when an author can legitimately use what seems to be coincidence. Think of the word itself: *co-incidence*, the joining of two incidents. In real life, coincidences do seem to occur, but the incidents were put into motion earlier and then crossed paths in the logical performance of the persons' activities. The same pattern applies when you use it in the mystery novel. Here is an example: A young man who walks home from work every day chooses to take an alternate route on a particular day because he wants to pick up his ski jacket at the cleaners. At the same time, a robbery is in progress at the bank on the young man's route, and he sees the robbers escaping. Later on, he is able to give a description of them to the police and then becomes part of the story. The robbery was an unexpected event for the young man, but not for the reader. Was the alternate route an author's convenience? Surely. Was it legitimate? Yes. One takes into account that the robbers had planned their heist for that day and that bank, and the young man needed his ski jacket. The plausibility of their reasons and the certainty of their meeting turned coincidence into encounter.

If you are going to use seeming coincidence, lay out its logical sequences first: the scene showing the bank heist, and the young man headed for the cleaners. Then the reader knows what you are up to and can share in the anticipation. Explaining the convergence *after* the events will involve you in tedious recaps and will be anticlimactic.

The Cliff-Hanger

A valuable tool in creating suspense is the cliff-hanger. This is a hazardous situation which the author takes his or her own sweet time in resolving. Even though the reader knows it will eventually be resolved, the anticipation lies in wondering *how* and *when*.

We have come a long way in using the cliff-hanger since Pauline—or whoever it was—got tied to the railroad tracks, but arousing anxiety by playing against time is still a page-turner. The cliff-hanger comes at the end of a scene or at the end of a chapter and it depicts a threat of harm of some sort, from either a person or the environment. The cliff-hanger is an example of the known being more suspenseful than the unknown. Say your heroine walks into her backyard just before going to bed. She is going to bring in the kids' toys or empty the garbage. The psycho jumps out from behind the cypress hedge, a garrote in hand. The heroine is shocked and the reader is surprised. And that is fine for a flurry of suspense.

But if it is known that the psycho has been casing the house all evening, then the reader wants to shout at the woman not to leave her house, and follows her activities leading up to the back door with mounting tension. In the beginning of the next chapter, you switch to the husband who has just watched the end of the ball game and who gets up, stretches, and realizing that his wife is tending to late-night chores, remembers that he did not put the lawn mower away. *Ah,* says the reader, *help is near.* But the husband thinks, *T'hell with it; I'll do it in the morning,* and ambles off toward the bedroom. The reader groans. The husband is sitting on the bed by now, about to take off his shoes, and the reader is furious with him. As if on cue, the husband remembers that he has an early appointment in the morning and decides to put the lawn mower away after all. He goes out to the backyard just in time to save his wife from the psycho.

In this scene, you have given the reader hope, then you have taken it away and, finally, restored it, all at the expense of the reader's blood pressure.

The cliff-hanger has to be a genuine part of the plot and not just an exercise in pushing the panic button. For instance, the backyard episode could be the latest in a series of the psycho's attacks against women and, because of the husband's fortuitous arrival, the last.

Please, though, do not fall into what I call the "idiot trap." This was a staple of gothic suspense which, I am relieved to note, has gone out of style. In the gothics there was always the mandatory scene where the governess walked bravely into the dark room, knowing too well that *someone* was lurking behind the drapes, and got herself into all sorts of unnecessary trouble. (I suspect the governess thought it was more palatable to risk rape or worse than to continue supervising those god-awful brats.) Watch out that you do not put your protagonist into a no-win situation, for the higher the idiotic anticipation, the lower the reader's credulousness.

You *can* put the protagonist into a situation recognized as dangerous if the person figures ahead of time that the goal outweighs the hazard.

Remember, however you set it up, the cliff-hanging sequence stops short at the realization of danger, or with the knowledge that the character is going into a dangerous situation.

The cliff-hanger can be followed up with a total shift of scene to another set of actions and characters whose story will eventually converge with the cliff-hanger (like the husband, above). This way, you are not only prolonging the suspense but adding material that will result in the resolution of the cliff-hanger. Or you can follow the cliff-hanger with a continuation of the scene from the threatener's point of view. This works if you feel more comfortable making the cliff-hanger one entire episode from its inception to its resolution. Your story line will dictate which of these follow-ups to use.

Subplots

So far we have discussed setting up your suspects and laying down clues and other peaks of interest that help to enliven the pace. Another way to keep up story momentum is by using a subplot.

The subplot constitutes a series of minor events that weave through your main story line and enhance it.

It can be put into motion before your story begins, to prompt the events of your story. For instance, the book opens in the middle of a storm—your subplot—which has marooned the island on which the action of the story takes place. Right off, you have set the mood: violence presaging violence. The storm continues through most of the book, cutting off radio contact and preventing anyone from leaving; and so besides setting the mood, the subplot serves practical uses for getting into your story and as an isolation factor throughout the story.

Incidentally, when an upheaval in nature is used as a subplot—a volcanic eruption, a tornado or, here, a storm at sea—its theatricality can overshadow the main plot. This is especially true if you project human emotions into it: the *anger* of a volcano, the *voraciousness* of a tornado. To keep a nature-on-the-rampage subplot in its place and still make it effective, you would do well to consult books on meteorology or volcanology (or whatever earth science) to learn about and describe the phenomenon's real traits, which are more overwhelming than our puny human emotions yet will not intrude on those human emotions in the main plot.

By the way, something of more than idle interest that you should know: Infusing human emotions into natural phenomena is called "the pathetic fallacy," and should not be confused with "anthropomorphism," as Dick Francis did in (I believe) *Banker*. Anthropomorphism is an infusion of human emotions into animals.

Usually the subplot arises out of the main plot, and if it serves as background, it involves institutions rather than the elements: the manipulation and results of a stock merger in the victim's investment company before or after the murder, the infighting of a theatrical group when the star is murdered. Examples like this might bring to light secondary motives for murder, and so here the subplot could incorporate red herrings as well as add color and vitality to the main plot.

You can use a subplot to give a broader delineation of your characters. One of your suspects or someone close to the sleuth might be trying to kick a drug habit throughout. Whether the effort succeeds at the end depends on the impact you want on the character(s) who will be affected.

The subplot could be a love affair that emerges during the investigation; its buildup and resolution will affect at least two of the characters. It has nothing to do with the cause of murder but it can be an impetus toward solving the murder, or it can get in the way of the solution: Painful emotions have to be sorted out to make sorting out the case easier.

You will have a tighter main plot if the characters in the subplot are connected to the main events of the murder, if only peripherally. They need not be suspects, but they should be affiliated to some degree with the main characters, if they are not main characters themselves.

A subplot can serve as a breather. If your story line is a grim one, subplotting a sympathetic character's (successful) endeavors to reach a goal can lighten the story line without detracting from it.

If there is a great deal of intense action going on, a cat-and-mouse game between warring factions, a main character's preoccupation with a hobby or an outside interest—like Rex Stout's orchids and Dick Francis's horseracing—can create a breather without cutting into the suspense. In fact, it might add to it by leaving the reader dangling for a short, entertaining interval; and constant tension—which is difficult to maintain anyway—makes your climax anticlimactic.

These examples work in tandem with delineating your characters. Subplots are automatically included in the police procedural novel. Besides the principal crime, the detectives are burdened with lesser crimes, and these form the subplots which add variations from the main plot and add life to the precinct.

Keep in mind that the subplot is essentially padding and seldom affects the outcome of the main story. What it does is to embellish and add to the entertainment. How much rein you give it depends on how it enhances the main characters, as well. It might be resolved long before the story ends, in which case you put in another subplot. As the mystery novel becomes looser in narration—modern-day readers accept more background color and broader delineations of character— the seemingly irrelevant subplot takes on a role earlier writers would not have thought of.

If solemnity is the key word for the opening gambit, *busyness* is the keyword for the early part of the middle game. How will the sleuth develop a case from the basic information? Obviously, by getting more information—facts and impressions and more facts and more impressions. These data, gathered by observation and conjecture, will be registered by the sleuth and filed away. Of course, they cannot be baldly set down in neat lists and diagrams, except in your outlines; a mystery novel is not like an Annual Report to the Board. Yet you have to show, directly or indirectly, connections among the data that will eventually tie together.

Viewpoint

How you arrange the data coherently depends upon two factors:

1. Your approach in handling the book by
   a) setting up a challenging puzzle with a clever solution, calling on the reader's thinking abilities. Will breaking a rockbound alibi, say, be of primary interest to you, so much that it becomes the dominant theme? This approach—close to the pure puzzle—does not offer much latitude while you are a beginner.
   b) developing a plot where you are more interested in the effects of the crime on the characters, especially the sleuth, and you want to appeal to the reader's emotions. This approach offers considerably more latitude and still allows for a puzzle.
2. The sleuth's approach in handling the crime by
   a) the value placed on his or her ability as a person and as a sleuth.
   b) the value he or she places on others.
   c) his or her attitude toward crime.

The first factor, the author's approach, will determine your structure. The second factor, the sleuth's approach, will determine your *viewpoint*, and this is the factor that needs to be discussed here.

Say your murder takes place in a jet-set environment: lots of drugs, scads of money too easily earned and rampant irresponsibility. And say your sleuth (your ideal self personified) is basically a conservative person, and is going to cast a jaundiced eye on the proceedings in this shoddy atmosphere and see the worst in everybody. In the worst will lie the clues. Amid more temperate, less flashy surroundings, the sleuth's eye will still have a glimmer of jaundice—after all, this is murder—but there will be compassion and caring for some of the characters, and the sleuth will look for clues based on more justifiable actions. Another example in which viewpoint is important is the case of the antiques dealer who was described in chapter 1. Not only was he intrigued by the cryptic message left in the Hepplewhite chest, but because there was a murderer at large within his professional circle, the honor of his trade was at stake, and by implication, his own.

When the sleuth has interviewed all the suspects, has filed away conjectures about their guilt or innocence, and has an idea of the kind of person the victim was, you have come to the first milepost in the middle game: The sleuth knows how to handle the crime.

Now the sleuth will follow up on information gathered from conversations and physical evidence and will begin tying them together by digging up confirming information, cross-checking and testing everything against the blueprint of experience learned in other cases. With the momentum well in hand, your secondary characters begin drifting in to play their roles and offer new voices and new challenges for the sleuth.

Do not make it easy for the sleuth. Put barriers in the way—small crises that create those needed peaks of interest. For instance, the sleuth has arranged a sub-rosa meeting with a character who has promised to divulge an "important" piece of information—for a price. The two are to meet in a secluded spot at some unearthly hour to protect the informant. The sleuth's hopes and curiosity have been raised. What is the information and what is the price? The sleuth arrives early to reconnoiter the area and finds nothing amiss, so awaits the arrival of the other. You can play this kind of scene in two ways: Either the price is too high or the sleuth is assailed by gunshots. It could be a less elaborate situation involving a courthouse clerk who balks at releasing vital records. A heated argument ensues but the sleuth leaves empty-handed.

In both instances you have added a nice piece of suspense and have heightened the reader's anticipation for a number of pages. Place buildup/letdown incidents like these wherever your plot can accommodate them, but be chary of overusing this device; this is a novel of detection, not a study in frustration. And be chary of the stress you place on these incidents. They are legitimate peaks of interest but they should not be higher than the final peak, the discovery of whodunit.

The most clock-stopping frustration for the sleuth is a second murder. Is it a cover-up for the previous crime? Part of a sequential plan? Or are there two murderers? This second murder looks as if it is going to gum up the previous work the sleuth has done. This is a fair-sized crisis. It is also the second milepost, and calls for a change in pace, one of revitalized *determination*, the prevailing mood of this new part.

The sleuth will now have to rearrange the picture in order to form a new way of looking at the case, but for the moment everything looks hopeless. How much you play up this despair depends on how much sympathy you want the reader to feel for the sleuth, by making it the sleuth's personal problem: Is confidence in the sleuth's ability on the line? As a result of the second murder, does the sleuth get into hot water with the client or the cops? Physically attacked or ethically compromised? Can precious time be used to resolve the personal crisis, or will the stigma hover like a dark cloud until it is resolved at the end of the book?* This is a discouraging juncture in the investigation: frustration

---

*A possibility for a subplot.

upon frustration, another tragic murder, and the sleuth's credibility at stake.

In real life, people are sometimes confronted with a hopeless situation in which they can feel compassion but do not necessarily feel responsible for finding a solution; they are not even sure there is a solution. They turn away regretfully. However, when they read of the plight of a beleaguered sleuth, no such dismissal enters their minds, only defiance: How is the sleuth going to get out of this quagmire? It is a low period for the sleuth and a high point of involvement for the reader.

Will the sleuth's reaction be to review assiduously the data in hand? Make frantic phone calls to client or cops? Think about suicide or go to confession? No. If your sleuth is human, he or she will more than likely hop in the hay with a lover, get drunk, or both. If the sleuth is a straight arrow, there might be a rugged fifteen-mile jog or a pruning session with the rosebushes. Whatever approach you choose, your sleuth needs a respite from disappointment and/or self-castigation, and even your sternest reader will allow this brief unburdening. But, please, watch out! Do not get maudlin about it. There is a not-so-subtle difference between manipulating a reader and willfully milking a situation beyond its value.

The sleuth passes this second milepost with renewed determination, and *now* can review data, make those phone calls and begin recovering from psychic and physical wounds. You can use this second murder to supply a new capability for action: a rearrangement of priorities of suspects and a fresh eye for clues not apparent before or newly surfaced because of the second murder.

It is legitimate at this stage to allow the sleuth a measure of serendipity; in pursuing one piece of evidence, the hero comes across another piece of evidence. Say the sleuth is in the lobby of a hotel, waiting to interview X, and picks up yesterday's newspaper lying on an end table. On page three there is a picture of X at a ribbon-cutting ceremony. But on the phone, X claimed to have been somewhere else yesterday. This new piece of intelligence will give the sleuth an opening at the upcoming interview, either as a confrontation or as a trap.

By now, the sleuth has gotten his or her second wind and commences to turn adversity into advantage.

CHAPTER 6

THE END GAME

THE MURDERER

BY NOW YOU HAVE PUT your characters in the places they will assume to the end of the book, according to their innocence or guilt. The innocent will turn out to have been where they said they were at the time of the murder, doing what they said they were doing, so you have narrowed the guilty down to one of the remaining suspects. Have all of your characters placed for the final outcome as naturally as possible. At this stage, do not let them surprise us—not the innocent ones, at any rate. Keep them portrayed in a way that is consonant with the habits we have come to expect of them.

You might want to add one character, though, who has been accounted for earlier but only appears now, to offer a final corroboration that serves to tie up the case. Say a long-sought-after witness, who has been holed up to avoid child support, finally comes back on scene (for whatever reason). His arrival stirs up interest because of his possibly important information (and it had better turn out to be important). Try to make his arrival interesting as well as a logical piece of the plot; it will seem less like manipulation to the reader. For instance, you would expect this defaultant father to grouse about his life or have a word match with his ex-wife. Readers will know that he has something to add (or you would not have referred to him earlier and have brought him in now), and by creating this little hubbub you turn him into something more than a convenient courier. For the moment you divert the reader from the purpose of his appearance, and in this vignette you will have created interest and, when the information is finally gotten across, a nice surprise.

A totally unacceptable surprise is introducing new characters in the end game. No *deus ex machina*, please! There is simply not time to develop and fit new characters into the scheme of things without wrenching the plot apart. At this stage, if you need an extra character to plug a hole in the plot, then you had better backtrack to see what you left out earlier. Then again, you may have thought up a cameo role, after your plot was fixed, that seemed too good not to use. It, too, will be another plot-wrencher. Grit your teeth and set it aside. If you really like it, it will wangle its way into another book.

The end game is a tight one and you cannot introduce superfluities; its mood is one of *intensity,* for by now you are playing against time—to prevent more murders or to prevent the murderer from getting away. Perhaps the sleuth is dealing with an impatient client, and time means money. But even if the intensity is low-keyed and no such dramatic imperatives are placed on the sleuth, you are subject to the reader's impatience: *Let's wind this up!*

And so you can. All the facts have been marshaled and the sleuth has arranged them into a discernible pattern that fits the actions and personality of one person—the murderer. The reader has been given everything the sleuth knows but is waiting to have the clues interpreted and linked up. This is the second highest point of the book,* for it is here that the sleuth's data and conjectures converge and prove to be correct. Most of the explaining will take place here, and the reader, anxious to know whodunit, is willing to sit back and listen. Not since the murder scene have you had such a captive audience.

You have prepared for this scene in your outlines in terms of the information you want to reveal. To get it across in the actual writing without a labored explanation takes a little thinking. Begin the scene by letting the reader know that it is a vital one. Build up to it by alerting the reader that the solution is in sight. No solution comes to the sleuth in a blinding flash, but it is legitimate here in the end game to have the sleuth observe that "everything fell into place"—though I hope you phrase it in a less clichéd way.

Be sure to have your sleuth, either by dialogue or inner thinking, identify the clues by their origins: "X claimed to have been (somewhere), but we know now that he was (somewhere else)"; describe *when* clues took on meaning; detail blind alleys and red herrings and how they were rectified; explain what seemed to be the truth and what really happened. The sleuth not only is illustrating the validity of the

---

*The first, if you remember, was the murder.

proof but is doing the reader a service by recapping; details that have a way of being forgotten during the narration, and in some instances have been camouflaged.

While you are working out this scene, keep these things in mind:

1. The solution has to be logical and arise out of the facts—the clues—which must be linked together.
2. The victim cannot have died by suicide—that is short-changing the reader's sense of justice (or revenge!).
3. Do not introduce parapsychological evidence—save ESP and poltergeists for your horror novel—because
4. All evidence should be easily recognizable once the sleuth brings it to the reader's attention.
5. The solution absolutely must explain motive, opportunity and means.
6. The solution should be contained within the book. This seems obvious to the point of absurdity. What I have in mind are those writers who think it doubles the value of the mystery element to leave the reader up in the air about a) whodunit, or b) whether the murderer will be caught. This Lady-or-the-Tiger ending will certainly baffle the reader, if that is what you are aiming for. It is also likely to infuriate the reader, which, I am sure, is not what you are aiming for.

Pay careful attention to this disclosure scene in your outline and in the writing. The reputation of a mystery writer rises or falls on working out a convincing and conclusive solution. Keep the plot of your first book relatively simple so that you do not have a cumbersome number of factors to deal with in your solution. The less you have to explain, the easier it will be to write and the clearer your solution will be. Remember, your readers will be convinced only if they can follow you.

If the solution calls for a lengthy explanation, there are several ways you can handle it without losing the reader's interest:

Do not save all the explaining for this scene. Try to clear up some of the clues toward the end of the middle game. Or break up the scene with stage business (lighting cigarettes, picking up an object-clue for display; having the sleuth's audience volunteer information or ask questions). The injection of humor (if it is appropriate) or references to the sleuth's manner of relating the findings are other ways of preventing the explanation from sounding like a lecture. If you have a really complicated point to get across, let the sleuth state it several times, using different approaches: This could be described as "repetition with variation."

Revealing whodunit is the climax of the mystery novel. It is what the reader has been waiting for. It would seem, then, that the remainder of the book is all downhill, anticlimactic, just so much mopping up. One way you can get around this is to have the sleuth confront, accuse and get a confession from the murderer in the last few pages of the book. A tour de force like this is easier to accomplish in a short story, where economy is mandatory. A novelist has far more space to work in, and there is a way to extend the story, and still keep up the suspense, without being anticlimactic.

The time-tested stratagem is to keep the solution and the capture pages apart. What you are doing then is shifting the emphasis from *who* to *how* and *when*. It is one thing to know whodunit and another 1) to prove it to the satisfaction of the authorities or 2) to catch the fugitive murderer.

1. Let us take the first possibility. The sleuth's conclusions are based on solid logic, but the murderer has covered his or her tracks so well that without a confession, the authorities' hands are tied, and it is essential that they have a court-sure case. What tactics do you use?

a)You set a trap. The sleuth can be cast as a judas goat, enticing the murderer into a situation that is similar to the tempting circumstances that led to the murder. A policewoman, for instance, is set up as bait for a psycho who has committed a series of crimes against women.

b) You lead the culprit into making a mistake by planting erroneous information. Say that you let the murderer know (by devious means) that he or she left a damning clue at the scene of the crime and the clue is still there. In the message, you include an address *two doors down* from the murder house. When the culprit goes to the right address, the authorities are there, waiting.

c) You play off one character against another. This is a tactic cops use in police procedural novels when they are dealing with a gang. They zero in on the weakest link by intimidation or promises of leniency. In civilian life, the sleuth also looks for a way to get at the criminal through someone else, but does it with more finesse. I consider it dirty pool to use innocent characters as leverage—kidnapping a member of the family or putting the squeeze on a blameless partner. This kind of tactic is bound to lower the reader's esteem for the sleuth.

d) You play on the murderer's weakness. If he or she is overly

fond of liquor, the sleuth sits down with the culprit over a full
bottle of Jack Daniels.

These four tactics involve entrapment. In real life, entrapment is illegal—often honored in the breach, considering that it is used even by
our federal government—but it is perfectly okay to use it in a mystery
novel. It may be a fine point, but the mystery writer is not tricking the
culprit into committing a crime but admitting to one.

If you are not confident about using entrapment, if it does not
seem fair or it seems like an easy way out, let me assure you that these
tactics have been used successfully in mysteries I have read or
published, to my great enjoyment.

If the Dr. Frankenstein in you likes the idea of them, then you will
think up your own entrapments—the *how* part.

Now let us talk about the *when*.

2. In adventure suspense, the pursuit frequently comprises a
healthy hunk of the story; in fact, it is often the theme. The appeal
of the mystery novel lies in the reasoning abilities of the protagonist. *Ratiocination* was once a popular word for the wind-up in the
manor library, where the immaculately groomed detective ex-
pounded to a tense and enthralled audience of six, also immaculately groomed. A further edict of earlier "detective fiction" was
that once the detective had solved the case, he (it was always a
"he") had no further business with the villain. It was enough that
the "little gray cells" had triumphed, and the constabulary removed the offender from the premises. For the detective to have
witnessed the subsequent hanging of the villain in Pentonville
Prison would have been bad form.*

Today's sleuth still expounds to a fictional audience, though the setting
has changed to the squad room or the sun porch. Contrary to the deli-
cate sensibilities of the earlier detective, the modern sleuth is often as
tough and streetwise as the murderer. And contrary to the neat dis-
patch of the villain to appropriate confines, today's murderer does not
automatically end up in the clink.†

Current tastes afford both sleuth and murderer a larger field of operations, combining pursuit with sleuthing, and there are as many set-

---

*If the miscreant was a woman, she was confined to Holloway Prison.
†"The Clink," by the way, was the name of a London (Southwark) prison in the fifteenth century.

tings for pursuit as there are writers—cars, boats, planes, waterfront alleys, building interiors or the murderer hides behind legal technicalities and behind hostages.

How and when the sleuth finds the murderer can produce more sleuthing. Where is the likely hideout? What have the murderer's habits been up until now? Whom can the sleuth contact to get a line on the murderer's whereabouts?

The time when the two finally confront one another is the last small climax. It may come at the end of the book, or you may still need a wrap-up. Either way, it is a scene that needs its own resolution. Here are a few options to consider:

a) The sleuth incapacitates the murderer physically, with a gun or by locking a door;

b) Reasons with the murderer by presenting what amounts to a Hobson's choice: a fair trial or a biased one, depending on the sleuth's testimony in court;

c) Appeals to the murderer's emotions—"Hasn't there been enough bloodshed already?";

d) Or executes the murderer, but only in self-defense.

e) Or the murderer dies by accident. Remember the situation when he sped off in the stolen car toward the washed-out bridge? The groundwork had been previously laid to account for this fatality. Here, the important characters must know of the death so they are assured that justice has been done.

You have a ready-made sensationalism built into fugitive scenes. Their melodramatic possibilities give you a chance to hone your suspense writing. I have had authors confess to me that even as they were writing these scenes, they themselves could hardly wait to see what happened! They said they took special care to find just the right words to put across the excitement they felt.

Something else they have told me that is worth passing on: It is very easy to get carried away by one's own excitement and turn the scene into a bloodbath, which changes the book into a horror tale, or to go on too long, which turns it into a chase novel. The original thrust of the whodunit gets diverted and the author ends up with a hybrid which satisfies no one.

The murderer dying a ghastly death is vengeful enough to please the most bloodthirsty reader. The prolonged pursuit can be equally enthralling. Both are fun to write. In the mystery novel, as authors have to remind themselves, the solution is the high point of the end game. Apprehension plays a valid part of, but should not overshadow, the real climax.

There is one final plot device I would like you to consider. It is a controversial one and will remain so as long as crime and punishment are the premise of the mystery story: letting the murderer get away with murder.

On the face of it, this is an outrageous miscarriage of justice. Because the mystery story *is* a morality tale, I would agree—ninety-nine percent of the time. As I observed about capers in chapter 1, once in a while it is satisfying to let the culprit walk away unscathed. In capers, the only loss is property and it is not destroyed; it just changes hands. A murder has more serious consequences than fencing a stolen Rembrandt; a human life is more precious than an assemblage of oil and canvas, or so most people would think.

Or so most people would think? Now there is an ironic statement for you, as it was intended to be. Irony plays a large part in that one percent of mysteries I would qualify as condoning unpunished murder. I have, on rare occasions in my reading, encountered a murder victim the world could well do without, done in by someone who deserved a medal for the deed. Obviously, the author thought so, too, but was aware that if he or she were going to break the rules, the reader had to be let in on the fact that the victim's public face was disturbingly different from the private one, and that to achieve true justice, the murderer *had* to work on the wrong side of the law.

I remember one mystery (*Beyond a Reasonable Doubt* by C. W. Grafton) in which a young lawyer kills his rotten brother-in-law, who has beaten his wife, the lawyer's sister, and in contemptuous tones announced that he was leaving her. In the heat of his anger, the lawyer picks up an oversized cigarette lighter and bashes his brother-in-law's head in. The police suspect the wife, so the lawyer confesses. The cops at first do not believe him (a piece of irony right there), but he is finally charged. Because it was a provoked and spontaneous act, the lawyer could plead guilty to manslaughter. Instead he not only pleads not guilty, but actually conducts his own defense and wins an acquittal. After the trial, he learns that the brother-in-law had engaged in shady business activities where the lawyer would have been the fall guy, another piece of irony.

Throughout the book, the lawyer is building up what will be the romance of his life, and he has had the moral support of his fiancée to help him through his ordeal. When the trial is over, he is looking forward to a much-wanted marriage and a bright future. The fiancée, who has attended the trial and has recognized the misuse of a piece of evidence—the lighter—walks out on him, knowing he is guilty. On the last page, the author describes a desolate young man with a bleak future. So, ironically, the lawyer is punished, though it is not commensurate with the crime—a double irony. However, the author had done such a skillful job of presenting black (the rotten brother-in-law) and white (accidental death) that it was an easy choice for me to sympathize with the lawyer; there were no moral grays to contend with.

If you ever choose to use this kind of plot, be sure the reader can agree to the justification of the murder. This means creating a protagonist who kills under extreme duress of the moment or who, after much thought, has no other choice. Your protagonist has to be a sympathetic character and the victim someone the reader can hate. If you can throw the processes of justice out of kilter as well, that is added ammunition to strengthen your theme.

THE WRAP-UP

The reader knows whodunit. The culprit is in custody or has met a fatal end. The story is over. The tension is gone. The book itself, though, still needs its own resolution, so you could say the tension is *almost* gone.

If you have used subplots, they must be resolved. You may have used them to throw light on the personal life of the sleuth—a romance, family affairs, a running battle with the income tax people. You may have used them to introduce colorful minor characters who played peripheral roles in the story. They may have been humorous episodes to lighten the main plot, or backgrounds to explain the workings of a precinct or the fashion world or a munitions factory. They have run through the book like novelettes and they deserve their own endings.

The minor characters have to be accounted for, unless they faded out of use in earlier parts of the book. The major characters need to be taken care of. Relationships formed throughout the story are firmed up or broken, if they have not been already. What are the emotional states of these characters? Has the murderer left a swathe of misery? Have some lives been unalterably shattered? Solving the case, however, does not have to mean that the characters' problems are solved, too. Have some characters come out on top—those on the murderer's list of intended victims, for example.

Will the sleuth have a wrap-up statement containing his or her point of view of the case? Is the sleuth wiser for the experience? Satisfied that justice has been done? Cynical about or reassured by the conduct of the people in the case? Is the world a better place now, or the same old grind? The sleuth has been the focal character throughout, has determined the direction of the case—and therefore the shape of the book—and has brought order out of chaos. It would seem fitting then that the sleuth have the last word.

This brings us to the final pages. How do you want your book to end? The plot, of course, will determine this to a large extent, but besides bringing your book to a logical conclusion, you want to leave the reader emotionally satisfied. Let us first discuss how you achieve the logical endings.

1. A conclusive ending. This would apply, say, to the John or Jane Citizen who has had to take on a nasty character to protect the family. An event like this will never happen again; it is a once-in-a-lifetime experience for the amateur sleuth and the sleuth's family, and the conclusion will be determined by the nature of the plot.

2. An open-ended ending. If you plan a sequel, using your main character or your setting again, you would let the reader know at this point. If it is a police procedural, you have built-in characters and settings. If your main character is a private eye, this is the place to mention the beginnings of a new case or to imply a continuance of the person's career or renewed contact with a sidekick. Your protagonist might be a professional amateur who has caught your fancy, and you want to be able to use this character again. This would be a character whose "other" career puts the new sleuth in touch with people all the time—a nurse, a charter boat captain, a priest—so there is plenty of grist for your mill. As with the private eye, you imply further sleuthing.

3. A surprise ending. You might have saved the identity of your murderer until the very end. Or one of your subplots incorporates a side conclusion that affects the characters in an unexpected way. This kind of ending can pack a wallop, but keep in mind that surprise is short-lived and loses its force almost as soon as it is written. You can get a fuller, more lasting effect if you think about including:

a) the murderer's under-the-surface feelings; you did not know (this) about that character;

b) an unexpected side motive that reveals yet another facet of the murderer;

c) information about another major character who was more involved than the reader realized;

d) unfinished business the murderer has left the sleuth, or someone, to cope with.

In chapter 4, The Opening Gambit, I stressed the importance of the opening lines to hook the reader. The last lines are equally important for letting the reader *off* the hook. What impressions do you want to leave to accomplish this?

Will your ending reflect your theme? Do you want to leave the reader thinking about the ironic ways justice is served? Or about a memorable major character who went through hell and came out intact?

Do you want to imply that there are unforeseen, though not insuperable, problems that can be taken care of later, or will *not* be seen until afterwards, even though the murder is solved?

Or does the story rest on the merits of the case? With the evidence presented, sorted out and neatly pigeonholed, is there nothing more to say?

These are three approaches: echoing back to the book, predicting what is yet to come, and stopping when the story ends. You will think of others.

What about the emotional satisfaction? The ending of the book has a life of its own, but it should reflect the tone of the book and therefore is an integral part of it emotionally as well as logically. Write so that the reader's sympathies lie where you want them to be at the end. Your characters have been worked out in advance, and you know where *your* sympathies lie, so it is a matter of making an ally of the reader *along the way* to ensure this final accordance on the reader's part.

I can tell when authors have had trouble ending their books. They tack on an into-the-sunset finale or a shock for its own sake. They did not think ahead, or they got tired. Just as an exercise, try writing the last chapter right after you have written the first one. See the two of them as skewers for the chapters in between. This will help you keep your in-between chapters in line. If you have the ending done at the beginning, you will write the rest of the book with a lot more confidence.

CHAPTER 7

CREATING MEMORABLE CHARACTERS

SOME FIFTY YEARS AGO, when the puzzle mystery was in ascendance, the plot was the thing and the characters were bloodless adjuncts to keep the story moving toward the author's solution of the puzzle. If the lord of the manor was the victim, then the banker, the solicitor and the gamekeeper were among the suspects. They were distinguished by their occupations, their speech and possibly their clothes—more to keep the classes identifiable than the characters themselves.

Another snobbish aspect of those early mysteries was their backgrounds—the estates, the quads of Oxbridge, the Inns of Court, all peopled by characters who were piloted into the murky waters of homicide by an author bent on testing the reader's cerebral acuity.

On our side of the Atlantic we had no such neat lines of battle. Authors mixed haughty dowagers with sniffling junkies; detectives could be erudite and impeccably tailored or bourbon-swilling street men as amoral as their prey. Here, as in England, characters were labeled and given backgrounds appropriate to their roles in the author's social structure. I would not be surprised if Mrs. Christie and Mr. Hammett thought up their backgrounds first and then dropped in their characters with the appropriate protective coloring! So the American characters were no more real than their English counterparts, and the emphasis on who killed Mr. Moneybags was essentially the same as on who killed the Fourth Earl of Fenleigh; the plot, in both countries, was more important.

The plots of the Thirties were very complicated, with convoluted solutions of who- and whydunit. Even as I find it difficult to follow their Byzantine reasoning and, halfway through their explanations, realize I could not care less, I have great admiration for the sheer brainwork of those earlier mystery writers.

And give them credit: They *were* masters of plotting. I am sure that a good many of our esteemed mystery writers of today cut their teeth on those early authors and absorbed their techniques of activating the story and moving the characters from place to place.

Shifting now from the first third of the twentieth century to the last third, how does the mystery novel stand in regard to the importance of plot versus character? Do characters still arise out of plot situations or do authors get their plot ideas after they have thought up their characters? I think this chicken-and-egg polarization is a futile kind of argument because the basic rules have not changed. Plot and characterization are still the primary staples of the mystery novel. What has changed over the last fifty years is that we have less complicated plots with a greater emphasis on characters. This makes a greater demand to develop them more fully and still keep the pace going.

Whether you kick off with a character you like or with a plot idea that strikes a chord depends on the kind of person you are: people-oriented or idea-oriented. But even these categories need qualifying; you have both impulses in you, and which comes to the fore depends on how alert you are to chance, what triggers your mind on a Wednesday afternoon in a shopping mall or a Thursday morning in the shower.

Authors writing on writing and authors I have worked with have claimed that character is the primary trigger for their books. Yet when I pinned down one of my authors, William M. Green, he analyzed his six suspense novels and found that three had been touched off by characters and three by events.

Those triggered by people:

1. Van Johnson, whom he saw in a Saks Fifth Avenue department store, "looking lonely and forlorn." The book, *Spencer's Bag*, was about an aging actor caught up in European intrigue.
2. Green himself, idealized into a young man of fortune (*Avery's Fortune*).
3. A retired British army colonel serving as a tour guide in Jamaica, who became a mercenary in his next book, *The Man Who Called Himself Devlin*.

Events which triggered his other three books were:

4. Learning that editors make yearly trips to England and the Continent scouting for books. His fictional editor is on the trail of a manuscript which turns out to contain real and dangerous information. *(The Salisbury Manuscript).*

5. J. Edgar Hoover's secret files, containing dirt on prominent Washingtonians, were brought to light after his death. (The author dreamed up the secret files long before they were reported by the media, and wrote *See How They Run.)*

6. A paragraph in *Time* magazine about Mountbatten's unsuccessful attempt to persuade George V to mount an expedition to rescue the czar and his family during the Russian Revolution. The author's book *The Romanov Connection* was about just such an expedition.

So it is my assumption that authors, when queried about their methods, find it pleasanter to describe their characters than to talk about the tedious process of structure. But, believe me, they are well aware of both.

Whether the trigger is a person or an event, the writer's alchemy will modify, expand or totally change the nature of the inspiration (British colonel into mercenary), but the initial impetus will still show up—the emphasis on one or the other. For example, there is a tendency to slight plot in order to make a showcase for a character. If the character is uppermost in your mind, you are liable to find yourself putting that character into a poorly thought-out situation and then relying on what you think he or she would do to get out of the situation. Your plot progresses by fits and starts.

If the plot is uppermost in your mind, you will find yourself forcing behavior on the character to make the person conform to the events. If your character is a weak one to begin with, this might work. If you have developed a strong character, making him or her react in a way that is alien to your original intentions will be more difficult.

There are no easy answers to this balancing act. You will learn by feeling your way: Characters will determine the kinds of actions expected of them and plot will dictate when those actions should be brought into play.

I have run into mystery writers who have said, "Halfway through my book, my characters took over from me and 'wrote' themselves." They said this with rueful pride, as if their conscious minds had played second fiddle to the rich, deep bubblings of their subconscious minds. I place such "inspirations" alongside of tarot cards and Ouija boards.

Granted, halfway through your book you will know your characters pretty well, and it is not likely that you will let them do anything that is opposed to their way of thinking, feeling and acting. But if the first half of your book was the product of your conscious mind, the second half will be, too—or you are going to be in trouble. The characters in a mystery novel are hand-held from beginning to end, as any pro will tell you. This is necessary because they share more or less equal billing with the plot. This means they are tailored by the demands of time. You can say only so much about them, so their every action, gesture and thought has to be worked out—and this takes conscious deliberation.

One way of accommodating yourself to the exigencies of a time frame is to keep the number of characters down to a manageable lot. Even with as few as six to ten, you will be surprised at the amount of juggling you have to do to give them their due time and space. And even with a small cast of characters, you will not be able to develop any of them in great depth, again because of the exigencies of the time frame. Yet they have to seem like real people in a real world. Because there is going to be an aura of fantasy about them—this *is* fiction you are writing—you do not have to think so much about them being real as being believable. The same guideline applies to their actions, which do not have to be real either, but do have to be plausible.

One author who succeeds with unbelievable characters and implausible actions is Ian Fleming. James Bond—Agent 007—provides a marvelous romp through a never-never fantasy land. It took talent to develop Bond and his highjinks. Fleming had to know what *was* believable and plausible in order to send these rules ass-over-backwards and get away with it.

The beginning writer would do well to learn the rules before attempting to break them. I hope that some of you *will* break them in the future. We need more James Bonds to shake up the mystery field, where we sometimes take ourselves too seriously. In the meantime, let us get back to being . . . serious. I am sure that Mr. Fleming was serious all the way to the bank.

How do you make your characters believable and their actions plausible? If you have a sound knowledge of your characters and the roles they play, it will not be too difficult to make them act the way they are supposed to. But how do you get that sound knowledge?

The first thing you do is get your prototypes—your standard character types—set up according to their functions. I classify these prototypes as primary, including the viewpoint character, who ties in most closely to the plot; secondary; and minor.*

The viewpoint character will be the one through whom the story is told. It could be a first-person narrator or a third-person observer who is the "eyes" of the author.

Other primary characters are the sleuth, the murderer and perhaps the victim.

Secondary characters are (again perhaps) the victim, and the suspects and nonsuspects whose lives will be affected by the death of the victim.

Minor characters are used as information passers, as reflectors of the sleuth's personality and background color.

You are long past the trigger stage, so you have your plot. How many of these prototypes do you need, aside from the primary figures, to fulfill the functions of the plot? How many suspects will your plot bear? Too many and the plot sags under the weight of numbers; too few and your plot floats away. What supporting characters do you need, other than suspects, to fill up your world and round out your story? What about your minor characters? Should they be assigned roles right off, or can you leave a space and fill them in later as the need arises?

Are you going to use the block outline to keep track of them, or 3x5 cards, or colored charts pinned on the wall? No matter which you choose, decide on one method, for until you get well into the book you are not going to keep track of the characters that well. Once you are thoroughly familiar with your characters, you can ignore your bios.† I have already given you examples of what one author did with biographies (see chapter 3). They were only thumbnail sketches meant to show one element among many in building a book. Now we must explore these prototypes in more detail.

I have covered at some length the characters' roles as they work within their genre. I did this in chapter 1 and in other chapters. Here, I think it would be well to zero in on particulars a little more.

---

*You might want to dream up your own classifications—whatever will work for you.

†You can always add to them on the way. The fact that you did not include "has a short temper in the morning" in your original bio does not mean that you cannot include it if a scene calls for an early-morning fracas. Small personality facets do not have to be explained—but they will be remembered.

THE PRIMARY CHARACTERS

The Viewpoint Character

Let us start with the viewpoint character because, as I said, who tells the story determines the linear construction of the plot. The stronger you make this character, the easier it will be for you to keep the plot line going, especially in that dangerous middle game where plots tend to sag. A strong lead character serves as a reference point for the rest of the characters and helps to keep them moving, too. As you will learn, all characters radiate from, and then circle around, the lead character.

First-Person Narrator

Let us agree that the focal character, and therefore the one through whom the story is seen, is the sleuth. And let us start out with the simplest way of using the focal character: as first-person narrator.

The advantage of using the first person is that the reader is an active participant. When the sleuth exults, ponders, bleeds, makes love or shoots, the reader has a ringside seat. This lends immediacy to the action and personalizes the feelings. That appeals to the reader. What appeals to the writer is that all of the other characters radiate from the sleuth; they do not appear on scene until he or she meets up with them. This makes it easy to introduce them and establish their parts in the story.

If you have a theme you want to get across—anything from child abandonment to capital punishment—your first-person narrator is the perfect exponent for it. These days the thoughtful, intelligent sleuth represents the norm rather than the exception, and this kind of interior buildup adds to the sleuth's personality and gives you a podium. Be careful that you do not make a talking puppet out of the sleuth. To stop the action so that the sleuth can expound on child abuse or the barbarism of the gas chamber is going to introduce a pompousness you did not intend, a hortatory note that could easily turn shrill.

Championing causes should be treated as a kind of window dressing or as a sly piece of self-indulgence for yourself. A much more important function for the sleuth is acting as a portrayer of people and a chronicler of their actions. This means that your other characters have to "cooperate" so that the portraying and the chronicling seem natural.

For instance, suppose your sleuth is investigating a murder in a theater and, here, he is interviewing an actress. The sleuth is trying to find out where she was at the time of the slaying (aptly) on stage:

> "But you were there. How could you not help but see it?" I asked.
> She shook her head. "How could I? The lights were dim and I was sitting in the back."
> I knew she was lying.

Okay, so the lady was lying and eventually we will find out why she was lying. But until we do, until the narrator discovers later on that she was actually standing in the wings, we have to take his word concerning her mendacity. This is because we, the readers, along with the sleuth, have been passive bystanders. But even a bystander is going to do some thinking. How does the sleuth know she is lying? Is he privy to information he has not shared with the reader? Not likely; the investigation has just begun. So where does he get off making such a snap judgment with no information to back him up? Between you and me, the sleuth should be wondering about this, too.

But you could write it this way:

> "But you were there. How could you not help but see it?" I asked.
> I watched as a flush rose to suffuse her neck and face. Her shoulders hunched forward and her hands stretched out like claws in a stance of attack. It was all over in a matter of seconds. She straightened her shoulders and dropped her arms to her sides. She looked at me and shook her head. "How could I? The lights were dim and I was sitting in the back."
> I knew she was lying.

And, by God, the reader knows it, too!

Do you see what a little cooperation produces? In the first version the sleuth, seemingly in a vacuum, *tells* us she is lying. In the second version, he *sees* that she is lying, and both characters come alive. She, with the author's connivance, changes from a faceless, formless "actress" into a gorgonlike creature grown ugly under the burden of her guilt. The sleuth, in turn, becomes the acute observer of her distress and has a lot more to go on in making his judgment.

The sleuth needs the author's cooperation in describing places, too. Say you want to get the sleuth from one destination to another and you do not want to take a lot of time or space to do it:

The sun had finally come out, so I decided to walk from my office to the Re-cords Building. When I got to Records . . .

In one sentence you have moved from Point A to Point B, and that is certainly economical. You have switched the sleuth to Off for the twenty-minute walk; no big deal.

But here is a small opportunity to keep the switch to On:

> The sun had finally come out, so I decided to walk from my office to the Records Building. The fountain in front of City Hall was shimmering with light and two kids were break dancing in its mist. When I got to Records . . .

By adding only one sentence you have let the sleuth respond to place (as well as giving substance to time).

Slipping in such throwaway lines is important in getting inside the narrator's head without stopping the action and without showing self-consciousness. Use them when you can so that by book's end the read-er knows this character intimately, seemingly without your having raised a finger.

The sleuth is going to want to describe things, too, in a way that makes the reader aware of them. For instance:

The rifle was loaded and cocked.

is more memorable than

I looked at the rifle.

And

It was a weird kind of thingamajig.

lends a better sense of confusion than

I couldn't figure out what it was.

The sleuth's descriptive ability will be only as good as the people, places and things the author offers for scrutiny, although the burden will seem to fall on the sleuth. In fact, as far as the reader is concerned, the first-person narrator does carry the burden.

Although this is the simplest form of narration, it has its drawbacks. For one, your sleuth has to be a damned interesting person for you to keep company with him or her for some 200-odd pages. You will put more words, actions, energy and thought into your narrator than you will into the rest of the crew combined. And because the narrator is on stage on every page, the character's constant presence tends to blur the edges. Now, on some level you will be aware of this problem even before you begin writing, because when you work up your profile you will have in mind that you must portray this character in a way that will keep the reader interested. You will probably think in terms of "colorful," "unique," "out of the ordinary" or interesting because of being "so ordinary." Somewhere in the back or front of your head you know that to get your readers to follow you, you have to create a Pied Piper.

Your Piper can be as colorful as you like, if the color is used only as highlights. Relying constantly on cute mannerisms or offbeat speech patterns is like hanging paper moons: Props are not personality. They are a lazy way to define character. Too often these props get in the way whenever the narrator refers to himself or herself, or when one of the other characters refers to the narrator (through the narrator's eyes).

Drinking and smoking were among the most abused props of the earlier first-person mysteries. They were "stage businesses" and took the place of thinking:

> I felt the need for a little encouragement so I pulled open the bottom drawer of my battered old desk and hauled out the bourbon. A couple of swigs that went down like fire and I was set to go.

and,

> To cover my surprise, I lit a fag. I took my time about it and waited until it was firing strong before I replied.

Nowadays, we would send these characters—no, caricatures—to Alcoholics Anonymous or Smoke Enders and send their authors to writing classes. A few bad habits do not a character make, regardless of how many fires are lighted.

If your sleuth is obese, walks with a cane, is gay or black, these are integral traits of the person and can be used in the plot. A good example of a character who has such an integral trait that meshes with the plot is Napoleon Bonaparte, a first-person series detective created by Arthur W. Upfield. Bonaparte is a half-caste aborigine whose anomalous role in Australian society works for and against him.

But if your sleuth sniffs cocaine or wears flamboyant ties, these are only garnishes, to be used with a light hand. You still have to get inside of your character.

You are going to need two sets of attributes to form a "whole" person. In compiling your bio, think first of all the bad traits your sleuth could have: amorality, sentimentality, sloppy personal appearance, alcoholism, recklessness, lechery, a readiness with arrogant, smart-ass comebacks, ad nauseam. When you have thought of so many black marks that you are ready to throw the character out, begin making a list of the person's good traits: smart, dedicated, resourceful, courageous, has a sense of humor, is capable of emotional distancing when necessary, is good with kids. Let both lists simmer a while and then go back to them. You will be surprised at how the two can meld to form a fairly rounded whole. If compiling the negative traits first seems too downbeat, then list the positive traits first. The order does not matter as long as you end up with both lists.

Another difficulty with first-person narration is in describing the narrator. You, the author, cannot step in and say, "He (or she) was so tall, with this color hair and wore . . ." Neither can your narrator, not without self-servicing awkwardness. You can avoid this forced narcissism with obliqueness. When your sleuth buys clothes, orders food and drinks, and gets tickets to the race track or the opera, you give indications of his or her inner and outer makeup; the person's size, shape and lifestyle will come through.

You can also let other characters point out the sleuth's attributes:

"You handle a gun well," the sergeant told me.

or

"You're pretty tall for a woman," he sneered.

Given openings like these, sleuths can respond with information about their own natures:

"You pick up a lot of skills in Vietnam," I answered,

and

"It gives me an advantage in dealing with creeps like you," I retorted.

There is a way of showing inner workings which is not as oblique but still does not push the reader's nose into information, and which seems to be a natural part of the narration. Here I am reversing myself: You *can* stop the action cold on occasions. Remember the sleuth going to the Records Building? Suppose the information he hopes to obtain is vital in an inheritance case that concerns the legitimacy of a child. Because you promise the reader an interesting revelation within the next two or three pages—a carrot—you can take time out to say a little more about the sleuth's inner workings:

> The sun had finally come out, so I decided to walk from my office to the Records Building. The fountain in front of City Hall was shimmering with light and two kids were break dancing in its mist. Carefree, unfettered, given the chance to live for the moment, how different they were from Davy Fenton. That kid was hemmed in by the family vendetta, used as a pawn in the brutal, grownups' game that left him feeling worthless, rootless and unwanted. Money aside, how many kids were there like Davy? Too many, I suspected. Too many Davys, too few dancers. I couldn't take care of the whole world, but maybe I could help this one kid join the others around the fountain.
>
> When I got to Records . . .

After reading this inner monologue, the reader has a better idea of what makes the sleuth tick. This is not some errand boy gathering pieces of paper to earn a fee, but a compassionate man who will be conscientious about what he is doing and cares about the person whom he is doing it for. With this glimpse of him, the reader cares, too, and is looking forward to a successful records search—which brings the action back into play.

As long as the sleuth's ruminations concern the case, you can write on for however long the thoughts are worth. If the sleuth, for instance, had produced a diatribe on Those Kids Should Be In School or a lecture on Fountains I Have Known, he would have lost the reader amid loud yawns.

If the sleuth's thoughts do not bear directly on the case but only on revealing personal slants, you are taking a chance on losing your audience. I may very well be in the minority here. Many published mysteries I read these days spend paragraphs on the sleuth's knowledge of wines, of explaining the pari-mutuel system or expounding on the superiority of London's Underground over New York's subways. These chunks of information thrust at the reader are a far cry from the throwaway lines that you can slip in gracefully. When I query readers about such morsels of didacticism, they counter with, "But it's so interesting, and I've learned something." Philistine that I am, I suggest that they would garner more from reading encyclopedias and travel books, but then they offer a second rejoinder: "Well, I find it makes the character more human." So! The identification factor we ask for in our modern sleuth!—and I did say earlier that personalizing is a plus. But look at some of the mysteries that have a lot of this instant expertise in them, and nine times out of ten their plots are thin . . . thin. These authors obviously had to do a lot of space-filling to meet their quota of 200-odd pages.

Yes, of course, there is more room in our modern mystery for character commentary, but not at the risk of making a stepchild of the plot.

The plot. Ah yes, the plot. If you have a one-person viewpoint, the plot takes special one-view handling. Nothing can happen that the sleuth does not take part in or does not observe. To put it positively, the sleuth has to be everywhere all the time. According to physical law, this is not possible—but you can get around it.

As with all murder mysteries, the sleuth will conduct interviews galore with the suspects and ancillary characters; no problem about his or her presence on scene. When the sleuth is following up on clues, again no problem; nor with eating, sleeping and other personal pursuits.

But the sleuth, after all, is not working in a vacuum. There are other characters out there who have information they are not going to conveniently volunteer. If they did, there would be no suspense, yet it is necessary for you to get their information into the book. How do you bring in off-scene information?

1) Let other characters do it.
   a) The sleuth has a network of snitches.
   b) Someone inadvertently lets something slip.
   c) Trade-offs of information.
   d) Pressure from the sleuth for information.

2) The sleuth uses inductive reasoning
   "If I see A coming out of the shack, I can infer that B is holed up there."

3) The sleuth uses deductive reasoning
   The sleuth catches a glimpse of C and D—an unlikely pair to be together—and figures out that they have joined forces.

4) The sleuth learns the hard way—by being put in an embarrassing position, double-crossed or shot at. (If a bullet is not an "information bearer," I do not know what is!)

5) Anonymous tips. Their sources have to be explained later on.

6) Media reports. This comes under chasing clues; if the sleuth realizes from a newspaper or from TV that suspects have soft-pedaled information, the sleuth wonders why.

It may have occurred to you that the first-person narrative is divided between 1) the sleuth relating his or her actions toward getting information and describing the other characters who supply the information, and 2) the sleuth's inner thoughts and impressions. An efficient way of balancing information-gathering and inner thinking is with dialogue, which is a form of action *and* thought running simultaneously.

A piece of advice about dialogue in a first-person mystery: When other characters talk with the sleuth, let them speak in their own way, not out of the mouth of the sleuth. If paraphrasing the conversation, the sleuth can deliberately mimic the way the other person talks. When it comes to the sleuth expressing his or her own thoughts, keep *that* vocabulary consonant with the kind of person the sleuth is. This applies to good or careless grammar, imagery, obscenity and speech patterns. (I will be covering dialogue in chapter 9, where I discuss style.)

The first-person viewpoint seems to be especially attractive to new writers. It is, I agree, the simplest, most direct way of handling a viewpoint character. You have a steady reference point from which all other characters and actions radiate, and to which they return. First-person makes a neat package, if you can accommodate yourself to its limitations.

Third-Person Narrator

Third-person narration, on the other hand, will give you more leeway because it is from an omniscient point of view. Characters will live on their own, as it were—speaking in their own voices, thinking their own thoughts, going wherever you want to send them, without any say-so from the sleuth. Scenes can be described as they happen, and the reader can have information that the sleuth does not get until later on. This puts the reader in a quasi-omniscient position, which can add to the suspense: *I have information the sleuth doesn't, and how is he (she) going to protect that blind side?*

In the third person, the sleuth can be described directly—and will not have a damned thing to say about it. If he or she has cloying moments of sentimentality, the reader, not the sleuth, will be embarrassed. If the sleuth performs an incredible act of bravery, there is no need for self-effacing modesty. And the author can ascribe private acts in third-person narration that no self-respecting first-person narrator would admit to.

If you remember, the first-person rendition of the sleuth's physical appearance is presented obliquely, in bits and chunks, and to some extent the sleuth will always remain as much a voice as a person. So a big plus of third-person narration is being able to describe fully—and up front—the sleuth's build, coloring, etc., and the impressions he or she makes on others. And then there are the affective touches the author can lay on the sleuth—the little mannerisms, the flits of emotion across the face, the instinctive moves a person is not aware of making.

Despite being one of many independent characters now, the sleuth is still the one you anchor your plot to. As a beginning writer, you would be wise to follow the sleuth's trail more often than diverging into scenes with other characters. In a sense, you are simply changing the construction from "I" to "he" or "she."

One way to get your feet wet, if you want to try diverging into other scenes, is to give the reader a breather from the sleuth's almost constant presence. To keep your plot tight, set up the divergent scene so that the sleuth is on either side of it.

Scene A	The sleuth discovers there is another sister of the recent victim, one whom the family has kept under wraps. She is in a mental hospital. Someone has clued the sleuth in that the woman is not as crazy as her family makes her out to be, and that she was a witness to the old man's murder some fifteen years ago. The sleuth, though, wonders if she is worth a trip.
Scene B	In the mental hospital—a portrait of the "crazy" sister, showing her to have in-and-out moments (talking to a nurse/orderly/other patient).
Scene C	The sleuth goes to the hospital. Gets information from the sister, catching her in one of her "in" moments.

In Scene A you have set up the groundwork for Scene B, leaving it up in the air whether the sleuth will go or not. Scene B convinces the *reader* that the sleuth should go. A moment of suspense! Go, sleuth, go! Sure enough, in Scene C the sleuth and the sister get together and she does have a piece of the puzzle.

Besides being breathers, where you still get your information across, the divergent scenes let you introduce other characters who contribute vitality to the book.

Multiviewpoint Narrators

I would like to wrap up the viewpoint section by mentioning the multiviewpoint, and to make an arbitrary statement about it: Do not try it for your first book. This form amounts to a tour de force that few experienced writers tackle. You still have a lead character who serves as an anchor, and it is usually the dead victim. All the suspects take turns on stage to articulate their feelings about the victim, and among those feelings are the clues to which of them is the murderer. It seems to me like a cross between "Show and Tell" and "Who Killed Cock Robin?" It is an interesting form, but there are dangers to it: The characters all sound alike or are so diverse in personalities that you get a splintered effect that does not add up to a whole. Try it for your fourth book.

However, if you would like to see how experienced writers handle multiview narration, I would recommend Michael Innes's *Lament for a Maker* and Philip MacDonald's *The List of Adrian Messenger*.

The Sleuth

The sleuth is the protagonist of the mystery novel, the one around whom the plot revolves and who carries the action. He or she will most likely be given one of the roles I described in chapter 1 on genres:

> Private detective
> Cop
> Professional as amateur sleuth
> John or Jane Citizen
> Romantic suspense heroine

Whatever role you choose, your protagonist has to be more or less likeable. A flawless sleuth is not a very human one so a few annoying habits are okay, but they should not be off-putting traits or you lose your reader's willingness to go along. Nobody wants to be in vexatious company for any appreciable amount of time.* So what will keep your reader sympathetic toward your sleuth?

1. To make your sleuth likeable, he or she should be *admirable*. This means giving your sleuth a) a challenging showpiece of a puzzle to solve and b) worthy opponents. By worthy, I mean other characters who will test the sleuth's mettle time and again—by lying, use of physical force, by manipulation. You use some of your other characters as antagonists to create conflict in order to give your sleuth backbone. There is nothing admirable about a sleuth who procrastinates or who rationalizes dangers away, not even under the guise of *I'm only human*. All of us say that—and few of us end up in books.

2. Nowadays, we also ask that our sleuth be *smart* rather than brave (if given a choice). We prefer him or her to ferret out information by using brain power rather than fists. I, for one, am not an admirer of the sleuth who careens around with broken ribs, chancing a punctured lung, to chase the murder car. That, to my mind, is pseudo-bravery—plain damned foolishness. A collapsed lung will damage your sleuth's effectiveness, and that is not very smart on your part. Surely you have enough challenges in the hopper to keep the sleuth in unapologetically good physical shape so those challenges can be met. Real bravery is confronting and dealing with unasked-for dangers.

3. Your sleuth must be *motivated* to solve the crime, and the greater the need, the more impassioned you can make the character. I have talked about the private eye's unique sense of justice as being the theme of that genre. Cops in police procedurals aim for societal order. The professional as amateur sleuth wants to wipe away a blot on his or her "world." These are the ideals they work toward. Their pragmatic outlooks are less sublime: The successful outcome of a case for a private eye offers a better chance for more cases coming along; a cop might be bucking for detective, first class; for the professional amateur, scared clients are disaffected clients. The personal stakes are minimal, which is just as well if they are to work efficiently.

Notice how much more affecting the motive is when someone close to the protagonist is murdered. Say that Jane Citizen has

* There are two exceptions that come to mind, two series characters, both created by Joyce Porter. Her Chief Inspector Wilfred Dover of Scotland Yard is as irascible as they come. Her other series character is the Honourable Constance Morrison-Burke (known as the Hon. Con), who plows her way through murder cases and pays no attention to the people she steps on as she plows. They are both so outrageous they are funny.

gotten a good look at her lover's murderer as he fled from the bedroom. Jane is in no position to go to the cops or her husband will
learn of her affair, and he is a mean one. Yet she feels deeply about
her lover's death. Hers is a very personal grievance that needs re-
dressing. If you have the kind of reader who can comfortably encompass both the woman's adultery and her sense of outrage and
grief, then that reader can sympathize with Jane's need to track
down the culprit herself and wreak vengeance on him. The citizen's bind need not be as controversial as adultery, and in any
case, the motive will always take precedence over the circumstances.

It is just as affecting if it is the protagonist who is in danger of
becoming a victim; there is no stronger motivation than self-
preservation. Private eyes, and cops even more so, are often in the
line of fire; it is a hazard of their trades and incidental to their roles.
There is a more personal sense of identification, however, if the
protagonist is an ordinary citizen, someone who could live down
the block from you, whose predicament is every bit as life-threat-
ening, but who has none of the resources of the professionals.
Take the woman and her lover. Suppose she managed to escape
before the murderer could shoot her; maybe she was in the bath-
room at the time and he was not aware of her presence, though he
was out to get her, too (maybe it *was* the husband). She is in the
dually difficult position of keeping the knowledge of the murder
to herself while figuring out a way of keeping herself alive by
somehow putting the murderer out of commission. You might
take another look at the suggestions I made about John and Jane
Citizen in chapter 1.

For any of these genres, the protagonist's motivation gets an
added boost if the murderer has killed before. There is no doubt
then in the protagonist's mind of the jeopardy he or she has been
placed in.

4. The sleuth must be *capable* of solving the murder. You might
think this goes without saying if your sleuth is admirable, smart,
brave and properly motivated. One would automatically assume
capability. This is not always the case. I have turned down manuscripts in which the author included these qualities and then, in
the clinch, let the sleuth down.

This happens when the author gets the sleuth in a tight corner and calls in the cavalry—some kind of *deus ex machina*—to save
a situation. The reader who is skimming the book while waiting
for a bus is not going to mind very much, but you should. If you
place your sleuth in a tight corner, provide a realistic escape hatch
before you set down another word. Make your sleuth capable of

extricating himself or herself in a rational way. If your heroine is tied up and guarded by three neanderthals, as one (unpublished) author staged this scene, there is no logical way for the heroine to have gotten away. The author, however, had one of the men pick up a dozen hot dogs at a local stand and, whaddya know? the dogs contained spoiled meat. They got sick and, as they passed out, one of them fortuitously dropped a mustard knife (yes) at the heroine's bound feet. Even the skimmer at the bus stop would have done a double take on this one.

Some authors have put their sleuths up against opponents whose expertise was far greater than their sleuths'. Here, a sleuth can show how capable he or she is by faking instant expertise and proving the villain to be a fraud, or in some fashion outwitting the villain at his own game. If your sleuth is only minimally conversant with a particular field—anything from pharmacology to spelunking—fine, as long as he or she can utilize the fundamentals of the field advantageously and, for the duration of the book, convincingly.

The most telling criterion of a sleuth's capabilities will show in the character's dealings with others—sizing people up: *This one seems innocent, this one does not* (and why); *this one is good for information, this one is a dry well gushing forth dust.* In a cat-and-mouse game the sleuth has to know the antagonist well enough to do some fancy second-guessing, often followed by some fancy footwork. The sleuth can be as artful at lying and manipulation as the antagonist, if the ploys produce results. The difference is that the sleuth will not feel good about doing it.

The sleuth is not all-seeing and all-knowing. If this were so, your book would end at chapter 5. There will be setbacks when the sleuth second-guesses erroneously or misinterprets someone's actions or reactions. This prolongs the suspense. Eventually, if you give your sleuth a chance, he or she will correct or neutralize the mistakes and will tie up all the cumulative facts about the antagonist and other suspects and arrive at the correct conclusions about all of them. This entails a combination of logic, intuition and experience. When your sleuth is an amateur, the experience is gained by doing; he or she grows by successfully coping with the criminal events.

5. There is another criterion regarding your sleuth that fits into plot as much as character: If you want the reader to pay attention to your sleuth, get the character into the story early, and make the person memorable from the beginning. If it is a private eye or a cop, the role will be established right then by virtue of his or her profession. If it is an amateur, you are going to need more of a

buildup. For instance, if you have a romantic heroine going into a new (and ultimately hazardous) job, the reader is going to need to know what kind of person would take a job like this and how she glommed on to it. Her bona fides has to be established as soon as she is introduced. Yet a long, careful description of the person and a lengthy explanation of the circumstances put you in danger of having a static beginning. Or put another way, the reader will have to plow through a lot of vital statistics. If you keep in mind that characters in mystery novels are more important for what they do than for who they are, then you can work out a dynamic opening for your protagonist.

A good way of explaining *dynamic* is to tell you an anecdote about George Bernard Shaw. An admiring fan asked permission to take a photograph of him. The old curmudgeon surprisingly agreed. The fan—an ardent but amateur photographer—posed him against a tree. Shaw shook his head forcefully. "No, no. Let me walk into the picture. It will seem more alive"—or words to that effect.

Let your protagonist walk into the picture. Let something happen that will establish him or her as a person of action—as you go along. Nobody is going to remember that the green dress matched her eyes or that he was only five feet eight inches tall. But if the scene opens with her handling a jade-green letter opener (that matches her eyes) or with him stretching his full five feet eight inches to turn off the alarm, then the reader will have a picture to remember.

These five criteria apply to all protagonists in mystery novels. How do you put a personal imprint on yours? I have been told by some authors that they (sneakily) use themselves—their ideal selves—as the basis for their heros or heroines. One of them, laughing, said it gave him a chance to activate his Walter Mitty complex: "It lets me daydream into the typewriter."

I am sure that all authors use their own values to determine the value of their sleuths—their compassion, their cynicism, their humor. When you put your sleuth into a situation, it *is* much easier to think, *How would I react?* Say your sleuth is driving along at night and sees a huddled figure by the roadside. He or she—and you—would stop to investigate. If the figure suddenly rose up and pulled out a .45, you would hightail it back to your car, but your Walter Mitty alter ego would disarm the figure in nothing flat. This is just an example, of course, but chances are your sleuth will be a combination of your sense of reality and your idealized wishful thinking.

The Murderer

The murderer is difficult to portray convincingly. The character who is a totally evil person will be one-dimensional. Yet if you introduce complexities and small foibles and kindnesses that round out the character, he or she seems less villainous. Fortunately, with today's emphasis on ordinary people, the murderer can have a lot of the values of the law-abiding citizen and seem quite normal on the surface. One school of thought says that almost anyone is capable of murder given strong enough motivation. I subscribe to this in part—certainly for murder mysteries. After all, the least likely suspect is often the murderer.

Whether your murderer is a bluebeard or a dishonest accountant, there is nothing so satisfying as to be presented with a villain you love to hate. This presents a problem in the murder mystery where the murderer is not known until close to the end. Until then, the character may have been disagreeable or uncaring but in no way seen to be murderous. So all the hate is focused and brought to bear in the revelation.

In the meantime, it is possible to hate the murderer in absentia: The crime he or she committed produces feelings of outrage and fear in the other characters—*What kind of person could have done this thing?* and *Which of us will be next?*

The reader will be asking these questions, too, so you need a profile of the murderer right from the start, but one that will not give the game away. At the beginning, we know the murderer only by the crime he or she has committed, but certain deductions can be made from the nature of the crime. If three or four old ladies are knocked off, we know that somebody did not love his mother. If it is a rich old man, one of the heirs is apt to be the culprit.

When and where the victim was killed will give some indication of how the murderer operated.

How the victim was killed will add to the profile.

In other words, you can build a profile of sorts by surmising a possible motive, the opportunity and the means, thereby giving the reader something to go by.

The characters in a murder mystery are living the drama that envelops their lives and are understandably too close to the events to recognize signs of the murderer. The reader is the semi-omniscient observer and can recognize signs if you observe the rules of mystery writing and place clues about the miscreant. By your slipping in clues in a "casual" manner, the final revelation does not seem to come from left field. Ways of playing fair are:

1. Placing the murderer in the wrong place at the wrong time so that he or she seems to be out of character.
2. Comments from the murderer that reveal a knowledge that only he or she could have about the murder.
3. Negative observations from others about the murderer's misdeeds having nothing to do with the murder.
4. References to the murderer's past that seem unimportant when they are mentioned.
5. Introducing other not-so-innocent characters he or she consorts with.
6. Getting the reader to hate somebody else in the meantime.

When I say, slipping in clues in a "casual" manner, I realize that it does not seem so casual when you are trying to fit these clues in. You have to walk a tightrope in order to supply a fair amount of information without tipping your hand.

One of the edicts of the older mystery school was that everyone, including the murderer, should be a suspect at least once. This would seem to take you off the tightrope. But I think that is overloading the circuits. I would settle for having the murderer suspected once, then cleared until the end, and have other suspects to throw sand in the reader's eyes. But it is not really necessary to have the murderer suspected at all. If you can pull it off, the least likely suspect is still the prize in the Cracker Jack box. But here again, you have to play fair. The murderer should prove to be a vital person, or at least have a substantial role, in the story—not some nut bearing a twenty-year grudge who sweeps in from New Mexico for this particular murder, but someone whose life intermingles with the other characters so it is inevitable that the spotlight will fall on him or her as a possible suspect. The inevitability of it takes some of the suspicion away from the murderer if he or she is just one among several.

It is possible to have a least likely murderer if he or she blends into the scene with a foolproof camouflage. Like G. K. Chesterton's postman,* he or she will never be spotlighted when the character is deliberately placed in the spotlight. Another kind of placement that is so obvious it goes unnoticed is when the murderer is a functionary on the

---

*In the short story *The Invisible Man*, the murderer dons a postman's uniform to gain access to the victim's lodgings in order to kill him. Just as important, the murderer was able to leave the scene of the crime "unseen." The ploy that Chesterton used for getting rid of the body should be taken with a grain of salt by the modern mystery writer; the victim is carried away in the "postman's" bag!

right side of the law—a cop, a prosecuting attorney, a judge or even a defense attorney. They can make the investigation of a crime go in any direction they want, with all trails leading away from them. You have to give them a motivation, as with any murderer, and you have to drop clues every so often. But until the end they are like Caesar's wife, so the impact will be even greater when the reader finds out whodunit. Make sure you have logical reasons for them committing the murder and for them being the investigating cop, prosecutor, *et al.*, in the case. Do you remember me talking about turning coincidence into encounter in chapter 5? Take another look at pages 91 to 93 to see how you can avoid using coincidences so that characters converge naturally and, in these examples, so that a minion of the law can work both sides of the fence.

A character who is not often used as a camouflaged murderer is the narrator. There have been few examples since Mrs. Christie stole the show. Though I think she was pretty fair about it, the flak concerning Dr. Sheppard in *The Murder of Roger Ackroyd* still goes on sixty years later. Turning the tables of justice (like the examples in the above paragraph) is an iffy business. Turning the tables on the reader, as Mrs. Christie did, is even iffier. However, caution never assured anyone of anything except boring longevity, and why were risks invented if not to be taken?

You will have thought out your murderer in the biography section, so you know whether the character has a strong or weak set of genes, whether he or she works from a sense of purpose or out of desperation. The murderer does not have to be a tower of intelligence, but had damned well better be clever. There is an old adage that says, "Chance favors the prepared mind," and your murderer has to be able to take advantage of circumstances as he or she sees them or, better yet, foresees them. Say that a member of the murderer's family is to be done away with. The family is at its usual Sunday night gathering from which only the victim and the murderer are absent. The victim is upstairs in bed and the murderer is "away" in Chicago (you can work this out easily enough). What cop or sleuth would rely on the family members alibiing each other? And so the murderer chooses his time wisely to sneak upstairs and murder the bedridden victim.

The murderer can leave a false trail at the scene of the crime, pointing to someone else; set clocks back; have a cohort serve as an alibi (a girlfriend or boyfriend, a tennis partner).

These suggestions apply to the planner. What of the murderer who strikes out in the heat of the moment? Is it possible to build a suspense novel based on a momentary flare of passion? I would think so. After all, murderous intent was there and the cover-up will be just as necessary for this murderer as for the careful planner. Does unpremeditated murder buy more sympathy for a murderer? If the victim was a rotten person, it might. Nonetheless, some kind of retribution has to be made. One cannot condone a vigilante action outright.*

I remember one lulu of a manuscript that crossed my desk in which the murderer, a mountain man, killed his uncle and eight cousins in a barn-burning. ("They warnt no good.") Because of the close tie between him and his "ole dawg Blue," the author let him waste away with "empasema" rather than sending him to the state penitentiary. In spite of the manuscript's hopeless illiteracy, I had a grudging sympathy for the mountain man; his relatives were pretty awful and they did him a lot of dirt, and he did love his dog.†

Is it possible, then, for your reader to have sympathy for a murderer, one who is not hated in the final revelation? Or if not sympathy, admiration? Suppose he or she were a scientist whose breakthrough research on a deadly disease was ignored by the university's department head. The department head had his own serum to push, one that the scientist felt could prove deadly to mankind. The scientist had appealed to other universities and to government labs, to no avail; his department head had an enormous amount of clout. So for the most altruistic reasons, he kills the department head with the latter's own serum to stop this dangerous charade and prove his case.

Do the ends then justify the means? Or, put another way, does the motive justify the ends? If the murderer is a wretched victim of circumstances, it is harder to make much of a villain out of the character; he or she is more to be pitied than censured. This might make the character more identifiable for the reader, but I am not sure that is a good idea, especially for a beginning writer who, I think, would be better off working with blacks and whites rather than to experiment with the ambiguous grays.

You can make a plausible murderer out of a character whom no reader could identify with. In fact, that should be your aim; otherwise, where would justice and revenge fit in? Where would the sleuth's challenge be? And it should be the sleuth, not the murderer, who is ultimately the admirable character. In the course of the story, the murderer should be a worthy opponent—as I said earlier—to test the sleuth's

*In chapter 6 I cited a case like this: *Beyond a Reasonable Doubt* by C. W. Grafton.
†I do not remember what happened to Blue.

mettle, but should definitely have criminal qualities that make him or her a danger to the other characters in the book.

As with the sleuth, the murderer appears on scene early in the book. I use "appear" advisedly, because if you open with a murder scene, the murderer is going to be a hand holding a weapon, or a threatening voice; not even the person's sex will be apparent. But even here, you can drop clues:

The kind of weapon used. If it is a garrote, for instance, you are depicting a coldly efficient, silent murderer, a scary type quite different from an emotional one who picks up a bronze statue and bashes in the victim's head.

What the murderer says; cursing or threatening the victim. Be cagey about this. If she yells, "You're some lousy brother," or he gloats, "Yeah, I cooked the books," you have given away the motive and have narrowed down your list of suspects at the beginning. Let your murderer make impassioned but vague statements that would fit anybody, like, "You have already hurt too many people." Or in third-person narration, you can simply state that there was a terrible argument.

Eventually—the sooner the better—you will introduce the murderer as a bona fide person who takes up his or her role in the story. You can do it as early as having the murderer "discover" the body. This was done in the locked-room mysteries of the thirties in order to let the murderer dispose of incriminating evidence. If you want to use this gimmick, you could have it be an employee in the plant, whose presence would be natural. By being the first to broadcast the news of the boss's death, the murderer would certainly throw the reader off, as long as he or she had a good reason for going to the plant office. Keep in mind that it might squeeze the time for the murderer's alibi, but this can work in your favor, if you think about it.

If your murderer is introduced later than the opening scene, follow the same dynamics you used for the sleuth: Let him or her "walk into the picture." Make his or her presence a natural part of the scene. With the sleuth, the role is apparent. Not so with the murderer, although the role will seem apparent: The murdered brother's sister, whom we get to know only later as murderously hating, might be helpful in settling the estate; the accountant is a kindly fellow who is clever in setting up tax shelters for his employer and meanwhile is cooking the books. The reader could even like the helpful sister and the zealous accountant, but do not overdo it or the wrench at the revelation will be severe.

Before we come to the revelation, let me caution you about one more thing: getting into the mind of the murderer. This is often attempted with the psychopathic murderer, and nine times out of ten it comes off as ludicrous. Why? Because the writer with a normal mind simply transfers normal, illogical—not psychopathic—reasoning to the disturbed murderer's mind. In one manuscript I read, the murderer was a sexual psychopath and his victim was a woman who reminded him of a "dreadful" teacher he had had in the second grade who had humiliated him "in a thousand ways." His victim, like his teacher, had frizzy red hair and wore a lot of junk jewelry. Bingo! (and here is the second mistake the author made) "Everything got dark, then purple lights flashed, her eyes loomed luminescently . . ." etc., etc., etc., which prompted him to plunge the knife into her "scrawny chest." The author took an unpleasant episode in the man's life and turned it into a big deal. Then the error was compounded by "painting" the psychopathic mind, using color as conflict. Believe me, it is easy to fall into this kind of melodramatic writing when you are dealing with the unknown and, perhaps, unknowable. Keep out of the psychopath's mind and just describe his or her acts, acts which no normal person would perform.

You will not fare much better—nor will your reader—trying to get into the mind of your normal murderer. Authors who do this produce what amounts to a hollow tease: *Which of my characters is thinking these thoughts?* Thoughts unattached to an unknown personality are, literally, disembodied; for my money, they might as well be coming from a *Star Trek* alien. This is a literary affectation I never encourage, for I have yet to encounter an author skilled enough to give the reader a ringside seat into a murderer's mind without being purposely vague, which does not help the reader, or without giving away vital information, which works against the writer. Until the revelation, let your murderer be portrayed through action and dialogue and any of the kinds of clues I listed on pages 85 to 87.

I would offer similar advice about dreams—for any of the characters. I have read manuscripts, and even published books, which opened with the protagonist or the murderer engaged in some scary action, a real cliff-hanger that got my attention, and then learned on page three that it was only a dream. I felt cheated. Other authors use dreams for beleaguered characters to show just how deep their emotional anguish is. It seems to me such a roundabout way to show stress, and it takes the reader one remove away. I would be more convinced of the anguish if the character threw a bookend through the window.

Now let us get to the revelation. The sleuth has discovered who-dunit and the reader wants to know why. What prompted this person to commit murder?

Well, first, the murderer will be sure that this final act was un-avoidable. He or she might give lip service to alternatives, like paying up or getting out or letting a lover go; there may even be remorse there. But the fact remains that he or she chose to kill as a solution to the prob-lem. This says something about the pressure the murderer was under, so the *why*, the motive, has to have been bone-deep.

I have mentioned several times that the murderer will not see the difference between desire and need. Put another way, he or she will not differentiate between mistaken self-interest and true self-preserva-tion. Somewhere along the line, the murderer's values went askew and he or she committed murder as a result of this jumbled thinking. It is up to you to straighten this out for the reader. You have the double du-ty of explaining the reason for murder and the murderer's reasoning, which may not be as simple as the reason.

Say a man murdered his wife for her money. On the face of it, that would satisfy the reader. But what if he married her in order to murder her in order to get her money? In other words, you have to bring to light the motive *and* how it was thought out.

There could have been a side issue that tipped the scales. Suppose the husband had a change of heart, but as the marriage went on, she became intolerable to live with; because of her own jumbled thinking, she became a castrator, and because murderers are self-justifiers, he re-newed his original plan. If he had been a virile-seeming, devoted hus-band up until the murder, these under-the-surface feelings will sur-prise the reader.

In fact, the only character in the book who will surprise the reader is the murderer, for this is the only character in the book who seems to change. But the murderer does not really change. It seems that way be-cause you have been holding back information, and when you reveal it at the end, you have simply thrown a new light on the person.

To make this seeming change credible, the revelation has to be built up from clues dropped throughout the story. If you do this, read-ers can thumb back through their minds and realize why this person had to be the murderer.

It is not a good idea, just for the sake of surprise, to bring in brand-new facts about the murderer at this juncture—say, along with plotting his wife's death, he ran an illegal bookmaking operation on the side. It might round him out a bit more, but you end up with too much explaining to do without appreciably adding to his profile. I have read manuscripts in which crime after crime was pinned on the murderer (or sometimes confessed to) to bolster this profile, including every murder in town since 1910. But there had been no—or insufficient—background buildup for these crimes. Writers who lay it on with a trowel have the mistaken notion that the more crimes, the more reprehensible the criminal. Three things go wrong here: The character gets distorted, the reader gets sated and plausibility goes out the window.*

In real life, most criminals are pretty dumb—our overflowing prisons attest to that. In the murder mystery, your criminal has to be caught, too. Not because he or she is dumb, but because of a fatal flaw in the character. He or she has to trip up in some fashion, either by being too smart for his or her own good or too complacent. It could be a clue overlooked or an action hastily devised as part of the coverup that seems to put the character out of character. As the net closes in, panic, fear or anger could cause the murderer to make a serious misstep. If you remember, some time back I said that the murderer often does not distinguish between need and desire, and so arrogance is among the most prominent of fatal flaws.

There are murderers who outstrip themselves in self-congratulations and self-admiration. It is this kind who fall apart most easily, who are the natural prey of panic, fear and anger.

Jonathan Swift described the flaw of arrogance very well:

> ". . . untroubled by the knowledge that he was a devil,
> [he] could not bear the suggestion that he was a dunce."

The Victim

Earlier, when I was listing prototypes, I listed the victim as either "primary" or "secondary." What I implied was, Just how important is the victim in your scheme of things? Granted, without the victim there would be no murder mystery, and, too, the victim *is* important, like the

---

*The greatest suspense writer of all time was guilty of all three when he had his arch-villain, Aaron, in *Titus Andronicus,* confess:
> I have done a thousand dreadful things
> As willingly as one would kill a fly;
> And nothing grieves me heartily indeed
> But that I cannot do ten thousand more.

other characters, for what he or she does—in this case, getting murdered. Thereafter, the victim appears only through the remembrances of others. So you must decide on how much emphasis you want to place on the victim-as-person and how much emphasis on the other characters' responses to the person-as-victim.

I would say that a primary victim is one who is not murdered right off but who has a chance to put his or her input directly to the reader. The reader gets interested in the victim as a live person and so becomes more involved when the person is killed. Remember, the more involvement, the more end-explanation is needed, so be aware of what you are doing. (To refresh your memory, end-explanations are covered in chapter 6.)

One popular mystery writer, Emma Lathen, seems to specialize in this delayed kind of action. Her murder often takes place halfway through the book. Her main thrust is to keep us entertained with the conniving power plays of all of her characters and to keep us wondering which of them is going to get it. So half the book is devoted to who gets it and the second half to whodunit. Sometimes the one we suspect is the one who gets murdered. Other times, the victim has only a peripheral role in the dishonest dealings, but it turns out to have been a pivotal one. It is an unusual way to construct a murder mystery, but it works. And with the victim on scene, alive and kicking through so many pages, the author supplies ample reader identification with the victim.*

What are some of the situations that would call for having your victim alive for a while?

1) If your victim "participates" in his or her own death:
   a) is being pursued;
   b) threatens the murderer;
   c) sets up an explosive situation for many others.

2) If you have the victim alive at the beginning, the reader can make up his or her own mind about the victim and so be able to evaluate the other characters' reactions later on.

3) A third reason, which ties in with the first, is that it gives you a chance

*Often Lathen has someone *report* the murder. Her murders are almost incidental to the intricate interplay of her other characters. One suspects that her detective, John Putnam Thatcher, Vice President of Sloan Guaranty Trust, looks upon corpses as awkward debentures to be cleared off the books as expeditiously as possible.

for a dramatic scene (or scenes) by letting the reader witness the buildup to the murder as well as the murder itself.

The victim as a secondary character is one who is already dead when the book opens or who is murdered early on, and whose death produces a different set of feelings. The closest identification the reader can make with the victim is as a who-was-it. The reader can sympathize but can hardly empathize. The act of murder is so final that the only realistic reaction is to seek out whodunit. Nonetheless, even dead, the victim has to be accounted for.

The Narrator's View of the Body

Some authors, in attempting to bridge the gap between sympathy and empathy, lay on the gore. They figure that desecration will arouse indignation. It will do that, yes. There will be horror in the reader's mind at the outrage that has been performed on the victim. This will produce a distant kind of empathy: *My God! I wouldn't want that done to me!* This can be terribly effective if it is a short description of the mutilation and if it is part of the murderer's plan and not solely the random action of a sick mind.

A brilliant example of gruesome death-dealing appears in the prologue to William H. Hallahan's *The Search for Joseph Tully*. The scene is set in Rome, 1498, in a swordmaker's armory where two fine Toledo blades are being forged. The final quenching of the red-hot metal is done by thrusting the blades into the bodies of two bound captives. And William Bayer does a superior piece of work in depicting the results of a psychotic murderer who decapitates his victims (and switches heads) in his mystery, *Switch*.

At the other end of the spectrum are the authors who prefer what I term "antiseptic death." The killing is done off-scene and the corpse never appears. (Could you call this a "tertiary victim"?) Or if we are allowed to view the remains, the appearance is a genteel one—a knife angled into the back of a tweed coat or a neat hole in an otherwise unblemished temple. These are not prudish writers, not by a long shot. They have set their sights on whodunit, not who-was-it. They are the puzzle-makers rather than the button-pushers.

Between the gore hounds and the antiseptics lies the broadest band of the spectrum: the philosophers. They fall into three groups:

a) The stoic viewer who describes the state of the victim as dispassionately as any coroner; a removed kind of person who keeps emotion out of it and notes the position of the body, the time and cause of death, any struggle that ensued, the victim's sex, clothes, etc. By showing no feelings the viewer lets the reader supply the commentary.

b) The humane viewer who sees the body as a once-living human being, who has respect for what that person was and compassion for what he or she no longer is. The viewer is angered by the brutality and saddened by the waste. These attitudes are the most sympathetic and, paradoxically, the most uncomfortable to deal with—the author is really striking home.

c) The callous viewer who is not at all fazed by the vulnerability of death. Back in chapter 4 I talked about this tough view, of seeing the victim as "a mound of inanimate tissue": "So Joe finally got his brains splattered; first I knew he had any." If you want to major in macho writing, you will be right at home with Joe's viewer.

The Other Characters' View of the Victim

In most mysteries, the victim is a secondary character and is killed off early. The reader may have a few glimpses of the person before he or she is killed, glimpses which offer only a fleeting kind of evaluation. It will be up to you to tell more about the victim through the other characters.

Has the murder sent shock waves through the community? Was the victim a powerhouse, so that his or her death starts off a scramble for new power? Did the victim leave a legacy of ruthlessness that the underlings want to emulate? Did they envy the victim's acumen while disliking him or her personally?

Had the victim been popular, so that the murder first numbs the community, then rouses it to anger? Is there a concerted wish to find the murderer? (A community, by the way, can be as large as an industrial complex or as small as a boardinghouse.)

Are there just a few who care? If so, they care deeply and in the most personal kinds of ways, when the victim was a spouse, a child, a lover or a very old and dear friend. They will be just as biased in their views of the victim as the power-hungry third vice president is in his.

Does the murder bring out second thoughts among people who

had been the victim's firm friends? Do they now see the victim in a new light, and does this affect their grief?

Almost as if the victim were reaching out from the grave, relatives and friends often feel guilty about what they could have done, or should not have done, that might have made a difference.

Do the facts that death has brought to the surface make the victim's death seem like a blessing for one and all? So that ultimately only the cops are interested in finding out whodunit? This kind of slant is difficult to take unless you can lighten it with humor, which usually turns out to be macabre. In any case, one ends up feeling more sympathy for the characters than for the victim, which is a reversal of the usual formula of seeking justice and/or revenge.

SECONDARY CHARACTERS

Secondary characters come in all sizes and shapes, but they have only two main functions: as suspects and nonsuspects. They share two things in common: They will have ties to the victim and their own lives will be affected, in varying degrees, by the murder.

Suspects

The suspects' roles are self-evident: Each of them had a motive for murder. How many suspects you have depends on your plot; as I have said, keep the numbers manageable. Remember, the sleuth is going to have to juggle this list until he or she comes up with the murderer, and you will make it unnecessarily difficult for yourself, and time-consuming, if you have a cast of thousands. You want to create puzzlement, not confusion. This means setting up adversarial relationships long before you begin writing.

Have your suspects be worthy adversaries. Profile them with hard, sharp lines, for, as supporting actors, they are ultimately meant to make the sleuth look good.

Nonsuspects

Your nonsuspects are important for the human interest that gives your story its soft lines. When a victim dies, those who care die a little, too. The reader's identification with the mourners can play a significant part in wanting to bring the murderer to justice. If the reader forms emotional attachments, you have added to the suspense. Go easy on the button-pushing, though. The reader has seen enough of life to know what grief is and would rather be led into tapping into his or her own experience than to be told what to feel. Laying it on with a trowel imposes an unwanted burden. It also interferes with the pace of your story.

You will need other nonsuspects who are not emotionally involved but who serve a purpose in the plot.

A sleuth's sidekick is one. This is a partner or a friend who acts as an active participant, a sounding board or, usually, both. Dr. Watson, of course, is the most famous prototype of the sidekick. Conan Doyle used him to describe Holmes' actions, leaving Holmes to perform with a free hand. Though Watson kept the reader apprised of events, he did not "give the game away." Holmes kept Watson in the dark, too, concerning the significance of what he observed. Even so, we know more about the great detective because of Watson's commentaries. Modern-day sidekicks serve exactly the same purpose—to give a particular slant to the sleuth and to serve as a bridge between the sleuth and the reader. In contemporary fiction, authors who consistently use a sidekick are Rex Stout (Archie Goodwin), John D. MacDonald (Meyer) and Marvin Kaye (Gene).

Secondary characters pivot around the sleuth; they also pivot around each other. This happens when you have a secondary theme. For instance, if you have put goals into motion before your story begins, goals in which the victim had a part—a budding business, a sports tournament, the rebuilding of a church—these goals serve as background for your "world"; you people them with secondary characters and place some of them in subplots. They will have known the victim, but aside from the hole he or she leaves in the project (goal), they are not affected by the victim's demise; they are used to fill out the victim's world by reacting to one another.

They can also be used for any expertise you want to bring in. For instance, if you are into church architecture, a knowledgeable minister would do some expounding as the foundations are being laid for the new church.* (The minister probably conducted the funeral services for the victim.)

How thoroughly do these secondary characters have to be described in order to be memorable? Because they *do* come in all sizes and shapes, I can only suggest broad outlines which you can tailor to your own needs.

*Remember what I said about using "expertise" simply to pad your book!

First, hold on to the thought that you are writing a novel of detection and not a character study like that of Raskolnikov in Dostoevsky's *Crime and Punishment;* and yet your characters have to be real enough to satisfy the roles you give them. Your work of characterizing will be simpler if you have thought through their roles ahead of time and make sure that they do not slip out of them as you go along. You will, with work and concentration, learn to sense that *No policeman would react this way* or that *She would not choose this kind of department store to shoplift in.*

Their roles will dictate their physical appearances, attitudes, personal backgrounds, ways of dealing with danger or with emotion (anger, love), mannerisms, prejudices—the list is almost endless.

There are three ways of depicting these roles. Use all three as situations call for them:

1. Up-front descriptions when the character is introduced. Try to include lifelike qualities, the way you would size up anybody you met for the first time—kind, aloof, nervous, apologetic, bubble-headed—however that person would be in that particular situation. This business of describing a character only by his or her clothes, for instance, is not worth a tinker's damn. Though she is not the only one, Margaret Truman does this quite a lot. Her men appear on scene and before they leave you know the cut of their suits, the color and quality of the material and the kind of neckwear they sport.* This is an age-old mechanism, tried and true, God knows, and a tired one. Introducing a character by listing only the obvious physical features—height, weight, coloring and clothes—is the mark of a hurried writer, one who wants to get on· with the story. But your story loses something if your character is plucked out of a pigeonhole. You learn nothing about the character's inner workings, no hint of what to expect from the person.

You do not have to go into lengthy, in-depth studies, but you are, by my lights, expected to nail down some singularity that distinguishes the person as an individual. Because you do not have much time, why not do it when the character first appears and will have the reader's optimum attention? Think about the character, hit the bull's-eye, and you will end up saving time!

2. Show him or her in action. This is the least self-conscious way of depicting a character. I do not mean the mindless knee jerks of a James Bond, entertaining as they are, but thoughtful actions done with an eye to the possible outcome. Suppose you had a mother in the playground. You could have her say, "We watch the children

*Haberdashery runs in her family, bless them.

carefully." Instead, what about having her stride toward a questionable-looking loiterer? The encounter will not amount to anything because it is not part of the plot, but you have shown a protective and decisive woman in action. This is a dynamic kind of portraiture, one that shows rather than tells. Another way of looking at this example would be if the now-angry loiterer turns up later in the story and proves to be a suspect. Then you would have the woman's portrait-through-action working hand-in-glove to forward the plot.

Another kind of portrait-through-action is to show a character on the job. Let a rookie cop work his crowd-control assignment for a bit, then let him spot an important witness heading for the bleachers. Show a swimming instructor, bamboo pole in hand, guiding a neophyte along the perimeter of the pool before you call her to the phone.

A little earlier, I suggested that you let the sleuth "walk into the picture." Here, let the reader walk in.

3. Through dialogue. I will be talking about dialogue in chapter 9, where I discuss style, but there is no harm in beginning the discussion here, so that I can talk about what fits here.

Secondary characters by their very natures will be upstaged by the primary characters and their dialogue will be feed-ins, especially to the sleuth. If you remember, starting on page 115, I talked about "cooperating" with the sleuth, noting that the sleuth's descriptive abilities were only as good as the people, places and things you offered for scrutiny. Now you are going to make the secondary characters cooperate with the sleuth. You are going to pull their strings so that they give the sleuth the answers that are needed to help the case along. Suspects will give clear-to-muddled answers and the murderer, of course, will give wrong answers.

Another kind of feed-in is to challenge the sleuth outright: by refusing to talk (a negative kind of dialogue!); circumlocution (lots of words to say little, another kind of negativism); apologies, smart-ass responses and proclamations of ignorance.

The secondary characters who care will offer what information they have in a straightforward way. They will describe how they feel (awful) and will in their pain exhort the sleuth—different from a challenge—to find the murderer.

All of them will tell something about themselves when they talk, if you keep them firmly in their roles.

MINOR CHARACTERS

Primary and secondary characters carry the plot and supply the emotions; both sets of prototypes work to form the fabric of the story. Minor characters are the selvage. So although their roles are small, they
are not as incidental as they might seem. They contribute their share by
being:

The information passers. They are live stand-ins for maps, tele-
phones and office-building directories. It is more interesting, for instance, if a character looking for a street in a strange part of the city ex-
changes a few words with a local about directions.

You can have racetrack touts, snitches, servants, cab drivers,
headwaiters and nosy neighbors—all of whom offer bits and pieces to
fill in the puzzle.

The information obtainers. A receptionist, an insurance clerk, a factory foreman are all useful for getting specific types of information not
readily at hand to the public. The sleuth's dropping in on an old newspaper buddy will expedite a clipping search in the newspaper's
morgue.*

These minor characters serve as painless ways of gathering the
bits and pieces. If you already have a heavy load of secondary characters, you might want to forgo these minor information obtainers and
use maps, phones and footwork instead.

Time passers. These are people observed in passing. I gave an example when I described the private eye walking to the Records Building (the break dancers). The time passer is used for a minute action that
does not necessarily forward the plot but gives the story a feeling of
busyness; it is a slender thread in the fabric.

Pace breakers. If your preceding scene has been an intense one and
your next scene will be intense, too, you can introduce a minor character to let the reader catch his or her breath, to provide a small air cush-
ion between explosions. An example would be the scene of the loiterer
at the playground (page 143). Say the loiterer has been shown to be a
menace, frightening the mothers and the babysitters into gathering up
the children and herding them to the safety of their cars. In the next
scene the loiterer is in pursuit. In between those scenes a mother recognizes a tiny discarded sneaker, stops to pick it up and makes a mental
note to return it to *that young Mrs. Haskell, so scatterbrained.*

Minor characters plop into the picture and just as quickly plop out.

*These days it is called the library. How drab.

Descriptions of them are brief, but they can be made memorable. The woman who picked up the sneaker, for instance: "One of the mothers, her two hundred pounds draped in a gaudy caftan, laboriously bent down to pick up a child's sneaker." (Then her mental note.) In one sentence you give the reader enough information to draw his or her own satisfying conclusions about the character. Perhaps later, the sleuth sees the same woman "turtling" (leaning on a windowsill) and yelling at the kids playing stickball on the hot asphalt below. Again, one sentence almost in passing tells the reader about the woman and her neighborhood.

Not all minor characters will necessarily be described this briefly. They may take up a paragraph or a page. What I am trying to get across is that they provide miniature actions and flecks of color that help to bind the fabric of the story.

I would like to round off this section by saying something about character-handling in general.

Characters should vary in terms of personalities and physical appearances, though backgrounds may be similar. If your sleuth is working on an industrial case, it would not be wise to have six redheaded machinists as suspects. It would be odd if your male sleuth were sleeping with three bosomy blondes, all with Ph.D.'s in biometrics, or your female sleuth were dating four N.F.L. quarterbacks.

Suspects, especially, should differ from one another—considerably. They are the ones the reader will want to keep track of, so make it easy to do just that.

Individual balances have to be set for the realism of the characters so that all of the characters can mesh in agreement or conflict.

The first type of balance, for realism, will not be difficult for your primary characters. You will probably develop them first anyway, then build the others around them. So you start with their inner balances. What traits are good for them? Which would work against them? Can your murderer love flowers? Love babies? Dote on bolo knives? Maybe the last one. Does your sleuth have keen sensitivity and a nasty temper? Not likely. Putting incongruous traits into a person verges on the absurd or the cute and burdens you with the confusion that will arise from the other characters.

In the second part, the balance among characters, you can be incongruous. The haughty dowager and the sniffling junkie I mentioned at the beginning of the chapter fit into the overall scene of their era and were comfortable being who they were; the author saw to that. For all that they might or might not have been important to the plot, they were unusual people.

Most of the people in murder mysteries are less so, otherwise there would be a constant fight for attention. You need contrast, yes, but in terms of grays and browns to offset the occasional vermilions. If any of your primary or secondary characters is portrayed in a continual dazzle of color, your reader will soon reach a saturation point. Save your vermilions for the minor characters, whose roles are not competitive and who appear on scene less often.

After you have identified the characters on their first appearances, reidentify them when they appear for the second time (maybe even the third time), so that you nail them down in the reader's mind. If a secondary character flits in and out, and these appearances are widely separated, tag that person *each time* with an identifying trait. Change the wording of your tagging each time, if you like, but use the same tag.

And speaking of tags, let me point out an onerous kind of tag that writers attach to themselves: the "male" point of view and the "female" point of view. No writer has to be confined to one or the other. In chapter 2 (on getting ideas), I wrote something to the effect that people who trigger any thought or emotion are good character material. Without thinking, I assumed that a writer's reactions will cut across sexual lines when that serves a purpose. If a man, say, were writing about a woman's hairdo, he might describe it as "a bouffant upsweep" or as "It looks like she's carrying a beehive around," depending on the kind of narrator he is using. A woman writer might describe a male character as wearing "bulging-tight jeans" or "dressing noticeably on the left," again depending upon the narrator she is using. Each writer has a choice of placing characters within or without his or her own realm of sexual identity.

Interestingly enough, more women than men use protagonists of the opposite sex.* I can only surmise that women do not feel threatened by "putting a man in power." Culturally, this has certainly been more acceptable (which is unfortunate). But you might be surprised at the number of men who write romantic suspense under feminine pseudonyms. I think the ideal author has an androgynous mind. To achieve a truly balanced set of characters, an author has to start with an

---

*Richard Barth, whom I mentioned in chapter 1, is one exception. His detective, if you remember, is a woman.

understanding of both sexes, go on from there to incorporate cultural attitudes toward sexuality, and then branch out into the psychological behavior that is common to both sexes.

There is one final consideration that I would like to bring up. I have mentioned it before in other contexts, and I may very well mention it again before I am through: the balance of character versus plot.

I am of the school that says *Yes!* to good characters in a mystery novel, but the plot is still the thing. Your characters' principal function is to keep the plot going. If you can work up a bunch of unusual characters serving a tightly knit story, more power to you, but I think it would be wise the first time around to concentrate your efforts on less-moving people in favor of keeping them moving. There need not be anything "ordinary" about ordinary people if you breathe life into them by giving them out-of-the-ordinary crises to cope with.*

*In his mystery, *Fletch*, Gregory Mcdonald did an outstanding job of combining polychromatic characters with the tightest plot I have ever encountered. He is an exception.

CHAPTER 8

BACKGROUND FOR MURDER

THE MYSTERY NOVEL, as we have seen, has four main components: plot, characterization, theme and background. It is time now to talk about the last of this quartet.

Background is tailored to fit the theme, to silhouette the characters and to provide a stage for the plot. It furnishes the "worlds" I talked about in chapter 1, where I pointed out that as the subgenres have proliferated, a growing number of authors with wider interests have been attracted to the mystery field and have brought new and different settings to it. Some of the settings have been exotic, and some so mundane that their very familiarity has created fresh interest. The best of these new authors have developed their backgrounds with three basic ideas in mind: 1) the construction of a realistic milieu, 2) the creation of mood and 3) the integration of setting and crime. Let us take each of these in turn.

1. To create a factual world for the story, the mystery writer gets material from the real world, then transmutes it into the "realism" of the book's world. Even though realism in the hands of a writer goes through a sea change, the facts on which the book's realism are based are real facts. The reader relies on the author's honesty in assuming this is so. Consequently, it is incumbent on you to know the facts, whether they concern gun calibers or hair dyes. If you are sure of your facts, you will write with greater ease, and the reader will sense your assurance.

If you already know your background well, if you are a cop or a doctor or a lawyer or an antiques dealer, your only problem lies in choosing the *pertinent* facts from your range of expertise. If you have not been trained in a specialty but are intrigued by it and know something about it, you have a harder task: to learn more about it and then to pick out the pertinent facts. There are cops and doctors, *et al.* who do use their knowledge and turn their talents to mystery writing, but the majority of mystery writers have no specialties other than the ability to write and *to do research*. I will be getting to these methods of research when I cover special backgrounds. What I want to get across here is that background is built on both feelings and facts.

What about including facts just for the fun of it? Will they interest the reader, too? As I noted in the last chapter, there are readers who enjoy learning "something new," and if the information is given to them as part of the entertainment, it beats going to the encyclopedia as far as they are concerned. The skillful author takes seemingly irrelevant facts and ties them in with the plot as a form of clue dropping. But if you go off on your own private hobby horse about wines or the pari-mutuel system, you take the chance of bringing the wrath of your readers down on your head: *Let's get on with the story!* they will say to themselves. Facts can be used as part of the entertainment if you have a strong plot line going for you and if the facts serve that plot.

One mystery novel I read recently, *A Cold Mind* by David L. Lindsey, handles facts-for-their-own-sake in a riveting manner. A brilliant virology student is killing off prostitutes with a deadly, time-delayed virus (when the victims begin to show fatal symptoms, he is long gone). The author devotes an entire chapter to a laboratory scene where we watch the student preparing the viral solution that will be injected into his victims. He begins by laying out his special lab clothing: bulky lab coat, plastic face shield and heavy-duty gloves. Then he lays out his scalpels, petri dishes and slides. First he has had to incubate the viral material in animal tissue, so he next brings out the head of an Irish setter, which he wedges into a V-shaped vise. We are then treated to the step-by-step process of extracting the virus from the dog's brain. At the end of each step, the student carefully cleans his equipment in an autoclave. The process takes hours, and I will spare you the rest of the necrotic details. It is a fascinating chapter that, in a sense, stops the plot cold. But it adds—does it ever add!—to the grimness that pervades the entire book. This scene, by the way, contains a vital clue that helps the cops to solve the case. I would like to point out also that the plot as a whole is a strong one, and this nine-page chapter does not weaken its thrust one iota. Another point I would like to make is that the details of the lab and the student's clinical processes sounded chillingly authentic and so made absorbing reading.

2. The second basic idea of background is to create feelings that permeate the story and give it its "tone"—a frantic pace or a calm detachment; grimness or lightheartedness. You could call these feelings "the emotional backdrop." Authors accomplish this by the way they delineate their characters, the landscape and the nature of the crime. The narrative styles and dialogue are slanted so that they, too, add to the mood.

One good way of setting the tone of the book is to have the victim found in a setting that evokes distinctive feelings. Fishing a body out of the sea produces a different reaction from finding a body behind an all-night drive-in. With both of these examples, the tone is set by the nature of the place, which has a mood of its own.

Another way to create mood is to make your characters and your landscape "real" but just enough off-key to remove them from their symmetrical, predictable, everyday appearances.

Think of a playground in a nicely kept park. The kids are busy in the sandbox, pumping away on the swings, squealing down the slides; the mothers are gossiping while keeping benign eyes peeled on their offspring; an ice cream vendor and a few fathers are there; sunlight, shouts, piping cries; a colorful blending of little dresses and minuscule blue jeans.

Now move the time on to the empty playground, the swings stilled, the children gone, a penumbra of twilight enclosing the park— and the legs of a supine figure extending out from under a rhododendron bush.

The playground is the same. The swings are still there; so are the benches where the mothers sat in the warm sun. But the gloom of the approaching night and the supine half-concealed figure have wrenched the happy scene out of its reality, and a distorted scene of murder has taken its place. Here, atmosphere has been created by *contrast*, which puts the reader off balance.

Another off-key way to create atmosphere is to put a character off balance. Say one of the fathers has come by to retrieve a forgotten toy (it was an expensive one), and stumbles over the victim's legs. His reaction will be the same as the reader's was in the first version, but this time the reader will have the added charge of sharing the character's shock.

Besides providing emotional furnishings for your world, atmosphere is an excellent tool for suspense.

The natural elements make good emotional backdrops, creating a mood that leads the reader into the story. In chapter 5, page 94, in the section in which I discuss subplots, I have described a way of using natural phenomena. I would suggest you take another look at those two paragraphs. Besides catastrophes—earthquakes, hurricanes, etc.— weather natural to its environment but catastrophic to the inhabitants can be an effective backdrop: bone-freezing cold, stifling heat, seasonal torrential rains. Extremes in barometric pressures set up tensions in humans that lead to emotional explosions.

3. The third basic idea is to integrate background with the book's structure, so that it would seem the murder could have taken place only in this particular environment. The crime, or the motive for the crime (once one or the other is revealed), will make this apparent: Murder on an army base, a ship at sea or in a small, inbred village would have happened only in those places.

You can be your own kind of specialist if you are at least familiar with your background. If you have taken a three-week cruise, you do not need to be an experienced mariner to know every deck of a cruise ship, the cabins' layouts, the engine room and salons that could serve as background. If you have lived in a farm community all your life you could walk the town's streets blindfolded.*

Mention of a cruise ship as a background brings up a point I want to stress: the pitfalls in using the picturesque for its own sake. A long, sleek liner, gleaming white under a Caribbean sun is a romantic notion, and there may be the temptation to use it. If you decide that your murderer is a nasty little oiler who is accustomed to sailing on Liberian tramps but who has connived to sign on the cruise ship to get at a purser he hates, then your ship is a logical choice. Using the ship only because it is exotic is like adding a colorful character who has no real role to play.

I can assure you that as a beginning writer your best plots will come out of familiar surroundings. You deal from strength on your home ground; you have a choice of sites that will spark you, the leisure to absorb the atmosphere, and the convenience of being close at hand. Background can more easily be made an integral part of your book if it is an integral part of your life.

---

*Even with the familiar, check your facts before you write. Walk your streets "with your eyes open." Your memory is inclined to deal carelessly with the overly-familiar.

Suppose you decide to stray from my hallowed suggestions and decide to use a background that is not embued in you bone-deep and, to be honest with yourself, you do not really want to know in mind-boggling detail. Yet the background has caught your fancy and you think you can work it into a necessary scene. You have talked with an expert, thumbed through a book or gathered some pamphlets on the subject. You know enough to wing it. Your reader may be aware of this improvisatory approach; handled right, however, you do not have to apologize for it. Let your sleuth—or whoever—come on this particular scene for the first time and ask questions, and let another character supply the answers. Maneuver your character into a position where he or she has to become part of the background for the scene.

John D. MacDonald did this skillfully in *Freefall in Crimson*, in a scene involving ballooning that culminated in a balloon escape:

"Give him a speedy balloonist's course, will you? He's going to substitute for Joe who has quit." Then: "I hope you are a quick listener [sic] because we don't have much time."

Having set this up, the author smoothly leads into a short lecture concerning burner, thermals, basket, canvas (ripstop nylon stored in accordion pleats, inspected when folded, inspected when unfolded), maneuvering vent, deflation port, melt holes, support frames, hooking the long cables to the blocks, blaster valves, and so on.

A few pages here of author's indulgence? Yes. Interesting? *Yes!* Or, *No! Damned show-off!* I would wager that half his audience liked this pamphleteering, half did not. You will encounter the same percentage with your improvisations. The point is, bring them in gracefully.

Remember, background is meant to enhance the theme. It, itself, is not the theme. If a murder occurs while a symphony orchestra is on tour, the towns they play, the number and kinds of musicians and the selections on the programs are background. The theme is murder within an unlikely group of people. The background is what makes them unlikely, not murderous—creating that off-balance.

SETTINGS

So your approach to background is one of presenting feelings, facts and relevance. How do you work them up to create the world you want? You do it with two simple methods: research and exposition.

Research will assure you of authenticity. Exposition will be the means of getting the fruits of your research across to the reader. Let us work with these two methods as I discuss background areas. Your first consideration is the book's setting.

The Foreign Country

You may think in terms as big as a foreign country; you grew up in Paris or spent your graduate school years in Bologna. You know the native language and the culture. You feel comfortable putting your American hero or heroine in this country. For an American audience there is nothing more exciting than a foreign background seen through American eyes—a shootout on the funicular ascending Montmartre, or a midnight stabbing in the Piazza della Signoria. Americans who have traveled from Afghanistan to Zaire—and millions have—get a kick out of recognizing places they have visited and enjoy "reliving" their visits under the dire circumstances of murder.*

If you are just a visitor yourself, but a quick study, you can learn enough about one part of a foreign city in a short time if you are aware of the limits of your knowledge and can absorb that small body of information thoroughly. Study the area around your hotel—the streets, the shops, the bus routes and some of the national attractions. While you are sitting in a sidewalk cafe, take notes; while you are strolling, take pictures. If you have come to the foreign country with an idea already in mind, then it is a fairly easy matter to record details that you can use later. (Forcing yourself to remember details when you have no idea for a plot will probably not work. If you are relaxed and receptive, details will come back to you.) Once you are home, you can haul out your photographs, maps and guide book to refresh your memory.

If you do not have a solid knowledge of the foreign language, do not fake it with the interjections of the few foreign words you have picked up. For instance, do not write about going to the *boulangerie* for coffee rolls. Instead, describe the French bakery, if you need to work it in, and how it differs from an American bakery, if it does.

An effective way of introducing a foreign background is to put a character in action against the background. Let him or her argue with a customs inspector or fumble over a seat reservation in one of those Orient Express-type European trains where nobody else in the compartment will admit to knowing English. You start the action going and introduce the background at the same time.

*Helen MacInnes specializes in mysteries with European backgrounds, and she has a sharp eye for pertinent details and local color.

I would venture to say that street names do not need translating; just about everybody will recognize *rue, via* and *strasse;* not many people would refer to Paris's main artery as "the Elysian Fields." For place names, use your judgment. If their meaning is clear in the original, then use them. They do add flavor.

There is a temptation to overuse a foreign background. You would like to include all of the wonderful sights, sounds and smells that differ so from your home ground. Use them only when they create a mood or are relevant to the action. Describing a sunrise over the Dolomites might be a welcome break if your protagonist was not sure, the night before, of ever seeing another sunrise. Or, if on your way to the Cotswolds once, you stopped to climb the Broadway Tower, which offers a spectacular view of the Avon and Severn valleys, you could later, in describing a pursuit, work in the tower as a landmark. In doing so, a small amount of its history would not be intrusive.

Intrusive is a warning word in exposition. *Windiness* is another. The background for a mystery novel set in a foreign country should not be half mystery and half travelogue, because then both halves will be slighted and the two halves will not make a satisfactory whole.

The City

Just as the setting for the English mystery has graduated from Upper Stokesbury in Devonshire to settings in Manchester and Liverpool, American settings have fanned out from New York, Los Angeles and San Francisco to include Wichita and Sioux Falls. The English village is still used and so are the big American cities, but the mystery map has expanded to encompass just about every area, certainly in the United States. The reason is simple: These are the places where writers grew up or where they live now. But there is another reason underlying this one: The mystery field is no longer considered to be a sacrosanct temple in which a few high priests and priestesses preside. As the mystery gained in popularity, thanks to inexpensive paperback editions, writers saw a chance to make money. As the number of copies sold rose, so did the genre's attractiveness. When a product becomes popular, it loses its original character—in this case, its sacrosanctity. It becomes less aristocratic and more democratic. It becomes a game in which any number can play. The proportion of good to not-so-good mysteries is probably the same, but the bottom-line figures differ significantly. The number of writers producing mysteries has increased many times over in the last five decades. Many of these writers have never lived in New York or San Francisco or Los Angeles, but they do need backgrounds, and what better place to work from than their own?

I imagine that you will base your settings in your own city, town or hamlet, or some place very nearly like it. If the town in your story is mythical, you can take liberties with the accuracy of your details, as long as you are consistent with them. If you use your real surroundings, this could be an opportune convenience, for you bring an extra set of "eyes" to your everyday background. Most people take their surroundings for granted. Oh, sure, if Delancey Avenue is torn up to lay a new pipeline, the residents are aware of the change because of the mess, but once the trench is filled in and topped with asphalt, the avenue is essentially what it was before, and the residents once again look inward—unseeingly, that is. A writer would continue to look outward. He or she would see Delancey Avenue as an artery leading from a middle-class neighborhood to the town's slums and drug scene. The old flatiron building that sits in the wedge where Delancey Avenue and Parsons Street meet is an eyesore left over from the 1920s, and contractors cast covetous eyes on the property. The writer casts covetous eyes, too; the wrought iron balustrades form perfect perches for murderous intruders.*

As I said a few pages back, "Walk your streets 'with your eyes open'." In order to do that, you have to educate your eyes. It would be a good idea to plan on which part of your city you intend to use—especially if your city is a large one—and to work from a town plat (you can get a copy at your city hall) or from a diorama like the one I described in chapter 1. In those pages I offered a suggested list to "furnish" a city area; here I will add only a few more suggestions: municipal buildings, museums, industrial plants, stadiums, campuses, green houses, cemeteries and funeral homes, docks, and department stores. Any of these places can be murder sites or fields of investigation or local color. If any of these sites is real, it would pay you to make a few visits to be sure it has not changed. There was one book I published in which a character who had business in Dallas, Texas, flew into Love Field from some distant point. I remembered Love Field well; I once lived just a few miles from the airport. The author surely knew it; he had gone to college in Texas. Several months after the book was published, the author got a

---

*A bizarre city background was used by David J. Michael in his murder mystery *Death Tour*. The book is set in a city sewage system! The events that occur are just as gruesome as the setting. His excellent research on the system gave his story plausibility.

letter from a reader advising him that the Dallas-Fort Worth International Airport had long ago superseded Love Field. Neither the author nor I had bothered to check on the changing times.

With any size area, you will know the layout, from a single backyard to the complexity of a shopping mall. This does not mean that everything you record has to be transmitted to the reader. What you do is shop your area cafeteria style: a street here, a building there. *Be specific without being laborious.* I have read mystery novels where authors devoted innumerable pages to a litany of streets, reading something like this:

> If I were going to catch Slocum before he deposited that phony check, I had better get up to his place right away. Damn him for not having a telephone! I figured the quickest way to Sherrill Heights was to take the interstate to the Cross County cutoff and sail down Jackson Boulevard. When I got past the cutoff, Jackson was so jammed that I switched over to Culver and then back down to Unitas. It was slow on Unitas, too, but it was better than if I had switched over to Tyson and . . .

This is what I call the Ungrand Tour. So *many* specifics, so *little* relevance, so *much* padding.

One author, who shall remain nameless (I would not want you to emulate him), does this quite a lot. He also pads in other directions. In one of his books he takes the reader through a famous old market. We stroll down those venerable aisles with him as he notes the myriad comestibles on display, everything from olives to pressed duck. I counted twenty-six categories of food that he felt it incumbent to list. Outside the market there was a line of shops. He listed those, too, according to the merchandise in each of them. No action took place in this chapter. Nor was the scene a setup for a later scene. In no way did it forward the plot. It did not tell us anything new about the protagonist. It did not even tell us anything new about pressed duck.

True, a reader will be more responsive to details if they afford a pleasant shock of recognition. We all have our Jackson Boulevards and famous gourmet marts and it is gratifying to encounter them in print. But chances are that only a small percentage of readers will recognize your landmarks, so keep a balance between reader identification and author's self-indulgence.

That old phrase *the telling detail* is especially important for mystery writers because they must work within a tight time frame. They must convince their readers of the importance of what they are writing about in as few words as possible. Did you gain any sense of urgency in that litany of streets or list of comestibles? Would either agenda give you a feeling for background that fits the theme of a murder mystery?

Using a background as large as a city or a town, you will find a plethora of detail to choose from. Select only those details that are telling. By *telling*, I mean capable of arousing feelings in the reader. You can do it by zeroing in on city sounds. The clack of heels on a sidewalk can be ominous. So can the swish of tires on wet pavement. Sirens. A cry from a courtyard. Sounds in the night are eerie because they are so clear, yet so difficult to pinpoint in the canyons of a city.

You can create a mood by how you describe night lights: the nervous flickering of neons, the soft, amber glow of sodium street lamps, the naked bulbs dimly illuminating alleyways. And, of course, the opposite of light: shadows, gloom, stygian black. Though have you ever noticed that nothing is ever really black in the city? There is always a dim glow coming from somewhere: an all-night drugstore, the glow from behind a half-pulled shade or the reflection from the sky itself.

Smells are a part of any city background. There are the good smells coming from the small bakeries or the chocolate plant or the pocket-handkerchief parks. Mingling with the good smells are the caustic odors of spilled garbage, canine detritus, incinerator belchings and gasoline fumes. It is a rare and welcome day when the west wind sweeps the city clean.

A city is man-made. The girders and cables, the generators and boilers make up the structure and the pulse of a metropolis. City people live by a plan of their own devising. When murder takes place within the confines of this plan, there seems to be an order to it. For instance, the lead paragraph of this news story could appear in any metropolitan daily:

> March 7. Early this morning the body of an unidentified man was found sprawled on the cement steps leading down to the basement of the Hanson Building at Third and Forsythe streets. The man's right arm was hooked over the wall banister. The night light over the basement door had been smashed and a nearby garbage can had been overturned. The night watchman made the discovery at approximately 3 A.M. . . .

Cement, bricks, steel, electricity, galvanized iron—the man died in an urban setting. Neither the site nor its apparatus causes an eyebrow to be raised; it is all so common, so familiar, that only the body gets a sec-

ond glance. You could say that the man died amidst his natural surroundings.

The Wilderness

Even in a planned environment like a city, there is a chaotic quality. Different parts of the city were built up at different times, one era of city
planning overlaying the next, so that the streets cross at peculiar angles
or peter out, and nineteenth-century granite-and-cast-iron buildings
rub shoulders with twentieth-century glass-and-aluminum skyscrap-
ers. But breaking down this chaotic scene, one can still recognize the
styles that identify each era, and the conscious thought that went into
each of them.

There is no such man-made, conscious thought in nature. For
most urban dwellers, wild country can be an awesome experience,
with its lack of human planning. We did not make the trees or gouge
out the limestone caves, and we had nothing to do with their placement. One pine tree looks pretty much like another and forest trails
were made by animals, not construction crews. For most of us there is a
more immediate recognition of a fire hydrant than there is of a wild
bush. We are mainly a nation of urbanites and suburbanites who admire the natural landscape yet are not totally at ease in it.

This does not apply to the minority who are at home in the wilderness, who can track their way through a forest or keep their bearings in
the depths of a mountain. If you are one of this minority, you are
among the privileged, as I see it; you can do something the urban majority cannot: You can combine mystery with what seems to our urban
eyes the truly chaotic.

Chaos itself has the earmarks of a mystery to the city dweller until
one realizes that, by the chance of a different upbringing, your eyes
have been educated in a different way. You have learned that it is not
"man against nature" so much as "man utilizing nature." You are able
to bring order into chaos. And here is where you educate your protagonist. In order to make the environment seem overwhelming—for the
sake of suspense—the protagonist gets lost, gets ambushed, or is the
hunted rather than the hunter, and it is through your educated eyes
that the protagonist makes educated guesses that get him or her out of
the predicaments and able to catch the murderer. If your protagonist
and antagonist are on equal footing in terms of wilderness lore, you
can create an interesting contest between them. If your protagonist is a

city slicker, a tenderfoot, so that for much of the book the contest is frighteningly unequal, you have even more suspense. This is doubled in spades if the antagonist is an unknown quantity: a man identified only by his red plaid jacket and Winchester 30/06, or one of three mountain sisters who has gone berserk (but which one?).

Treat your country/mountain milieu as you would a foreign country; stake out an area and get a handle on it—a lake, a section of a river, an abandoned Boy Scout camp, a mountain motel. For most readers, a wild country setting is almost as exotic as a foreign country, so the caveat I cited earlier applies here: Do not let your book turn into (in this case) a nature guide that competes with your plot, or once again you will have two shaky halves.*

The Rural Area

Between the city and the wild country lies the rural area, the farmland of America. The farmer has a lot of the conveniences of the city dweller and the individuality of the mountain man. Set against his Toyota pickup and air-conditioned tractor are the fickleness of the weather and the depredation of moles and locusts. Within the time span of one television sitcom, a tornado can wipe him out. As any farmer can tell you, farming is a life set on the razor's edge. Yet driving mile after mile through Iowa corn land or Nebraska wheat fields gives one a sense of place and order. The sturdily built windmills and cattle chutes and silos and combines that silhouette the flatness of middle America are affidavits of its solid communal character.

When violence erupts in these bucolic landscapes, it is not like city violence, where the nameless killer attacks the hapless stranger whose fingerprints have to be sent to the FBI before a name can be put to the body. Within hours after a murder in the farm country, the entire county knows that Ephraim Hartnett has been murdered and that Sheriff Goodrich is holding Ephraim's brothers-in-law, Will Brody and Tim Appleton, as suspects. The shock is both societal and genealogical; the Hartnetts and the Brodys and Appletons have farmed together and intermarried for generations.

Of course, in a murder mystery, the brothers-in-law would not be the murderers—that would be too easy, too quick, and where is your

*There is an interesting piece of nature lore in James McClure's mystery *The Caterpillar Cop*. The detective brings in an ecologist to examine the murder scene, a section of woods. By observing the activity of ants and their disposal of a caterpillar, the ecologist determines several time sequences that occurred during the murder.

plot? But somebody with ties to Ephraim has done it. The ties might go
back a long way, unknown to family or friends: some youthful indis-
cretion in the next county, which caused a long-smouldering resent-
ment that finally flared up. Or it could be traced to a fight over a crooked land deal or an attempt to finagle water rights. Any of these reasons
would fit neatly into the background. For every kind of problem inherent in an agricultural setting, there is a corresponding reason for
murder.

Those of you who know this background of farmland and small-
town granaries and general stores have rich material to work with. Like
the mountain people, you have it all over the urbanites who think the
world begins, is centered around and ends in their neoned cities. But
surely you know that provincialism is a state of mind more than the effect of a place.*

Smaller Areas

Once you have chosen your overall site, it is time to think about the
smaller areas. Say that, in looking over a promising neighborhood, you
have found a rundown hotel that would be perfect for an assignation
that leads to a murder you have in mind. If you really want to go for
broke, give yourself a cover story† and take a room for a day and a
night. Then you can examine the premises at your leisure and gain the
confidence of the staff. Check the lobby, your room, the john (if it is
down the hall), the condition of the elevator (if there is one). Check the
quality of the linens, whether there is enough soap, if the glasses are
clean (if there are any), if the windows are unwashed. If you have a
good cover story, you can talk to the desk clerks (there will be two in
the time you are there) and the maid on your floor. They can tell you
about the hotel's history and the type of clientele it gets.

If this seems too ambitious, then streamline your plan and stand
across the street and imagine how this seedy hotel, one fit for illegal
trysts, ought to look inside. Think back to a few such places you might
have been in yourself.

What I am trying to get across is that you have to supply the fodder
for your narrator, and what better way than to let him or her see the ho-

---

*A good murder mystery with an agricultural background is Stephen Greenleaf's Fa-
tal Obsession.
†Not as a reporter, for heaven's sake! Be a wide-eyed visitor from out of town who
was just "lucky" enough to stumble upon this "marvelous little hotel." The simpler the
lie, the better the chance you have of being believed.

tel through your on-scene eyes?

This kind of Operation Snoop applies to everything from tract houses to bus stations to race tracks. If you take an inventory of the ordinary details of whatever site you are looking at, you will be surprised later when an image of the whole coalesces from this list—and it should give you a feeling for the place. After all, what are feelings but well-considered facts that sit well within you?

I say "ordinary" details because they are the telling ones in the long run. But it is the unusual details that first catch your eye. Certainly they put a stamp of uniqueness on a place. But keep in mind that they are unique because they are surrounded by the ordinary, which provides a setting for them.

There are several ways to make the ordinary and the unusual work hand-in-hand.

1) Announce the unusual right away:

It was a pleasant little house, except that the windows were all painted black.

Then add:

They contrasted starkly with the whitewashed walls and the red-tiled roof.

2) Or lead up to it:

It was a pleasant little house with whitewashed walls and a red-tiled roof. The windows, however, had all been painted black.

Or you can let the unusual usurp its setting; no mention of the walls or the roof. Once the narrator is in the house, the unusual may (or may not, right then) be explained. If you mean to startle with the unusual, then it is worth leaving the reader dangling for the time being in order to drive home the effect you want. The effect, of course, is based on jarring contrast, and that is what you want to let sink in: the beautiful racehorse is seen limping in the paddock; the clock tower is a tall, handsome edifice that dominates the busy, affluent downtown area, yet the clock itself has stopped at 10:21; the imposing mansion sits on a wide sweep of *brown* lawn.

Even Smaller Areas

Just as important are the details of even smaller areas. A lovingly built grotto in a corner of a garden tells you something about the person who owns the garden. A junked car rusting away beside a disused well tells you about another kind of person.

These smaller scenes afford a sense of mood, just like the bigger scenes. They also contribute something else: a sense of the people associated with them. Rooms come to my mind first for they are the settings that tell you the *most* about the people who live in them. It could be a dank boiler room with the superintendent's pinups tacked to the wall studs framing an army cot; a living room containing Renoirs and Queen Anne furniture, with the damask drapes drawn to keep the sun off the Brussels carpet. Each room tells you about the lifestyle of the people who inhabit it. Eventually, if not then, the narrator will introduce the reader to these people, and when they appear on scene the reader already knows something about them. You can, of course, introduce the people and the places at the same time, i.e., in the same scene.

Describing intimate background scenes serves another purpose: to lay clues. And here we come to the unusual detail again. An elegant sewing box on a dusty shelf in the superintendent's quarters or a cheap cigar smouldering on the Brussels carpet would be alien to their scenes and would give the reader pause for thought.

A device that is used fairly often but never seems to lose its appeal to writers nor its impact on readers is a description of a room and its contents, with everything as normal as it should be except for the last item noted: the body. The very blandness of the inventory leaves the unsuspecting reader unprepared for the shock.

If you are using a first-person narrator, your sleuth will be sensitive to small surroundings. He or she would grumble at walking through a hollow of ankle-sloshing mud, or would shift uncomfortably while sitting on a splintery orange crate. These actions are immediate and personal. Less personal but just as immediate would be the sleuth's descriptions of the insides of buses, telephone booths, elevators, confessionals—mini-landscapes that bear the imprint of the public and lend a sense of the anonymous traffic of life that surrounds us all.

Earlier I stressed that your background details should be based on accurate, on-scene sightings. This is not always possible and it is not always necessary. In your wanderings you have undoubtedly stored impressions of many details of many places. The origins of the details may be hazy by now, and impressions have a way of blending into one another; but if your original sightings were accurate, and the facts well digested, then you can create a site from what seems to be whole cloth. You can make up a room or a hotel or a grotto. For instance, say you want a scene that takes place on a sailboat, but at the moment you are living in Fort Collins, Colorado, and the nearest marina is probably on Lake Powell. You think back to remembered sailboats. As long as you feel confident that you still know the difference between a transom and a bowsprit, and remember what lies in between, then write from memory. Part of the joy of writing is pulling out of yourself stored knowledge you did not know you had. It is also a joy to have the creative freedom to work that knowledge into any shape you need it to be.

Minutiae

Details are the fine-tuning of a mystery novel, whether it is for a character, an action or a background. One way for an author to fall flat on his or her face is to include erroneous or misplaced details of background material. That Love Field incident I mentioned on page 155 is a good example. The author could have had his character's plane land, period. But no, it seemed like a good piece of fine-tuning to have him land at a specific field. The result was that the reader who wrote in asked if the author had ever been in Texas. I read one manuscript where an entire city was misplaced. I remember wondering how Kansan readers would have felt about finding *their* Manhattan transported to an area between the East and Hudson Rivers. No amount of tectonic activity could have explained this displacement, only a careless author.

Authors who fault on their details often do so because they become absorbed in the big picture and neglect to check the small details that eventually contribute to the whole. This is understandable and no great crime; a good copy editor usually catches what the author and (sometimes) the editor have missed. But readers are not so kind, and believe me, they catch the smallest damned things, like Coors beer spelled with a *K*, and the fact that a revolver does not have a safety catch.

Readers' irate letters can be shrugged off if you have a thick skin. What should not be ignored, though, is the implied message the readers are sending: their potential loss of faith in the author. *If the author is wrong about this detail, how can we believe anything else in the book?*

The kind of book you are writing is a morality tale with overtones of fantasy. You hope the reader will suspend disbelief as you spin your tale, and to do that you must make the reader think that this fantasy is for real. You do this by putting in touches of real things: identifiable objects. They are the breadcrumbs you scatter along the forest way to leave comfortable, recognizable signs. For instance, the petite widow would shoot her husband's murderer with a lightweight Llama .32 automatic, not with a cumbersome Colt .45. The benign, pipe-smoking college professor-cum-sleuth would puff away on a sedate-looking Stanwell rather than a flashy Ben Wade.

These are the little touches that subtly say "authentic." There is no need to take them further in order to establish their legitimacy. By this I mean you do not have to go into the ballistics of firearms, that the grooves in the gun barrel are so many millimeters in depth and have a right- or left-twist spiral; nor do you have to explain the curing of the pipe bowl and the manufacture of its stem. I have run across instances of both and, as you know by now, I get impatient with such didactic nonsense. If you are of the school that loves to show off soon-acquired, soon-forgotten information just for the hell of it, you will always find some readers who will go along with you just for the hell of it. All I can ask then is that you be sure that your gun, or your pipe, or whatever, is real and that you have your facts straight.

The important thing to keep in mind is that details—in this case, facts—are used to give your story sharp little reliefs, and you will use them most effectively if they are kept in their place. If you let them strut on stage like mini-starlets, they will interfere with, not enhance, the action.

SPECIAL BACKGROUNDS

Everyone knows these backgrounds: churches, PTA meetings, bowling clubs, political rallies, auctions, and the like. We all have easy access to them and they are the mainstay settings for many mystery novels. But have you noticed that less common backgrounds add a fillip to any story? I do not mean murder in Tanzania or some other far-out place, but backgrounds that are right in our midst—courtrooms, hospitals, art galleries—in which the participants possess special knowledge. In chapter 1, page 10, I listed forty-five such backgrounds, culled from mysteries I have read. There are a few professionals, among them doctors, lawyers and clergy, who can write and who have produced some very good mysteries. But there will be many of you who want to use an expert's background and who feel that encyclopedic knowledge is not necessary, that you need only one scene in a courtroom or one visit to an art gallery. Nonetheless, you want that scene to appear authentic. This means doing research.

No, groans should not be forthcoming. I do not envision you surrounded by stacks of heavy tomes in a badly lighted library nook, round-shouldered and bleary-eyed. Such heavy research, best left to doctoral candidates, would take up more time than writing the book—if you did not falter on the way and give up the idea entirely. No, there are ways of streamlining your research by tailoring it to the needs of your book.

The first thing to consider is that a first mystery novel is going to keep you very busy. You will have plenty of juggling to do with plot, characterization and theme without bringing in an overly complicated background, which can so easily overwhelm your theme. And, to speak in personal terms, it could overwhelm you. So think not only in terms of tailoring your research to your book but of tailoring it to your burgeoning abilities.

If you have chosen a special background for a chapter or a scene, I assume you have done the initial field work. You have looked the place or profession over. Now choose those elements within the field that you need and that interest you. The next step is to get books out of the library (a well lighted one!) and read up on those elements. Choose books that have been written for the layperson, for you are writing for the lay reader. Once you have put particular pieces of information together, check your grasp of them with an expert. Be prepared to ask specific questions, not "Tell me everything you know about your field." Experts get to be experts by dealing with specific facts and then filing them into their proper places in the scheme of things. To be sure your expert keeps explanations simple and relevant, describe the kind of scene you have in mind so the answers can be framed for your needs. The real experts will know how to talk to the point if you tell them what the point is. Some of them may give you information that sounds pretty impressive, so much so that you want to use it. Just remember that information is not knowledge—be sure that you understand it yourself and that you do not go over the heads of your readers when you use it.

Choosing an expert requires a little research unto itself. Do you need a criminal lawyer or one who deals with probate litigation? Do you need to check your facts with an internist or with a radiologist? With an art dealer who specializes in modern acrylic paintings or one whose field is nineteenth-century etchings? An air controller of a small airport or a large airport? The more specialized your expert is, the sooner you can zero in on the information you need.

There are ways of dealing with special backgrounds that need little or no research except for on-site observations. For example, everybody has been in a hospital, either as a patient or as a visitor. Yet how many will have noticed the soft-soled tread of a nurse as she makes her rounds; or how television sets hang like stalactites by the beds; the rattle of the dinner carts; the moans and whispers in the night? These are details you would associate with a hospital.

Not long ago, I accompanied a friend to one of the lower courts, where she had been summoned to answer to a misdemeanor. It was a nineteenth-century building and the courtroom's decor had not been altered since the place was built. It had a thirty-foot ceiling painted sky blue and festooned with rococo moldings; the benches were like church pews. On the wall behind the judge's bench was a fresco of Justice holding her scales. The scales had half peeled away. The waiting defendants slouched in their pews, the court attendants slouched around the bench, the judge slouched in his high-backed swivel chair. The voices of the participants were muted, the actions were slow-motion. I was surprised at the casualness of the court's manner. Granted, the cases were small potatoes, yet I have sat in on hearings concerning serious crimes where the atmosphere was highly charged but the same slow, measured proceedings were the order of the day. Would Perry Mason's pyrotechnics fit into these surroundings? Not at all. And this is what has impressed me the most about courtrooms: the *ordinariness* of the people, carried along on the *inexorableness* of the process.

So you do not necessarily have to crack a book or query an expert to gather material from arcane fields. Sometimes, if the scene calls for it, just pointing out what is *there* will make a reader see with new eyes.

CHAPTER 9

THE STYLISH MYSTERY

IN EVERY CLASS and every symposium on mystery writing that I have attended, students have been lectured on plot, characterization, red herrings and all of the other components that go into structuring a mystery novel. Not in any of them have I heard the lecturer talk about how to put these components down in passable, preferably good, English. These lecturers assumed, I suppose, that if students could read, they could write—a fallacy accepted by far too many would-be mystery writers. And there may have been a jaundiced eye or two among the lecturers who followed the precept of John Lyly, a sixteenth-century writer:

> If one write never so well, he cannot please all;
> and write he never so ill, he shall please some.

Courses in novel, journalism and technical writing devote at least a quarter of their time to style, emphasizing that good style is a great persuader and bad style turns people off. Why should this not apply to mystery novels? Or should Lyly's cynical observation be germane *only* to genre writers? Does this not smack of second-class citizenship?

There is a truth here to explore. Memorable mystery writers have an above-average command of English. Popular mystery writers are not necessarily good with the written word and count on volume to create their niche in the mystery field. In this sense, they *are* second-class; their fifth books cannot be distinguished from their first. As Truman Capote said about Jacqueline Susann, "She types her books; she doesn't write them."

The most ingenious plot in the world is dragged down by ungrammatical, unimaginative prose; characters become stereotypes; narration and description are leaden and teem with clichés. If this makes heavy going for the mystery reader, think of what it does to the author who shuffles along with an inadequate, colorless vocabulary. It would be like a sculptor working on a marble statue with a handleless mallet. Without a command of words, and a joy and ease in using them, writing is a tough—unnecessarily tough—business.

I was fortunate enough to go to a country school when I was a kid: Grady County Consolidated Schools in Amber, Oklahoma, for the eighth grade. Those were poor times in the dust bowl, and there were no frills to the school. There were no unionized benefits for the teachers, and they were, bless their hearts, still in the nineteenth century. We had reading, writing and arithmetic, and basketball in an unplowed field after school. I loved it. I loved the red-haired teacher, with straw coming out of his ears, who taught grammar and writing. We had weekly spelling bees, we learned declensions, we parsed sentences until straw came out of *our* ears. We learned the structure of the English language. He taught us to appreciate its logic and its beauty. I still remember him saying, "Clean writing means clear thinking. Clear thinking produces clean writing."

In the intervening years, twentieth-century usage has found its way into my vocabulary, and it is a rare day on the podium that you will catch me saying, "It is I." Nonetheless, I still keep my singulars and plurals straight, my verb tenses in line and my prepositions and adverbs where they ought to be. I have yet to put the proper reins on qualifiers and punctuation, but knowing this keeps me—more or less—alert to these violations. I cannot stress enough the need for a good grounding in grammar for ease of expression. Syntax is what lubricates the sentences.* Along with a dictionary and a thesaurus, get yourself a book on basic grammar. Spend a day or two with it. Then keep it on your desk with Webster and Roget. It will bring back a lot you thought you had forgotten and, believe me, it will improve your cerebral muscle tone.

---

*Yes, I know. Syntax is that which lubricates the sentences.

STYLE

If syntax is the lubricator, style is the enchanter. Random notes banged out on the piano by a ten-year-old hardly grab you. Those same notes coming from Pan's pipes have created myths; from the Pied Piper, disrupted a town. A storyteller is an enchanter, and convincer, too, and to accomplish this, a writer uses a deceptively simple formula: the choice of words and their placement. But the burden of it all! If a manuscript is two hundred pages long, the writer has made sixty thousand—*sixty thousand*—individual word choices, and another sixty thousand choices in deciding where to put those words. But the writer is lucky, too. English is so plentiful a language and so rich in variety and nuance that sixty thousand is an infinitesimal portion of the words that are available. You have a wide and fruitful field to play in, so let us talk about some of those choices and where they go.

Style may be consciously contrived or may flow out of you from who knows what nether regions of your mind. If it comes from the nether regions, let it flow. Most of us, though, deliberately choose a style to match our characters' personalities and the mood of the genre. Let's take some copy from a detective novel as an example.

The flat style

> I walked out of her apartment and down the street. What a mess! I kept my hands in my pockets. When I got to my car, I saw a ticket under the wiper. I thought, *That will place the time.* I drove away. When I got home, I'd call the cops. I'm good with handkerchiefs.

The author has told you the bare necessities, only what he felt you absolutely had to know. Now either he has already described what happened in the woman's apartment, and the sparseness of the information is enough, or if it's an opening scene you will find out more when he phones the cops.

The rococo style

> I stumbled down the stairs. I had to get away from her blood-spattered apartment. *Oh my God, those eyes! Those staring eyes!* I kept my palsied hands deep in my torn pockets. I scampered as fast as I could down that windy, rain-smeared street. After what seemed years, I reached the old wreck and checked to see if the tires were still cooperating. I saw a memento under the

wiper from the neighborhood boy-in-blue. *Nice timing, buster,* I thought. *Thanks a heap.* I drove off in a muddy spray. When I got home, I'd call one of the dum-dums at the precinct, using one of my cleaner snotrags to disguise the old vocal chords.

This piece of floridity tells you that there has been a violent murder and that our seedy narrator is pretty well shaken up about it: blood-spattered, *those eyes,* palsied, torn, rain-smeared. The author has given you a little more information, but you would have learned that from the scene before or the scene after. His object was to throw you into an emotional bath. The destructive elements here are the barrage of adjectives and the strained noun and verb replacements which the author felt compelled to use, either because of bad taste or unsureness about the power of ordinary words.

The straight style

I left her in her torn-up apartment. As I walked down the rain-swept street toward my car, I kept my hands in my pockets to hide their shaking. When I reached the car, I saw a parking ticket under the windshield wiper. *This will pinpoint the time for me—one way or the other,* I thought. As I drove off, I decided that I would call the precinct when I got home, figuring that I could disguise my voice.

This includes the same amount of information but with only two elements highlighted: the shambles he has left behind and the kind of night it is, economical mood setters. The verbs do unobtrusive duty to describe the action, the unadorned nouns are strong enough to stand for what they are. Two highlights for color and the rest of the prose carries itself to move the story forward.

Watch out for overblown verbs and nouns and adjective-noun combinations. Be frugal with the seething, grinding, panting, sweating, slithering, sidling, moaning, shrieking, screaming, sobbing, and the like. Keep your nouns simple. *Vaticination* tells you what it is all about, but *prediction* will reach your readers quicker. *Desuetude* has its honorable roots in Latin, but try *disuse* for understanding. For the triple whammy you could write, "She was afflicted with thoracic kyphosis," and a few of your readers might realize that the old lady had dowager's hump.

Just as Julius Caesar fought the Gallic Wars, you should be fighting the Great Syllabic War. Tintinnabulation worked fine for Poe—but in another literary form and in another time. Polysyllabic words are like flagstones in a garden walk: decorative but easily tripped over.

Clichés

We all know what they are. They come tripping from our tongues a hundred times a day. They are facile little conversation oilers (the weather being the most called-on), and stand in good stead for casual encounters. Among editors, they are called "clitches," a deliberate mispronunciation to show scorn. In writing mysteries, they are Typhoid Marys (there's a clitch for you). Like any genre, the mystery can be easily ridiculed, in part because there are lazy mystery writers who will settle for the easy thought, the time-worn phrase.

There was a parody written some years ago (by whom, I do not remember) of Mickey Spillane, the arch duke of the cliché. A deliciously buxom blonde has turned out to be a no-good spy and Mike Hammer's indignant response is, "So I worked her over with a rusty knife because I wanted a clean America." The parodist was right on the mark. None of you is going to write a mystery that is one long cliché (it takes a peculiar talent to do that), but unless you keep your cerebral muscles flexed, clichés are going to slip in. A particularly dangerous area is dialogue. It usually happens when you have not pinned down a scene or have not worked out a character. You get impatient, or tired, and do a quick wrap-up with a golden oldie (clitch). What do you do about it? You wait until you are fresh and then rework it. Here is an example: When I encountered the sentence "It's a small world," I suggested to the author that she coin her own cliché or rearrange the present one. She changed it to "It's a small, circular world," which produced unexpected echoes for her.

Clichés abound in physical descriptions. You must have read innumerable times, "He tented his fingers" and "He made a steeple of his fingers." These are always preludes to pronouncements. Other sets of fingers "pluck nervously," usually at napkins. Shrugs are "eloquent." The raised eyebrow is "supercilious," which is a redundancy. There are sharply drawn breaths, scuffing toes, narrowed eyes, haughty hips (seen from the rear) and lips. Arms flail, sometimes "like windmills," although windmills do not flail. Authors write impressions like these from having read other books rather than from observing people firsthand.

Similes, Metaphors, Hyperboles, Oxymorons and the Misused Onomatopoeia

Here is where you can have fun with style and do some interesting writing. This quintet represents legal outlandishness. Each member of the quintet produces electric shocks; twists new meanings out of old meanings; changes the ordinary into the exciting.

A simile telegraphs itself by starting, "Like . . ." or "As . . ." and then goes on to compare unlikenesses.

> The numbers man was a sad little fellow, about as attractive as a mangy dog and as pathetic.

> When she came into the courtroom, she walked like a fallen queen, disheveled but proud.

A metaphor is more sophisticated. It, too, involves comparison, but because it is less explicit, it makes the reader think more and so is more provocative. You use one word in place of a dissimilar one, taking for granted that the reader will bridge the difference as well as see the connection. For instance, with a simile you could say:

> He ran through the parking lot like a hurricane.

With a metaphor:

> He tore through the parking lot.

Another simile:

> His mouth shut like a sprung trap.

The metaphor:

> His mouth sprang shut.

In the first example, the comparison is between the velocity of the man running and the velocity of a hurricane. In the second, it is between the snapping motions of a mouth and of a trap. Each example combines two dissimilar objects—man and hurricane, mouth and trap—to create a new and independent image. The metaphor, as you can see, has more economy and, unlike the telegraphing simile, catches the reader by surprise.

Hyperbole is the nth degree in exaggeration. All stops out with a vengeance. It is a bombastic reaction.

"Hotter 'n hell." "Lower than a skunk." "High as a kite."

In a mystery it works to depict fear.

> The young girl peered from behind the tombstone at the man striding toward her. His shadow, silhouetted by the peripheral lights of the cemetery, was eighty feet high. The man himself was a looming giant.

The oxymoron (from Greek *sharp-foolish*) is not as well known or as often used, but it can be a sleeper! It contains two totally disparate elements that are perversely contradictory. Everyday examples would be

> bittersweet . . . cruel kindness . . . fiery cool

Here is one that is a little more complicated.

> The cheerful country folks pressed around her, overwhelming her with their vicious good will.

Oxymorons provide wry shocks. Use them sparingly.

The misused onomatopoeia is a concoction that is called the Critic's Delight. Using a verb that suggests the sound of the action it describes gives dimension to both the verb and the noun: the *hum* of the bee, the *roar* of the train, the *moan* of the wind. But the fancy-action writers leave themselves open to the critics' brickbats when they use the onomatopoeia erroneously: " 'Be quiet!' she hissed." Where is the sibilance in this sentence? " 'Goddamn you!' he groaned." Poe excepted, how does one groan an imprecation? Can one really growl, "Gimme a beer"? Chuckle a six-word sentence? Or, barring a cold, sniff an answer, as in, " 'I really couldn't say,' she said sniffily"?

The Crab-Wise Approach (a/k/a Hesitation Marks) and the Admonishing Negative

Too often when I have picked up a manuscript, I have found right off:

> It wasn't that Tracy didn't like her husband, but he did interfere in the long search she had been conducting to find her mother, missing for so long.

The author is packing too many pros and cons into that opening paragraph by over-explaining. Vaguely sensing this, she shoehorns the reader into the story with a denial. The second paragraph compounds the error when the author, still hesitating to get into her story, writes:

> Her husband was a nice person. He was kind and thoughtful and she loved him dearly. But the search for her mother seemed, somehow, more important right now, even after so many years.

She has just repeated the information stated in the first paragraph, actually apologizing in the second for throwing so much into the first!

Time and again, I have seen the second paragraph work only as a recap for the first one. It is a sure sign that the author has not marshaled his or her facts according to their priorities and is trying them on for size, as it were. The first paragraph of a mystery is a mean one, I know. You have to catch the reader's interest right off. But negativism is not conflict and the crab-wise approach is not a clever ambush.

Dialogue

Dialogue stitches the narrative together. It portrays the characters directly—out of their own mouths. It lends a sense of naturalism. With dialogue you can have an interplay of ideas between characters, a give-and-take that is much more than simple remarks by alternating speakers. And—very important—it forwards the plot.

A good example of moving the story forward with dialogue is found in the private eye novel. The P.I. gathers his information by moving from one suspect to the next, and the plot builds as he moves. Here is an example:

The P.I. interviews the matron whose jewels have been stolen. She gives him a hazy description of the thief. He tackles the maid, who has nothing but hysterics to offer. Then the cook, a dour old soul, who had "warned the missus not to wear all them joolz to that fancy shindig." From the social secretary he learns more about the shindig and gets a guest list. Then he's off. . . . The dialogue is interspersed with narration of quick stops at the diner, stops at his apartment for a clean shirt, romantic interludes, philosophical thoughts about the nature of evil while he is driving to the next interview. At each stop he picks up more information—some of it misleading—until he discerns a pattern or until somebody makes a slip. Then he backtracks for second interviews and nails the thief.

There is a lot of talk in detective novels, and it is a field day for the author who is a good dialoguist. For one thing, the P.I. is going to meet many types: the matron's banker, the secretary's boyfriend, the host of the shindig, the host's gardener, the social-climbing guests. Each will have his or her social position and vested interests, and they will reflect in the speech of each of them. It is one form of an author's scorecard. The gardener may drop his *g*'s while the nervous banker will salt his talk with *Uh*'s. Their vocabulary and speech patterns will vary widely. So will the tones of their voices—excited or low-keyed or measured (with the help of body language). Even the rhythms and lengths of their sentences will differ. Here we have the detective talking to the gardener.

> P.I. Were you around when Mr. (Host) left the party to take a call in the library?
> GARD. Nope.
> P.I. What time did you leave?
> GARD. 'Bout six.

Then to the banker:

> P.I. Mr. (Banker), were you aware that Mrs. (Matron) had taken her jewels from her safety deposit box that afternoon?
> BANK. Let's see. That would have been, uh, last Friday. Yes, the sixth. I was with the state auditors that afternoon. Now let me think, uh . . .
> P.I. She came in just before three.
> BANK. Just before three. Uh. We were getting to debentures. The state isn't too happy with us, you know, Uh, three. Three?

This may not be the way real gardeners and bankers talk, but the author has created his or her own rules of "naturalism," and as long as the characters are consistent in their speech patterns and their word levels, they will pass for the real thing between the covers of a book. And, too, it is a pretty safe bet that the dialoguist has heard people talk somewhat like this, and has shaped their speech to suit his or her ends.

I remember working with one author on his first book. The leading characters were lovers, a young black man and a young white woman. The manuscript began with them in bed and the woman had the opening lines, with words to this effect:

"You are one handsome black stud. I dig your ebony eroticism, man."

I stopped right there and asked the author if he had ever slept with a black woman. He hesitated and then said, "Well, yes." "Did you," I asked, "in your wildest moments of passion ever refer to her 'ebony eroticism'?" He dug back into his "natural" references and toned down the lines.

Diatribe, a kissing cousin to hyperbole, is an effective way of letting characters reveal themselves. It should be used cautiously and should be interrupted occasionally so that it doesn't turn into a boring harangue.

> Mr. Stinson waved his hand toward the door. "What do you mean, when did I see my daughter last? I'll tell you when I saw my daughter last. She was fooling with that no-good creep, that—"
>
> "Can you give me the man's name?" the patrolman asked.
>
> Mr. Stinson shrugged. "How do I know his name? How do I know any of their names? I've brought her up strict and right and—and does she appreciate what I've done for her?"
>
> The patrolman frowned impatiently. "Sir, can you tell me this man's name, the one she went out with last night?"
>
> "Sure. Sure, why not? Mr. Creepo, that's his name. They're all creeps."
>
> "We're not getting anywhere this way, sir."
>
> Mr. Stinson drew in his breath, then let it out slowly. "I guess not. But you won't get any sense out of him. He wasn't born with any. Always a wild kid, always into—"
>
> It was the patrolman's turn to sigh. "Mr. Stinson . . ."

The father has given absolutely no information that the cop can use, but he has told the reader something about himself and, by inference, about his daughter. A bitter, strict father, a rebellious daughter, and though only God knows *what* has happened to her at this point in the story, the reader does have an inkling of what precipitated the situation.

Brogues and burrs and broken English. These are anathemas to typesetters and sources of irritation to readers. I will not attempt to duplicate these kinds of speeches. Suffice it to say they require large quantities of single quote marks and hyphens.

Tell the reader that the character speaks with a brogue or a burr,* that the immigrant stumbles over his pronunciation or searches for the right word. If you have heard enough talk from the lately landed, you

*And, please, do not refer to an "Irish" brogue or a "Scottish" burr. That is like calling a millionaire rich or a fire hot. *Tautology* is a word worth adding to your vocabulary.

can pick up their grammatical errors and speech and cadences, and use them. If you have not, better not try it.

Rules of grammar, by the way, do not have to apply to dialogue. But be sure your readers are aware that you—through your characters—are deliberately fracturing speech. For instance, it would be as perfectly natural for one character to say, "I ain't," as for another to say, "I'm not." Incomplete sentences are also acceptable in dialogue. They are usually followed by ellipses or dashes to indicate incomplete thoughts.

Word choices. Those sixty thousand word choices. In dialogue, of course, they must fit in with the characters. The gardener would not know what a debenture was. The banker, with his Harvard Business School background would not say, "Nope." The bitter father is most likely a bluecollar worker or a clerk. Here again, listen to people talk, preferably where you can be the outsider, sitting in an aisle seat on a train or listening in on a party line (if they still have them). See if you can spot professions, social levels and places of origin. Listen for special vocabularies, cadences, accents and word inversions. Do not look to television for dialogue. Most TV writers are a harried lot pushing deadlines, and they often fall into dreadful clichés and rotten grammar. It is better practice to draw from the raw material of your surroundings. The more directly you are involved (although an aisle-width away), the fresher it will be and the better chance it will have to stick. Carry a notebook—small and unnoticeable—and record odd phrases and choice words. Sometimes a word or a sentence out of the blue will trigger a whole scene, or even the idea for a book.

Imitation

Imitation may be a sincere form of flattery, but it is not good for writers. It does nothing to build your self-confidence if you admire someone else's writing more than your own. Granted, as a neophyte you will not turn out flawless prose, but neither did the admired one at the beginning. It does nothing for your confidence if you aim too high too soon by making unrealistic comparisons.

If you like the way an author has handled a particular sentence, sort out the elements we have been discussing. Substitute your own words for the author's words using the author's structure. It will not be the same and you probably will not like it. This is a good exercise in learning that style comes from within, not from without.

Nevertheless, one way of learning style is by osmosis; a wide range of reading cannot help but have an effect on how you ultimately write. Let your mind absorb with pleasure those elements that fit you, that will filter through your mental sieve and will stick, to become your own.

However, be careful of faddish styles. They are so very easily imitated you may not even realize that you are doing it. You might be intrigued by the hard-boiled school, with the tough guy talking out of the side of his mouth. He will throw out phrases like, "Ya see what I mean," and "Like I said"—all very macho, I am sure. These are shades of the thirties. Today, the tough guy will throw out a lot of four-letter words to let you know he is nobody to fool around with. He has altered his vocabulary, but the same effort is in evidence: He is trying too hard. If you write like this, you are perpetuating a stereotype, and fads are stereotypes the first time they are set down on paper.

Another genre that abounds in exaggerated reactions is romantic suspense, where there is a lot of pulsating, throbbing, trembling and gasping. It is not enough that the heroine is frightened out of her wits or is seized in sexual ecstasy, prompting her to do something about her feelings. No, every quiver must be carefully recorded before she takes any action.

Both of these examples prove their authors have character problems as well as style problems; they are letting the style create the characters, not the other way around. The tail is wagging the dog.

Obscenity

There are many shibboleths in the publishing world. "Give the reader a break." "Little words, little words." "Will it travel?" (from England or the Continent). "Does it turn the page?" The one that applies here is, "Treatment transcends taboo." Since this was coined, many of our word taboos have lost their power through sheer repetition of use. Those words are no longer confined to back fences. Why, even on television you will hear *hells* and *damns* now, and on public television, considerably stronger stuff. We are no longer as schizoid about "bad" language. If you hear it in the pool hall, chances are you will hear it in the living room. Art, as usual, has been slow in imitating life. In the last two decades, novelists have been catching up with a vengeance. Mystery writers have been more reticent. This is surprising, considering that mystery writers specialize in, yeah, a helluva lot of seaminess.

Perhaps their values are different. Perhaps having a character say "Shit!" is worse than having him murder someone. They have loosened up, though, as they see their audience loosening up—and I think that is the clue. In the last ten years, mystery writers have thrown in four-letter words, raunchy sex, and even a little bit of torture. The good ones don't flail it; they keep it in character and in context. In a mystery now, the frail octogenarian is probably going to continue to say "Shoot!" when the screen door slams on her fingers. A truck driver with two flats on his semi or the cop who watches the tail end of a burglar scoot over the fence will, by *their* natures, be liberal with the strong stuff.

Obscenities lend color to dialogue. They sharpen emotion by shocking. Even the single expletive has enormous punch. Overused, they draw impatience from the reader and sometimes—rightly so—disgust. Nobody wants shock after shock. However, if you do not want to shock, then do not use the strong words at all. There are other ways of showing anger and contempt that will not offend and bore, and that will actually catch the reader's ear, and echo. Remember the tag line of the joke about the little old Quaker lady and her altercation with the tough truck driver? "I hope when thee gets home thy mother comes out from under the stoop and bites thee." Insults without strong language are often more effective. The targeted one definitely gets the message and cannot defuse the insult by attacking the *way* it was said. The Quaker lady calling the truck driver a son-of-a-bitch would have had as much effect on him as telling him his socks did not match. For all of their touted shock value, the strong words too often become—yes—clitches.

Foreign Words

An incident in my prepubescent days put me off of foreign words forever; foreign words out of context, that is. A little chum and I found a copy of Dr. Marie Stopes's *Married Love* (1917) in her grandmother's cedar chest. Talk about hot stuff! It was pretty vague hot stuff, but we imagined the worst. I still remember the buildup in the chapter entitled "The Wedding Night."

> The bridegroom should disrobe in his dressing room, so that the size of his organ will not frighten the bride.

Wow!

The bride must be sure to pare her bunions before retiring.

Phhtt.

The rest was phhtt, too. All the juicy words were in Latin.

Dr. Stopes's use of Latin was accepted practice in the medical literature of the time. It was more of a hang-up than an affectation. I wish I could say the same of mystery writers who lard their dialogue with foreign phrases. They undoubtedly feel that it gives them *panache*. It gives me a pain. Here's an example of what I mean:

> "Am I to understand that you suspect me, Inspector?"
> "I'm the one who asks the questions, *monsieur*."
> "You don't really think that I—"
> "*Zut alors!* I don't think anything. I'm still looking. There is no such thing as—*comment dit-on?*—a perfect crime. Except in detective stories."
> "You don't have any evidence against me."
> "That is true. At the moment, I have no clues. *Mais parbleu!* You had a motive. Murderers always give themselves away by their motives."

The French interjections lend a Gallic flavor to the dialogue, *oui?* Sprinkling the inspector's speech with high-school French lends authenticity to his role, *n'est-ce pas?* Well, that sprinkling is about as legitimate as a prospector salting a mine. You do not agree? You like those little French touches? Let us reverse the process and see how it stands up in French.

> —*Hey now*, dois-je comprendre que vous me suspectez, monsieur le commissaire?
> —C'est moi qui pose les questions, monsieur.
> —Mais vous croyez vraiment que je . . .*Come on, ole buddy!*
> —Je ne crois rien. Je cherche. Les crimes parfaits n'existent pas. Sauf dans les romans.
> —*But damn it!* Vous n'avez aucune preuve contre moi, *Jack*.
> —C'est vrai. Je n'ai aucun indice pour l'instant. Un coupable se démasque autant par ses mobiles que par les indices.*

Do you see? It is like wearing one brown shoe and one black shoe.

---

*Excerpted from *Voulez-vous Tuer Avec Moi.* by Fred Kassack. © Presses de la Cité, 1970. Translation by Barbara Norville.

I hope that this has given you some sense of the basics of style. I have not included such elements as allusion, synecdoche, ellipse, ambiguity and mixed figures. There is time for these later, once you have decided on your style.

In the section on imitation, I might have added, "The way to develop your own style is to put one word down after another, and to do it again and again until you are satisfied." There are no short cuts to good writing, but the long way can be a pleasurable one, and the hours spent in writing can be rich ones.

Something I cannot stress enough: Do not throw anything away. Hold on to every scrap while you are starting. In chapter 2, "The Realm of Ideas," I suggested that there might be a good idea lurking in fuzzy prose. It also works in reverse: An incomplete idea may be expressed with a well-turned phrase that you can later wrap around a better-thought-out idea.

Whether it is fuzzy or felicitous, keep the writing going while the thought is there. Sometimes, certainly at the beginning, it is better not to worry about how you are saying it *while* you are saying it. You are dealing with two separate entities simultaneously and, until you are more practiced, one will likely take precedence over the other. If a small voice tells you that either the style is not right or the thought is not clear, keep writing. Later on, isolate the miscreant and a stronger voice will tell you what is wrong, and then you can take the time to fix it. In the meantime, you have not interrupted that all-important flow.

CHAPTER 10

LAUNCHING YOUR MANUSCRIPT—AND YOURSELF

EDITORS OFTEN CALL the books they publish their "babies," and some-times refer to themselves as "midwives." Once a book is edited to the satisfaction of the author and editor, it is ready—or almost ready—to be sent out into the world. First it is tuned up by a copy editor, who catches grammatical and factual errors. Then it is outfitted by the book designer and the jacket artist. Meanwhile, the production staff over-sees the setting of galleys, which are then turned into pages. These, in turn, are sent to the bindery which produces the finished book. Final-ly, in conjunction with the publicity and sales departments, the editor is assured of the book's reasonably safe passage into the world, and the baby is born.

In spite of the care the book receives before this momentous entry, the editor still has pangs of anxiety: How well will the baby make its way? Will the reading public appreciate the qualities that the editor and the rest of the staff have seen? Will critics be perceptive (read: kind)? Will book clubs and/or reprint houses want it? With every launching, an editor's taste and reputation are on the line.

Imagine, then, what an author goes through! The hard work, the anxiety and the alternations of hope and doubt are a thousand times more intense than those of the most dedicated editor, for the author's is the first launching—from head to typewriter to envelope to post office. Each step calls for heroic measures. The first-mystery novelist has yet to develop a reputation to lay on the line; instead, it seems as if one's very being is about to be exposed to the world's praise or censure. It is a scary proposition, and I never cease to marvel at the first-novelist's gutsiness.

But sometimes, I must add, the baby travels in ill-fitting swaddling clothes. I remember the first time I spoke before an audience of hopeful mystery writers. I was very nervous, and when the first question was directed at me, I blew it. The question was, "What is the first thing you look for in a manuscript?" and I blurted out, "A return envelope!" Everybody laughed, including me, but there was more truth than humor in my reply.

The return envelope, of course, is more than a courtesy. Can you imagine the publisher's postage bill otherwise? But this is a mere bagatelle, the lack of return postage, compared to the state of some manuscripts when they cross an editor's desk. If there is anything that will turn an editor off, it is a manuscript that is—to be polite—less than presentable. Among the no-no's are dog-eared pages, pages out of sequence, coffee stains—any indication that the manuscript was delivered by mule train via Tierra del Fuego, or worse, that fourteen publishers, all with sticky fingers, have already seen it and turned it down.

Another item that upsets editors is receiving a bio and a snapshot of the author. Being compulsive readers, editors are at the mercy of their compulsion and actually read the bios and scan the photos, then shake their heads at their own slavishness. A one-paragraph cover letter containing your name and address and a list of any writing you have published is sufficient; though, of course, you should mention that this is a mystery novel. If you know the editor's name, by all means use it. In fact, check in the latest edition of *Literary Market Place*, which is published annually, to see which editor handles mysteries for each house. You can find a copy of *LMP* at the reference desk of any public library. If your book is taken on, the publisher will send you a bio form and ask for a photo.*

I used to feel uneasy about photocopied manuscripts. *Where was the original? Buried in a time capsule? How many copies were with how many other publishers?* The copies were heavy to handle and hard to write on. Times have changed and editors are now comfortable with photocopies. The paper quality has improved immensely. The paper is now 20 lbs.—the same as bond—and the surface takes markings well. Those of you who have word processors will print your own copies on paper

*I mention *LMP* because it is so easily obtainable. You can find considerably more information in *Novel & Short Story Writer's Market*. This book will give you detailed information on every aspect of the writer's market, much more than I can cover in this brief chapter.

that is also acceptable now. A word to those of you who do not have word processors: Starve the kids, forget your income tax if you have to, but get one. They are worth their weight in plutonium in terms of organizing your manuscript and of time saved.

You should have at least one clear copy of your manuscript stashed in a safe place, preferably your original.

One ploy that amuses me is the one in which the author submits half a dozen titles and, bowing to my "expertise," exhorts me to choose among them. If I opt for *Death's Doomful Draft* over five equally memorable titles, my interest is supposedly then vested in this authorial company; I now "own" shares and it would profit me to publish the author's book.

In all fairness and with ploys aside, titles are stinkers to deal with. A phrase containing one to five words carries the burden of the following sixty thousand to seventy thousand words. This phrase is the first thing the editor sees, and eventually it shares space among hundreds of others in bookstores, so it has to be an eye-catcher.

Gone are the days when titles like *Murder Stalks the Moors* or *Death's Gory Hand* were good coinage at lending libraries. Words like death, murder and killing seem to appear in perhaps only one out of every six titles I see on the shelves. The fronts of the jackets do not always identify the books as mysteries—though this is sometimes rectified by the jacket designs—but libraries and bookstores set up special sections for mysteries so hard-sell titles can safely be the exception today rather than the rule.

Titles should still be intriguing by way of implying some conflict, but even this rule is observed more in the breech than in the doing. For instance, what would you think of this for a mystery title?

ROAST EGGS

If I had not seen it on a mystery shelf, I would not have known what it was. Even so, it sounded like a barbecue in a henhouse. I was intrigued, and when I opened the book to the front matter I read:

> It is the nature of extreme self-lovers, as they will set a house on fire, and it were but to roast their eggs.
>
> Francis Bacon

and I knew that the story would be about death by arson. So it was, and exceptionally well done.*

If it seems to be reaching to get a title from a seventeenth-century essayist-philosopher, remember that mystery writers are a well educated group, and so are their editors! I published a mystery in which the author used a line from Ecclesiastes as a springboard.† I am sure there are titles taken from other parts of the Bible and from Shakespeare, to name the two most popular sources.

A line or a phrase that seems ideal for a title can actually spark an idea for a story. An author friend of mine recently lost a lover through death just as they were about to take a long-awaited vacation. "She's on a long vacation now," he told me dolefully, then paused and murmured, "The long vacation." He looked off in the distance and I could almost see the phrase coalesce in his mind. I think a book will come out of that phrase when his grief has lessened.

Titles are important, but they are, in publishing terms, the first item to be looked at and the last to be considered. Like contracts, they are written to be changed. Even the least promising titles never turn an editor off completely, for editors earn part of their keep by changing them.

What about submitting outlines and sample chapters? Are these no-no's, too? When you have had two or three mysteries published by the same house, you can probably get away with them. In fact, I have given a couple of my established authors contracts on the basis of a paragraph of intent: the theme and estimated due date. With a first mystery, I would strongly recommend submitting the entire manuscript. You are going to write the book anyway, so why not put your best—and strongest—foot forward?

It is true that the editor can get some notion of your book from an outline and sample chapters. He or she can see the kind of story you have in mind and can get an idea of how well you write. Usually the sample chapters I have seen are 1 through 3, the opening gambit. But no amount of outlining is going to tell me how you are going to maintain the vigor of the middle game and how you will wrap up the complexities of the end game.

Some outlines I have seen deliberately leave out the solution, with the intention of intriguing the editor. Believe me, this has the opposite effect, and if you *do* include the solution set down as bare fact, the who-

*The author is Douglas Clark.
†*More Bitter Than Death*, by Kate Wilhelm.

dunit element is shot to hell. In other words, you are damned if you do and damned if you do not when you submit an outline.*

But wait. Perhaps you want to play it safe and get an agent rather than chancing the whimsies of an editor (and editors can be whimsical). Agents *do* know the houses and the editors in them, and an agent can make sure your manuscript is presentable. He or she can do more than that, for an agent wears two hats: as a business person and as an editor. An agent can point out the rough edges in your story, or tell you that it is fine as it is.

If this is the route you want to try, then your first step is to find an agent who is willing to take you on and with whom you can get along. You may have to work this out by trial and error; after all, you do not know the agent and the agent does not know you. However, this applies to any two people getting together for the first time, and each party will understandably have questions for the other. You will, of course, open the discussion by telling the agent that yours is a mystery novel, giving a brief resume of its theme and a little about the characters, especially the protagonist, and indicating the novel's length. The agent will probably ask about your other writing credits, if you have a track record, and whether you intend to go on writing. An agent, like a publisher, is always looking for a long-term investment. You, in turn, can ask for the agent's credentials: how long the person has been in the agenting business and does he or she have an authors' list, especially of mystery writers, that you could see. Be wary of agents who offer to "critique" your novel for a price. If they thought it was marketable, they would simply take it on and charge their usual percentage when they sold it. Falling for their blandishments is, as one wiseacre put it, "paying to be rejected."

Some agents will write back, "Not interested." Do not get into a tizzy over one rejection or even more. Curse them out for *their* missed opportunity and go on to the next name on your list.

Once you get an agent, it may still take time to interest a publisher, but if your agent thinks your manuscript is marketable, he or she will have enough faith in it to send it out on innumerable rounds, if that proves necessary. In turn, have faith in your agent. Check in every so often if you like, but keep in mind that publishers can be slow in responding even to agented manuscripts. In cases of rejection, your agent should level with you and tell you what the publisher said. There

---

*Romantic suspense houses have their own rules about outlines and/or finished manuscripts. I would suggest writing query letters to them. See chapter 1, page 38.

are times when a rejection can be instructive, and if enough rejection letters offer the same criticisms, you and your agent should do some rethinking.

There are five sources I know of that will supply lists of active literary agents. They are:

The Society of Author's Representatives, Inc. (SAR)
10 Astor Place
New York, NY 10003

Literary Market Place
(At the reference desk in your public library)

Independent Literary Agents Association (ILAA)
432 Park Ave. South
New York, NY 10016

Guide to Literary Agents & Art/Photo Reps
Writer's Digest Books
1507 Dana Ave.
Cincinnati, OH 45207

Literary Agents of North America (LANA)
Author/Aid Research Associates International
340 East 52nd St.
New York, NY 10022

According to Mystery Writers of America, owning a copy of this publication could prove to be a worthwhile investment for you:

This fine reference work has come out in a fourth edition that has been updated and expanded to include a third more listings. The 1991 edition of LANA has information on over 1,000 agents and the policies of most of them. You will be able to tell whether your prospective agent charges reading fees; gives editorial assistance; wants to see unsolicited manuscripts, especially from beginning writers. You will notice that quite a large number of literary agents do handle mysteries. The editors have also provided an excellent introduction that gives authors some idea as to what it is a literary agent can (and cannot) do for them, as well as suggestions on how to contact the agent of their dreams.*

*Quoted from *The Third Degree*. Reprinted by permission of Mystery Writers of America, Inc. Copyright © 1985, and updated by LANA in 1991.

There are two publications you might want to subscribe to that are specifically published for writers; they contain market news and advice from published authors. They are: *Writer's Digest*, 1507 Dana Ave., Cincinnati, OH 45207, and *The Writer*, 8 Arlington St., Boston, MA 02116. In addition, *The Romantic Times* gives current information about the romantic suspense market. The address is: 55 Bergen St., Brooklyn, NY 11201.

It helps to know that there are others who are experiencing the same anxieties and hopes that you are, and that there are still others who came before you and succeeded. You can take courage from one group and learn from the other, and there is an organization that will allow you to do both. It is Mystery Writers of America. It has a large membership that extends from coast to coast, with chapters in every section of the country. Each chapter holds monthly meetings in which authors get together and swap information and invite guest speakers. Every spring, the New York chapter plays host at a week-long conference and invites members from all the chapters. The week's activities culminate in the annual Edgar Awards dinner, where busts of Edgar Allan Poe are given for the best writing of the year in half a dozen or so categories. Even if you have not published anything, you can still join as an affiliate member. The annual fee is $50. You can write to MWA headquarters to join, and to find out the location of the chapter nearest to you: 17 East 47th St., New York, NY 10017.

Canada has its own mystery writers' organization, Crime Writers of Canada. For information about joining, contact Howard Engel, 281 Major St., Toronto, Ontario M5S 2L5.

Earlier, in chapter 2, I suggested that you read other mystery novels to get ideas for your own book and for what you can learn from other authors. So there is one other meeting place that is well worth mentioning, and that is your local mystery bookstore. There are forty-two of them in the United States and five in Canada. Their inventory is almost entirely mysteries. Many of them put out their own newsletters, conduct workshops, and pay special attention to local authors. Most handle mail orders. I would imagine that they are good places to meet other authors and feel that you have a home away from the typewriter. (This is the latest update I could get.*)

Footprints of a Gigantic Hound, Ltd., 16 Broadway Village, 123 South Eastbourne, Tucson, AZ 85716. (602)326-8533 (Elaine and Joseph Livermore).
Foul Play, 780 Arlington St., Cambria, CA 93428. (805)927-5277 (Laurence Goldberg).
Fahrenheit 451 Bookstore, 540 South Coast Hwy, Suite 100, Laguna Beach, CA 92651. (714)494-5151 (Dottie Ibsen).
Sherlock's Home, 5624 East Second St., Long Beach, CA 90803. (213)433-6071 (Beth Caswell).
The Mysterious Bookshop, 8763 Beverly Blvd., Los Angeles, CA 90048. (213)659-2959 (Otto Penzler).
Vagabond Books, 2076 Westwood Blvd., Los Angeles, CA 90025. (213)475-2700 (Patricia and Craig Graham).

Book Carnival, 870 North Tustin Ave., Orange, CA 92667. (714)538-3210 (Ed and Pat Thomas).

Grounds for Murder, 3287 Adams Ave., San Diego, CA 92116. (619)284-4436 (Phyllis Brown).

Fantasy Etc., 808 Larkin St., San Francisco, CA 94109. (415)441-7617 (Charles Cockey).

San Francisco Mystery Bookstore, 746 Diamond St., San Francisco, CA 94114. (415)282-7444 (Bruce Taylor).

The Book Stalker, 4907 Yaple Ave., Santa Barbara, CA 93111. (805)964-7601 (Michael Van Blaricum).

Scene of the Crime, 14450 Ventura Blvd., Sherman Oaks, CA 91423. (818)981-2583 (Ruth Windfeldt).

The Mystery Annex of Small World Books, 1407 Ocean Front Walk, Venice, CA 90291. (213)399-2360 (Terry Baker and Mary Goodfader).

Book Sleuth Mystery Bookstore, 2423 West Colorado, Colorado Springs, CO 80904. (719)632-2727 (Lyman Mark).

Murder by the Book, 1574 South Pearl St., Denver, CO 80210. (303)871-9401 (Shirley Beaird and Chris McPhee Benight).

Rue Morgue, 946 Pearl St., Boulder, CO 80302. (303)443-8346 (Tom and Enid Schantz).

Snoop Sisters Mystery Bookshoppe, 566 North Indian Rocks Rd., Belleair Bluffs, FL 34640. (813)584-4370 (Linda Tharp and Susan Rose).

Science Fiction & Mystery Bookstore, 752½ North Highland NE, Atlanta, GA 30306. (404)875-7326 (Bill Amis and Mark Stevens).

I Love a Mystery Bookstore, 55 East Washington, Chicago, IL 60602. (312)236-1338 (John Morginson).

Scotland Yard Books, Ltd., 556 Green Bay Rd., Winnetka, IL 60093. (708)446-2214 (Judy Duhl).

The Raven Bookstore, 8 East 7th St., Lawrence, KS 66044. (913)749-3300 (Pat Kehde and Mary Lou Wright).

The Mystery Bookstore, 7700 Old Georgetown Rd., Bethesda, MD 20814. (301)657-2665 (Jean and Ronald McMillen).

Spenser's Mystery Bookshop, 314 Newbury St., Boston, MA 02115. (617)262-0880 (Andy Thurnauer).

Murder Undercover, AKA Kate's Mystery Books, 2211 Massachusetts Ave., Cambridge, MA 02140. (617)491-2660 (Kate Mattes).

Murder for Pleasure Mystery Books, 2333 Minneapolis Ave., Minneapolis, MN 55406. (612)729-9200 (Steven Stilwell).

Once Upon a Crime, 604 West 26th St., Minneapolis, MN 55405. (612)870-3785 (Steve Stilwell).

Uncle Edgar's Mystery Bookstore, 2864 Chicago Ave., Minneapolis, MN 55407. (612)824-9984 (Don Blyly).

Big Sleep Books, 239 North Euclid, St. Louis, MO 63108. (314)361-6100 (Chris King and Peter Simpson).

Mystery Lovers Ink, 8 Stiles Rd., Salem, NH 03079. (603)898-8060 (Joanne Romano).

Murder Unlimited, 2510 San Mateo Place NE, Albuquerque, NM 87110. (505)884-5491 (Tasha Mackler).

Borealis Book Store, 113 North Aurora St., Ithaca, NY 14850. (607)272-7752 (Douglas Anderson).

Foul Play, 302 West 12th St., New York, NY 10014. (212)675-5115 (Wendell Huston).

Murder Ink, 2486 Broadway, New York, NY 10025. (212)362-8905 (Jay Pearsall).

The Mysterious Bookshop, 129 West 56th St., New York, NY 10019. (212)765-0900 (Otto Penzler).

Escape While There's Still Time, 488 Willamette, Eugene, OR 97401. (503)484-9500 (Bill Trojan).

Murder by the Book, 3210 Southeast Hawthorn, Portland, OR 97214. (503)232-9995 (Jill Hinckley and Carolyn Lane).

Mysteries From the Yard, 101 Cemetery Road, Yellow Springs, OH 45387. (513)767-2111 (Mary Frost-Pierson).

*This list, dated September 20, 1991, was supplied by Sarasota, Florida, mystery novelist Lary Crews.

Gene's Books, King of Prussia Plaza, King of Prussia, PA 19406. (215)265-6210 (Gene Massey).
Whodunit, 1931 Chestnut St., Philadelphia, PA 19103. (215)567-1478 (Art Bourgeau).
Murder by the Book, 1281 North Main St., Providence, RI 02904. (401)331-9140 (Kevin Barbero).
Murder by the Book, 2342 Bissonnet, Houston, TX 77005. (713)524-8597 (Les and Martha Farrington).
Booked for Murder, 2701 University Ave., Madison, WI 53705. (608)238-2701 (Mary Helen Becker and Mary Monkmeyer).

Shamus Books, 183 King St., London, Ont., Canada N6A 1C9.
Prime Crime Books, 891 Bank St., Ottawa, Ont., Canada K1S 3W4.
Ann's Books (Mostly Mysteries), 225 Carlton St., Toronto, Ont., Canada M5A 2L2.
The Handy Book Exchange, 1762 Avenue Rd., Toronto, Ont., Canada M5M 3Y9.
Sleuth of Baker Street, 1592 Bayview, Toronto, Ont., Canada M4G 3B5.

All of these suggestions are meant to show you how to ease the suspense of the waiting game. And you will wait. Depending on whether you use an agent or send the manuscript out on your own, the waiting time can be anywhere from three weeks to two months. These are not inordinate time spans for publishers, but they can seem like an eternity to an author.

When you have gone through the arduous feats of writing your book and launching it, and are waiting for the results, what are your chances? How many first mysteries are published? Count up the number of published mystery writers—somewhere in the thousands—and you have your answer. Even the most popular, the most long-lived started with Book One. And that is the only realistic answer anyone can give you.

Yes, a first mystery novel is considered a risk, but you have to start somewhere and editors know that. Besides, there is more often than not a built-in sale for mysteries, to hedge the publishers' bets. Libraries account for the bulk of sales, but a lot of bookstores have standing orders. There is always the chance of a reprint sale and/or a sale to one of the four mystery book clubs, Mystery Guild, Detective Book Club, Mysterious Book Club (distributed by Book-of-the-Month Club) and The Crime Collector's Club. Foreign sales are in the picture, too. By American standards they are modest, but they are found money and publishers from Lapland to Australia do buy American mysteries.

The domestic market is a healthy one. It accommodates fads and momentary trends and still continues to publish the mysteries that have a timeless quality. You may not make a fortune in the mystery field, but you could become part of its timelessness.

A FINAL WORD TO THE ASPIRING WRITER

WRITING A MYSTERY novel is a challenge to your talent *and* your fortitude. To decide on a crime, to work out the solution, to delineate your characters and create their backgrounds take equal amounts of inspiration and concentration. Putting all of these elements together to produce a page-turner takes time and more time. Except for some of your research, your time will be spent alone, in hours of thinking, accruing, discarding and writing —right down to the last page.

I assume you would not attempt this unless you really wanted to write a mystery, that you are willing to put up with the long hours, the frustrations and the loneliness that all writers go through. I think you will find that one hour at the typewriter is comparable to a week spent building a stretch of highway across the Arctic. As in any field of endeavor, there is no gain without pain, but if you stick to your guns, the gain will eventually outweigh the pain. The satisfaction of *having done it* will be there, and you will be surprised at just how much you have learned from writing this first book. The *doing* is your day-by-day goal; the final accomplishment is the patient accumulation of those days.

Appendix

(Continued from chapter 3.)

I   *Monday night—10 P.M.—Victor's home*
    1) Victor's den
    2) Victor
    3) His angry voice, saying?
    4) X answers angrily
    5) Gun shot
    6) Karen's voice in hall
    7) X flees—how?
II 1) Karen
    2) Discovers Victor's body
    3) Mrs. Roth (housekeeper) comes downstairs
    4) Scene with Karen & Mrs. Roth
    5) Karen calls Bergson
    6) Karen & Mrs. Roth sit—stunned? Crying?
III 1) Bergson in his apt.
    2) Phone call from Karen
    3) On way to Victor's apt. Remembers 15 years with Victor. Flash-back?
    4) Examines crime scene: Victor's body and open safe
    5) Finds small Mayan medallion—(on chain?)—CLUE!
    6) Calls cops. Comforts Karen
    7) Police lieutenant—name? with cohorts?—arrives. Friend of Bergson
    8) Preliminaries—lab crew, etc. Bergson gives medallion to lt.

IV   *Monday night still—around 11 P.M.—Katie's apt. in Berkeley*
      1) Party going on
      2) Katie, Damien, Tony & other guests—pretty high—drugs/booze?—Alibis for Tony & Katie.
      3) Call for Tony from Bergson
      4) Tony's reaction—make it convincing—guests gather round
V   *Friday morning—11 A.M.—Funeral home*
      1) Victor's funeral
      2) Karen, Bergson, Tony (hung over?), Katie, Helen, Mrs. Roth, friends & employees, minister, ushers
      3) Establish Bergson's relationship to Tony & Katie & Helen
      4) Police lt. takes Bergson outside to tell him medallion has been identified (by whom?) as belonging to Felipe Mendez, former employee and Victor's once protege. Felipe supposedly moved back to Mexico 4 years ago. PRIME SUSPECT! Bullet came from .32 gun.
      5) During service, Tony rushes outside, vomits. Bergson, already outside, figures Tony is hung over. Tony mumbles, "That bastard!" Bergson too intent on what police lt. told him to have Tony's remark penetrate. CLUE! Bergson's thought: Felipe had worked with Brannigan up to the time Brannigan went to prison.
VI   *Friday afternoon—cemetery—time? Mid-morning?*
      1) Tony, Katie, Helen, Bergson, Karen and hardcore group of friends—few
      2) Bergson drives Karen away from cemetery. Learns more about her (loving but tough)
      3) We learn more of Bergson's feelings toward her (love)
      4) She asks Bergson to drive her to plant. Bergson shocked. "Victor would have wanted me to."
      5) Bergson figures he can't compete with memories
VII   *Late Friday afternoon—San Jose*
      1) Plant—Karen goes to her office
      2) Bergson sees Brannigan in hallway. "What are *you* doing here?" "None of your damn business!" Brannigan leaves.
      3) Helen packing up her office (next to Victor's). Bergson comes in, sees what she is doing. Ambles into Victor's office till she is done. Bergson reminisces about Victor with Helen. She breaks up. Offers to take her out to dinner, to cheer her up.
      Friday evening—Sausalito (Valhalla Restaurant—change name?)
      1) Both of them get tipsy. Bergson tells Helen of his love for Karen. Helen, getting drunker, turns her mourning into vituperative bitterness against Victor.
      2) Tells how she sympathized with Brannigan & Felipe (innocent

bystander); Victor too hard a taskmaster, forcing Brannigan to steal. Admits access to .32 which Victor kept at plant. Says she was home night of murder.

3) The way she defends herself—Bergson doesn't believe her. SUS-PECT!

VIII *Saturday morning—Bergson's apt.*

1) Recap of dinner with Helen. Remembers (for reader's benefit) her defense of Brannigan. Remembers Brannigan at plant the morning before.

2) Calls police lt. for Brannigan's parole officer. Gets Brannigan's address.

3) Goes to Brannigan's hotel. Talks with desk clerk, re: Brannigan's alibi murder night. Feels that clerk is covering for him.

4) Goes to Brannigan's room: "What were you doing at plant?" "None of your business!" (again!). "Where were you the night of the murder?" "In my room!" Bergson brings up Felipe. Brannigan says to leave Felipe out of this, he moved to Mexico.

5) Brannigan takes a swing at Bergson, Bergson knocks him out.

IX *Saturday afternoon—Berkeley*

1) Bergson drives to Tony & Katie's apt. to get more background on Felipe. Knows that Victor took Felipe into his house when both boys were young. (Good side of Victor.)

2) Tony not at apt. Katie and Damien are.

3) Learns that Katie supports˙Tony's drug habit, so Tony not strapped for money. Suspicions about Tony abate.

4) Takes a good look at Damien: prissy fellow; dresses too well for college instructor's salary; seems close to Katie.

5) Katie invites Bergson to party following Saturday night. "Life must go on." Tells him Tony is at Victor's house, "looking over his new estate." Bergson leaves, bad taste in his mouth over the whole scene.

6) Damien: "Why did you invite him? He's past it." Katie: "He's kind of sexy." Damien: "Tony won't like it." They both smile. CLUE!

7) Bergson sees Ferrari in drive. Thinks it's Katie's. CLUE!

X *Later Saturday afternoon—Victor's House*

1) Greeted by Mrs. Roth. Remembers her reaction to Mayan medallion on murder night. Reluctantly she admits knowing it belonged to Felipe. Defends him. CLUE!

2) Tony comes in, hears description of medallion, agrees it is probably Felipe's. CLUE! Speaks of Felipe as a "scrounge" on Victor's good will. Jealousy? Bergson asks himself. Tony adds. "And a thief." Felipe has stolen valuable ring from Tony and Victor had

fired Felipe. Tony smirks. Bergson thinks there is more than jealousy, but what?

XI   *Saturday afternoon—even later—North Beach Bar*

    1) Bar scene. Orders sandwich & beer.

    2) Phones Helen, who would have background knowledge of Felipe's & Tony's younger days. Learns (from whoever answers phone) that Helen has gone to Mexico.

    3) Tries Brannigan's hotel. Learns from smirky clerk that Brannigan has checked out. Calls parole officer: Brannigan got permission to fly to Mexico on business deal.

    4) Has sandwich & beer. Heads for airline office.

XII   *Sunday—San Francisco & Mexico*

    1) Bergson flies to Mexico City. Takes bus to Cuernavaca.

    2) Helen & Brannigan staying with Felipe. Learns that H & B are going to try to make a go of it (explains Brannigan's presence at plant). They were together night of murder at Helen's. Had kept in touch while he was in prison "as friends."

    3) Felipe comes in wearing ring he "stole" from Tony. Says Tony had given it to him in exchange for medallion as boyhood friends. Left Victor's home when Tony got too possessive. Tony, in revenge, told Victor of "theft" and Victor fired Felipe when he refused to admit to theft. Felipe then returned to Mexico.

    4) Bergson & Brannigan apologize for fighting in hotel room.

XIII *Monday—Mexico & San Francisco*

    1) Bergson feels he has been neglecting his work. Goes to plant from airport (had left his car at airport).

    2) Sees Karen, who was concerned about Helen. Tells her of his trip but not his suspicions.

    3) Karen says will is to be read on Friday. Says she knows what is in it. "I think you will be surprised." Bergson wonders silently.

    4) Takes Karen to lunch. She is very sweet to him. He becomes hopeful.

XIV   *Friday morning—lawyer's office*

    1) Tony, Karen, Bergson, plant foreman, lawyer, secretary.

    2) Karen gets 55 percent of Saybrook Tectronics stock; Bergson gets 15 percent; plant employees get remaining 30 percent.

    3) Karen gets house & personal fortune.

    4) Tony gets allowance only.

    5) Felipe gets allowance (guilt money for kicking him out).

    6) Tony blows up at Karen; name-calling, accusations, physical threats; Bergson intervenes.

XV   *Saturday night—Berkeley—Katie's party*

    1) Bergson driving over Bay Bridge to party on fishing expedition,

though has a good idea of what he is looking for.

2) Along with party cars parked on street, sees Ferrari in driveway along with two other cars. CLICK!
3) Party in full swing: UC students and instructors. Tony morose, half drunk (drugs?). Ignores Bergson.
4) Katie flirtatious. Damien amused. Both seem edgy. Keep looking at Tony.
5) Bergson remembers their studied casualness when he was here the Saturday before. Tells reader? No, wait for wrap-up. CLUE!
6) Overhears lovers' quarrel between Tony & Damien. CLICK!
7) Asks Katie if she bought Ferrari for Damien. She laughs. CLICK!
8) Corners Tony & softens him up with news of Felipe & medallion; puts him on the defensive. Then implies that Katie and Damien are lovers.
9) Tony confronts them, they deny it ineffectually. Tony blows up at Damien: "After all I've done for you!" (Ferrari & clothes) "I was even willing to . . ." Bergson: "To what, Tony?" ". . . to murder my uncle."

WRAP-UP

Two weeks later—Cuernavaca

1) Bergson on vacation at invitation from Helen, Brannigan and Felipe.
2) Recaps party scene & aftermath: what is to happen to Tony, Katie & Damien, plus detailing the will (and Tony's forfeiture).
3) Explains how he solved the crime:
   Started with question: for whom would Victor open the safe?
   Tony, to give him money; Helen, to give her company records; Ed, at gunpoint. Narrows list of suspects after Felipe is cleared. Tony's lie about ring, his possessiveness with Felipe, his largesse toward Damien—a vindictive person & bisexual.
   Damien blackmailing Tony or threatens to tell Katie whom Tony is dependent on (surrogate mother).
   Katie and Damien are lovers, so Katie aware of blackmail, unknown to Tony. Tony needs more money as blackmail gets more expensive. Damien persuades Tony to kill Victor (how?) so he will inherit the lot and keep Damien in style. Katie in on plan.
4) Bergson surmises:
   Katie would have persuaded Tony to marry her.
   After decent interval, Tony would have "accident."
   Rich widow & lover would live off inheritance, or
   Damien might also, later, have "accident"—rich widow becomes black widow? (Title possibility?)

5) Helen reminisces about Tony as angry young boy.

6) Felipe reminisces about Tony as sad, angry young boy.

7) Bergson, by himself, thinks of Karen: Not only is she better educated than he, but now she is a lot richer, too. Figures there is no chance at all with her.

8) Will he stay at plant? Probably. He has share in it now and has fond memories of Victor as well. Silently, he toasts Victor: "Thanks, old friend."

This first "buildup," I thought, was a good start. I could see where the author, beginning with three fairly brief outlines, had escalated them into workable chapter sections. And as the sections unfolded, his ideas for the book expanded. He:

introduced three new key characters: Mrs. Roth, Felipe Mendez and the police lieutenant;

added the two Mexican scenes;

put in clues;

laid out the book's time span and where his characters would appear by using chapter headings;

thought of a title possibility and the last line of the book;

There were still questions to be answered:

What was the argument between Victor and Tony?

How did Tony get out of the house unseen?

What was Brannigan's business enterprise? Could he leave the country legally (as a parolee)?

What about probating wills and legal language?

These questions and others that surfaced as he got into the book could be answered as he went along.

He would also be confronted with the challenges of dialogue, scene transitions and chapter endings, which would come to him more easily now that the book had its initial shape—thanks to his outlines.

BIBLIOGRAPHY

Bibliographies are important for two reasons. They list books on subjects you want to know more about, and they introduce you to a fellowship of like-minded enthusiasts and scholars. It is comforting to know that there are others out there who share your interests, and it is gratifying to know that they want to share their knowledge with you.

I have listed some of the books I think might help you to join the fellowship. In some instances, I have not been able to track down publication dates, but be assured that the books' contents are as valuable as they are dateless. My list is far from being a complete one, so for more titles on specific subjects—ballistics, pathology, law, medicine, etc.—check the *Subject Guide to Books in Print* in your library. And, too, some of the books will have their own bibliographies that will send you off on new trails.

I would also suggest that you make up your own bibliographies in the form of mystery fiction. *Read, read, read!* In Chapter 1, I cited William D. McElroy's estimate that 50,000 mystery stories have been published since the genre's inception. So you have an enormous selection to choose from, and what could be a more enjoyable way of learning your craft?

As of this writing, some of these books may be out of print. If so, try your second-hand book stores for copies. They are worth looking for.

Writers on Writing

Adventure, Mystery and Romance: Formula Stories as Art and Popular Culture, by John G. Cawelti. University of Chicago Press, 1976

The Art of Creative Writing, by Lajos Egri. Citadel Press (paperback)

The Art of the Mystery Story: A Collection of Critical Essays, edited by Howard Haycraft. Caroll & Graf, 1983 (paperback)

Aspects of the Novel, by E.M. Forster. Harcourt, Brace, 1956 ed. (paperback)

Becoming a Writer, by Dorothea Brande. Torch, 1981 (paperback)

Hillary Waugh's Guide to Mysteries and Mystery Writing, by Hillary Waugh. Writer's Digest Books, 1991

How To Write Mysteries, by Shannon OCork. Writer's Digest Books, 1990

Making Crime Pay: A Practical Guide to Mystery Writing, by Stephanie Kay Bendel. Prentice-Hall, 1983

The Murder Mystique: Crime Writers on Their Art, by William K. Zinsser. Harper & Row

Mystery Writer's Handbook, by The Mystery Writers of America. Edited by Lawrence Treat. Writer's Digest Books, 1981 (rev. ed.)

Plotting and Writing Suspense Fiction, by Patricia Highsmith. The Writer, Inc., 1966

Writing Commercial Fiction, by John Stevenson. Prentice-Hall, 1983 (paperback)

Writing Detective and Mystery Fiction. Edited by A.S. Burack. The Writer, Inc., 1977

Writing Mysteries: A Handbook by the Mystery Writers of America. Edited by Sue Grafton. Writer's Digest Books, 1992

Books for Background

Armed and Dangerous: A Writer's Guide to Weapons, by Michael Newton, Writer's Digest Books, 1990

Bouvier's Law Dictionary and Concise Encyclopedia (8th ed.), by John Bouvier. W.S. Hein, 1984

A Catalogue of Crime, by Jacques Barzun and Wendell Hertig Taylor. Harper & Row, 1971

City Police, by Jonathan Rubenstein. Farrar, Straus, and Giroux, 1973

Deadly Doses: A Writer's Guide to Poisons, by Serita Deborah Stevens with Anne Klarner, Writer's Digest Books, 1990

Detective and Mystery Fiction: An International Bibliography of Secondary Sources, by Walter Albert. Brownstone Books, 1985

Fundamentals of Criminal Investigations, 5th ed., by Charles E. O'Hara. C.C. Thomas, 1981

Firearms Encyclopedia, edited by George C. Nonte, Jr. Harper & Row, 1973

Handbook of Forensic Science. Compiled by The Federal Bureau of Investigation. Government Printing Office, Washington, D.C. Order No. J1.14/16: F76,1975

Homicide Investigations: Practical Information for Coroners, Police Officers and Other Investigators, by Le Moyne Snyder. C.C. Thomas, 1977

Legal Medicine and Pathology and Toxicology, by Gonzalez, Vance, Helpern and Umburger. Century-Crofts

Manual of Police Report Writing, by Frank M. Patterson. C.C. Thomas, 1977

Modern Criminal Investigations, by Harry Soderman and John J. O'Connell. Revised 5th ed. by E.O. O'Hara. Funk and Wagnalls

Techniques of Crime Investigation, by Arne Svenson and Otto Wender. Elsevier, 1980

Who Done It: A Guide to Detective, Mystery and Suspense Fiction. Compiled by R.R. Bowker, 1969

Wild Justice: The Evolution of Revenge, by Susan Jacoby. Harper & Row, 1986 (paperback)

The Writer's Complete Crime Reference Book, by Martin Roth. Writer's Digest Books, 1990

Investigating the Marketplace

Fiction Writer's Market. Writer's Digest Books, 1986

Personalities in Crime
(Fact and Fiction)

Agatha Christie, by Janet Morgan. Alfred A. Knopf, 1985

The American Private Eye, by David Geherin. Frederick Ungar, 1985

Art Cop Robert Volpe: Art Crime Detective, by Laurie Adams. Dodd, Mead, 1974

Coroner, by Thomas T. Noguchi with Joseph Di Mona. Simon & Schuster, 1983, Pocketbooks, 1984

Crime on Her Mind — 15 Stories of Female Sleuths from the Victorian Era to the Forties, edited by Michele Slung. Pantheon Books, 1975

Deadlier Than the Male: Why Are Respectable English Women So Good at Murder?, by Jessica Mann. Macmillan, 1981

Detective Marie Cirile: Memoirs of a Police Officer, by Marie Cirile. Doubleday, 1975

Jay J. Armes, Investigator, by Jay J. Armes as told to Frederick Nolan. Macmillan, 1976

The Lady Investigates: 19th and 20th Century Lady Detectives, by Patricia Craig and Mary Cadogan. St. Martin's Press, 1981

The Making of a Woman Cop, by Mary Ellen Abrecht. William Morrow, 1976

Mystery and Its Fiction: From Oedipus to Agatha Christie, by David I. Grossvogel. Johns Hopkins University Press, 1975

The Private Eye: 101 Knights, by Robert A. Baker. Bowling Green State University Popular Press, 1985

The Professional Fence, by Carl B. Klockars. Free Press, 1974 (paperback)

Secrets of the World's Best-Selling Writer — The Story Techniques of Erle

Stanley Gardner, by Francis L. Fugate and Roberta B. Fugate. William
   Morrow, 1980
Sons of Sam Spade—The Private Eye Novel in the 70's, by David Geherin.
   Frederick Ungar, 1980
The Unknown Thrillers of Louisa May Alcott. Edited by Madeleine Stern.
   William Morrow, 1975
Varnished Brass: The Decade After Serpico, by Barbara Gelb. G.P. Putnam's
   Sons, 1983

Style

A desk dictionary, either Webster's or Random House, latest edition
The Elements of Style, 3rd ed., by William Strunk, Jr. and E.B.White.
   Macmillan, 1979 (paperback)
A Handbook To Literature, 3rd ed., by C. Hugh Holman, Bobbs-Merrill,
   1978 (paperback)
Roget's International Thesaurus, latest edition
Words into Type, 3rd ed. rev. by Marjorie E. Skillin, Robert Gay, et al.
   Prentice-Hall, 1974

INDEX

Other Books of Interest

Annual Market Books
Guide to Literary Agents & Art/Photo Reps, edited by Robin Gee $15.95
Novel & Short Story Writer's Market, edited by Robin Gee (paper) $19.95
Writer's Market, edited by Mark Kissling $25.95
General Writing Books
Annable's Treasury of Literary Teasers, by H.D. Annable (paper) $1.00
Beginning Writer's Answer Book, edited by Kirk Polking (paper) $13.95
Discovering the Writer Within, by Bruce Ballenger & Barry Lane $17.95
Freeing Your Creativity, by Marshall Cook $17.95
Getting the Words Right: How to Rewrite, Edit and Revise, by Theodore A. Rees
Cheney (paper) $12.95
How to Write a Book Proposal, by Michael Larsen (paper) $10.95
Just Open a Vein, edited by William Brohaugh $15.95
Knowing Where to Look: The Ultimate Guide to Research, by Lois Horowitz (paper)
$16.95
Make Your Words Work, by Gary Provost $17.95
Pinckert's Practical Grammar, by Robert C. Pinckert (paper) $11.95
12 Keys to Writing Books That Sell, by Kathleen Krull (paper) $12.95
The 28 Biggest Writing Blunders, by William Noble $12.95
The 29 Most Common Writing Mistakes & How to Avoid Them, by Judy Delton
(paper) $9.95
The Wordwatcher's Guide to Good Writing & Grammar, by Morton S. Freeman
(paper) $15.95
Word Processing Secrets for Writers, by Michael A. Banks & Ansen Dibell (paper)
$14.95
The Writer's Book of Checklists, by Scott Edelstein $16.95
The Writer's Digest Guide to Manuscript Formats, by Buchman & Groves $18.95
The Writer's Essential Desk Reference, edited by Glenda Neff $19.95
Fiction Writing
The Art & Craft of Novel Writing, by Oakley Hall $17.95
Best Stories from New Writers, edited by Linda Sanders $5.99
Characters & Viewpoint, by Orson Scott Card $13.95
The Complete Guide to Writing Fiction, by Barnaby Conrad $17.95
Cosmic Critiques: How & Why 10 Science Fiction Stories Work, edited by Asimov
& Greenberg (paper) $12.95
Creating Characters: How to Build Story People, by Dwight V. Swain $16.95
Creating Short Fiction, by Damon Knight (paper) $10.95
Dialogue, by Lewis Turco $13.95
The Fiction Writer's Silent Partner, by Martin Roth $19.95
Handbook of Short Story Writing: Vol. I, by Dickson and Smythe (paper) $10.95
Handbook of Short Story Writing: Vol. II, edited by Jean Fredette (paper) $12.95
How to Write & Sell Your First Novel, by Collier & Leighton (paper) $12.95
Manuscript Submission, by Scott Edelstein $13.95
Mastering Fiction Writing, by Kit Reed $18.95
Plot, by Ansen Dibell $13.95
Spider Spin Me a Web: Lawrence Block on Writing Fiction, by Lawrence Block
$16.95
Theme & Strategy, by Ronald B. Tobias $13.95
The 38 Most Common Writing Mistakes, by Jack M. Bickham $12.95
Writer's Digest Handbook of Novel Writing, $18.95
Writing the Novel: From Plot to Print, by Lawrence Block (paper) $11.95
Special Interest Writing Books
Armed & Dangerous: A Writer's Guide to Weapons, by Michael Newton (paper)
$14.95

The Complete Book of Feature Writing, by Leonard Witt $18.95
Deadly Doses: A Writer's Guide to Poisons, by Serita Deborah Stevens with Anne Klarner (paper) $16.95
Hillary Waugh's Guide to Mysteries & Mystery Writing, by Hillary Waugh $19.95
How to Pitch & Sell Your TV Script, by David Silver $17.95
How to Write Action/Adventure Novels, by Michael Newton $4.99
How to Write & Sell True Crime, by Gary Provost $17.95
How to Write Horror Fiction, by William F. Nolan $15.95
How to Write Mysteries, by Shannon OCork $13.95
How to Write Romances, by Phyllis Taylor Pianka $15.95
How to Write Science Fiction & Fantasy, by Orson Scott Card $13.95
How to Write Tales of Horror, Fantasy & Science Fiction, edited by J.N. Williamson (paper) $12.95
How to Write the Story of Your Life, by Frank P. Thomas (paper) $11.95
How to Write Western Novels, by Matt Braun $1.00
Mystery Writer's Handbook, by The Mystery Writers of America (paper) $11.95
Powerful Business Writing, by Tom McKeown $12.95
Successful Scriptwriting, by Jurgen Wolff & Kerry Cox (paper) $14.95
The Writer's Complete Crime Reference Book, by Martin Roth $19.95
The Writer's Guide to Conquering the Magazine Market, by Connie Emerson $17.95
Writing Mysteries: A Handbook by the Mystery Writers of America, Edited by Sue Grafton, $18.95
Writing the Modern Mystery, by Barbara Norville (paper) $12.95

The Writing Business

A Beginner's Guide to Getting Published, edited by Kirk Polking (paper) $11.95
Business & Legal Forms for Authors & Self-Publishers, by Tad Crawford (paper) $4.99
The Complete Guide to Self-Publishing, by Tom & Marilyn Ross (paper) $16.95
How to Write with a Collaborator, by Hal Bennett with Michael Larsen $1.00
How You Can Make $25,000 a Year Writing, by Nancy Edmonds Hanson (paper) $14.95
This Business of Writing, by Gregg Levoy $19.95
Writer's Guide to Self-Promotion & Publicity, by Elane Feldman $16.95
A Writer's Guide to Contract Negotiations, by Richard Balkin (paper) $4.25
Writing A to Z, edited by Kirk Polking $22.95

To order directly from the publisher, include $3.00 postage and handling for 1 book and $1.00 for each additional book. Allow 30 days for delivery.

Writer's Digest Books
1507 Dana Avenue, Cincinnati, Ohio 45207
Credit card orders call TOLL-FREE
1-800-289-0963
Prices subject to change without notice.

Write to this same address for information on *Writer's Digest* magazine, *Story* magazine, Writer's Digest Book Club, Writer's Digest School, and Writer's Digest Criticism Service.